John Groth's World of Sport

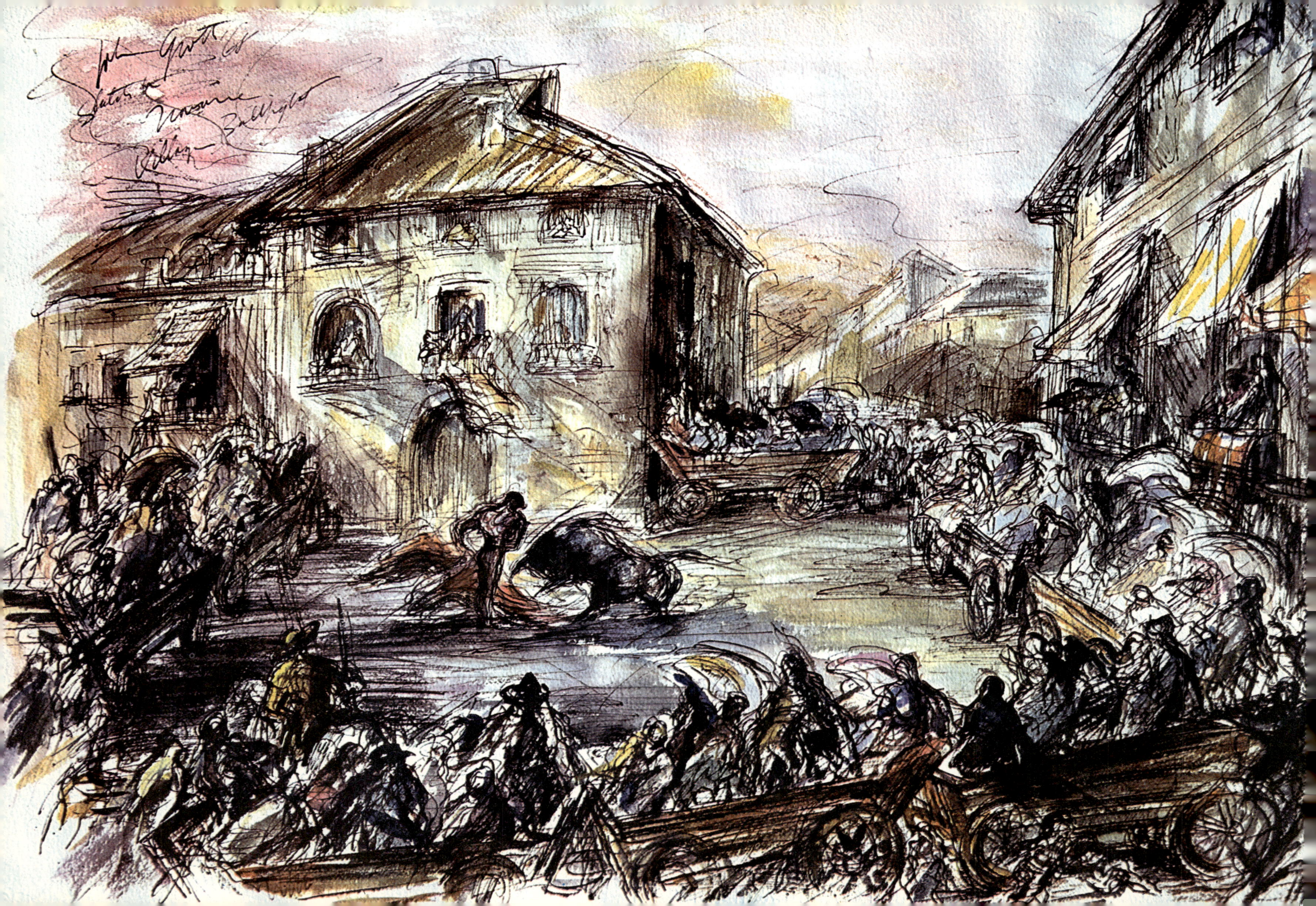

by John Groth

John Groth's World of Sport

Foreword by Arnold Gingrich

Text by Pat Smith

Winchester Press

Acknowledgments

This book had its beginnings fifteen years ago when *Sports Illustrated* sent me to Afghanistan to record the legendary *buz kashi*. Since then I have traveled thousands of miles and have been helped by hundreds of people as I have witnessed and sketched sports events of all kinds. It would be impossible to mention here all of the individuals to whom I owe a debt for the work included in this book. But it would be a callous omission not to thank the editors of *Sports Illustrated*, especially Sid James, Richard Johnston, Percy Knauth and Andre Laguerre, and two *SI* art directors, Jerome Snyder and Richard Gangel. Other magazines also sent me on assignments that resulted in drawings and paintings reproduced on the following pages. Thanks go to *Esquire, Fortune, Holiday* and *Sport,* along with the Hudson's Bay Company. Roy Attaway, Merrill Lindsey and Jim Rikhoff offered aid and encouragement in the early stages of shaping a ton of artwork into a manageable book. It goes without saying that I am proud to have my name on the same title page as Arnold Gingrich and Pat Smith.

J.G.

Copyright © 1970 by John Groth
Text copyright © 1970 by Olin Corporation

Many of the paintings and drawings in this book were
executed while on assignment for *Sports Illustrated,*
and are reproduced with permission.
Library of Congress Catalog Card Number: 72-127958
ISBN 0-87691-013-4
Published by Winchester Press
460 Park Avenue, New York 10022
Printed in the United States of America
BOOK DESIGNED BY EMILIO SQUEGLIO

Foreword

In Chicago in the days of the great depression we used to have a simple definition for a successful artist: one who has managed to accumulate bus fare to New York.

John Groth achieved success faster than anybody had a right to expect in those days; he made it to New York before he was thirty.

I first knew him before he was halfway through his twenties, and I was in the last year of my own. I met him because I was looking for him, or at least for somebody like him.

It was the late spring of 1933, a matter of weeks after the Bank Holiday, and I was confronted with a very strange emergency, for those times. I was trying to put together this proposed or projected new magazine for men, to be called *Esquire*, and I suddenly discovered that I had made a grave miscalculation in the first issue's physical specifications. I had thought all along, since we had first planned it, that it was going to have twenty-four color pages and learned within the looming shadow of the first deadline that it was going to contain a dozen more color pages than I had counted on. At the moment of this sudden realization I hadn't even managed to fill the twenty-four color pages that I thought I had, and now in what seemed like less time than the shake of a leg I was scurrying around trying to find a way to fill thirty-six.

I needed somebody, preferably good, but certainly fast, who could fill a lot of color pages in one hell of a hurry.

I was walking up Michigan Avenue from the Art Institute, where I had gone with my peculiar problem, thinking they could send me to somebody who might solve it. This was naïve of me, because in those days all the artists they'd ever heard of at the Art Institute were dead.

I was passing the open space in Grant Park just south of the Lorado Taft fountain of the Great Lakes when I saw they were having an outdoor art fair, and I turned in to take a look. Almost the first thing that caught my eye was a sign over one of the exhibits that read "Speed-line drawings" and I thought, "Hey, boy, just what I need."

They looked like what they were called—quick sketches done in a variety of colored inks, with a lot of fast-flowing lines—the line looked fast as the speed of light, though of course I had no way of knowing how long it took to make it look that fast—and in many instances, except for the different colors of the inks, I'd have sworn that the line was continuous, that the artist had not once lifted his pen from the paper after starting the first stroke.

The subject matter, appropriate to the times, was the seamy side of big city life, the ghetto and the slum, the breadline and the soupline, and the lineup for handouts at the missions on the West Side. But though the subjects were grim, the treatment was compassionate, and an air of puckish and impish humor pervaded the inherently gloomy scenes, like sunlight breaking through the bars of a jail cell. I'd have said that in its strangely paradoxical blend of cheerful cynicism it suggested that some sort of a share-the-work plan had been evolved between those improbable collaborators, Daumier and Disney.

I looked to see if there was an address given along with the name of the artist, and there was. It said the speed-line drawings were the work of John Groth and that his studio was on North Michigan Avenue, at an address that I recognized as being up near the old Water Tower, one of the few structures to survive the Chicago fire and, in those days, the symbol of the Near North Side neighborhood known as Towertown, the nearest Chicago equivalent to New York's Greenwich Village. I was headed that way anyway, going back to my office in the Palmolive Building, so I stopped in to look him up, and in my eagerness I walked up there at a near-trot.

Studio was a pretentious term for the upstairs rear room in the rooming house at the number given, and when I found him I mistook him for his son.

He was a scrawny towheaded tousle-haired kid, barefoot with faded khaki pants and a venerable looking black jersey gym shirt, and he was leaning over a table, from which he was engaged in pulling off, from an apparently very sticky surface, a large piece of white paper. He looked disturbed, if not annoyed, at being interrupted in what he was doing, which looked to me very much like an attempt to pick up a piece of flypaper which had by inadvertence been placed on the table gummy side down. So I stifled the impulse to ask, "Say, sonny, is your old man around?" and waited for him to finish.

He began to explain, as I waited for him to finish, that what he was making was a monotype, and as he continued lifting it I saw that there were colors on the underside of the sheet, and it dawned on me that, whatever a monotype was, this was the artist himself and not his little boy.

John Groth was rising twenty-five at the time, but he could have passed for a teen-ager. This dampened my hopes that had been building up as I had rushed there from the outdoor art fair. Another disappointment was that I had constructed an advance mental image of some guy tearing off colored sketches at the approximate speed of a flatbed printing press, and here was this youngster engaged in what seemed one of the slowest processes I had ever watched.

But my spirits rose again when he finally got the thing off, not the table, to which I had thought it was stuck, but a piece of glass, on which he had made a composition in oil paints, and from which he had now taken an impression with such painstaking deliberation.

"So that's a monotype," I said, and I've been learning things from him ever since.

I took him right back to the office with me, as soon as I'd explained my problem and as soon as he could find his shoes, and barely let him out of my sight for weeks thereafter. He filled seventeen of those pages in that first issue of *Esquire,* with monotypes and aquatints and drypoint etchings and speed line drawings, served up in the form of both cartoons and story illustrations, and to explain why one man happened to fill such a measurable portion of the magazine's space we both decided it would look a little better if we called him the art director. I don't think either of us quite knew what an art director was, or did, but John's interpretation of the second word of that title seemed to be "one who goes off in all directions." Before I knew it he was off to Mexico, coming back with drawings of soldiers keeping house on the tops of railroad cars, and hardly had he got back from there before he was off again, to Germany and to Russia—and all this before the magazine was a year old.

I soon saw that it was not for mere whimsy that he had been working barefooted the day I met him—he had an itchy foot, and in the three and a half decades since then I've seldom seen him that he wasn't planning to be off for somewhere, or that he wasn't just back from somewhere else.

He was in Berlin on the first of July 1934, the "night of the long knives" when Captain Roehm got jettisoned from Hitler's intimate entourage, and he thus early set the pattern that he has followed with astounding consistency ever since. Two samples, out of many: he just "happened" into both Paris and Berlin, during World War II, ahead of the main body of American troops.

And it was equally early evident that no one magazine is big enough to fetter for very long a spirit so roving and venturesome. John Groth beat *Esquire* out of Chicago by better than a decade, and the wide world has been his beat ever since.

But though he soon went on to bigger and better things, to world-girdling assignments and to projects for the illustration of world-famous books, over the years and through all the travels John Groth has never forgotten a favor, never left anybody with anything but a smile, nor ever quit a place that they haven't kept his chair warm for his return. He has a genius for friendship and is, quite simply, the kindest and most considerate human being I've ever known. But he also enjoys more aches and pains than a ward full of invalids. An almost daily habitue of health clubs, he can hardly get through an afternoon without encountering some new ailment, yet by morning he'll be ready to take off for the other side of anywhere if you make him an interesting enough proposition tonight.

This book, which is a by-product of his almost constant travels, is a revelation of but one facet of a many-sided personality, for John Groth is a denizen of many spheres of interest, and a catalyst of many enthusiasms. He talks and writes as well as he draws, as those who have attended his classes at the Art Students League and those who have read his books *Studio: Europe* and *Studio: Asia* will be quick to testify.

The hair is white now, that once was tawny, but the hand that draws, with those music-pens that composers use, is still as quick as an adder's tongue. And the zest is—well, seemingly endless. I never saw so many drawings in one place at one time as when he was working on *War and Peace*. But after that, when he was working on *Gone With the Wind,* and the drawings flew all over the studio like sparks from a scissors-grinder's wheel, I began to think I hadn't seen anything yet.

Now obviously no man can go on like that forever, but who's going to keep up with him to find that out? I've been trying to keep abreast of his work, with the hope of sometime saying something about it, for a long time. In fact, in the forematter of my first book, in 1935, there was the announcement of a forthcoming work (in preparation) entitled *John Groth: A Monograph.* I think that was another word he taught me, along with monotype. At any rate, try as I will to chug along, puffing and panting, every time I think I'm catching up the least little bit, I find I've lost him around the next turn ahead. So I'm afraid the monograph is still in preparation and still forthcoming. But there is some progress to report. I've finally got the first sentence done:

John Groth is an original, in everything he says and does and touches.

Arnold Gingrich

Introduction

The essence of war is violence.
Thomas B. Macaulay

Mister Macaulay could have applied the same definition to the world of sport, especially John Groth's world of sport. For what is sports, really, if it is not a relatively civilized form of war, one without its grim outcome, one in which points are counted rather than corpses, and cups and money and pride are wagered rather than countries, economies and national identities.

But if the stakes are less vital in sports, the presence of violence is just as pervasive. In order to make this violence acceptable, however, it is sometimes necessary that it be dressed in various disguises. Is not violence suggested, for example, when a pitcher intentionally fires one—"high and tight"—at a batter he decides is crowding the plate? Nearly always, the batter eludes the missile, but the so-called "brush-back pitch" nevertheless represents a stern warning: Get out of my strike-zone, man-with-the-bat, enemy, or you will be knocked senseless. Is not violence symbolized when an archer's arrow punches into the center of a bull's-eye, or when a fencer's foil strikes the heart sewn on his opponent's uniform? And does not potential violence dominate the Indianapolis 500, when over 100,000 people fill the stands, their eyes glued to the ghosting autos and their hearts anticipating that ultimate moment when an exhausted driver misjudges a turn and sends his car barreling into the concrete barrier—wheels scaling free of the axles, engine exploding into a fiery ball, gas and oil spewing onto the track, setting the stage for still more spills and thrills?

But most often the violence of sport is as kinetically real as a right cross—or a sniper's bullet. When football linebacker Sam Huff once described his job as "get the quarterback," was he not expressing the same basic tactic taught every infantryman: "Eliminate the highest-ranked enemy officer"?

This preoccupation with violence is by no means limited to the stadia of America. In fact, of the forty-three sports included in John Groth's exciting world, no less than forty-one are violent—and not one was born in America. From the frozen slopes of the Hindu Kush in Afghanistan, where as many as a thousand men on horseback flay one another with lead-tipped whips in a primitive form of polo called *Buz Kashi*, to Port au Prince, Haiti, where every Sunday afternoon red-eyed fighting cocks are unleashed in the pit, violence is the name of the game.

Yet, despite the violence of his two major artistic worlds—sports and war—John Groth remains one of the most nonviolent men I have ever known. How, you ask, can this seeming duplicity exist within one man—and what does it make John Groth? Well, in a word, it makes him honest, for as most critics would agree, an artist's basic responsibility is to be true to his work. Sometimes, this search for honesty—or accuracy, as he himself would have it—has led John too close to the action. Covering the Scottish games at Aboyne in 1955, John narrowly escaped being brained when he unwittingly placed himself directly in the path of an airborne hammer in order to capture a close-up of the thrower. In a similar effort in 1948, John was rudely interrupted from his work when his subjects—the Notre Dame backfield—ran over him on one of their patented end sweeps. And during a Brooklyn Dodgers exhibition game in Cuba, in 1948, John was cut short in a chat with the third base coach Ray Blades by a line drive in the groin. "I wore the imprint of the National League on me for days," he recalls.

Evidently Groth is at least as enterprising in his war coverage. Ernest Hemingway—a very tough man to impress—once said after World War II, "I never saw him go off . . . that I did not expect we would be burying him that night or the next day. But he always came back with the sketchbook full of lines we could not understand. If John would have made them from any closer up front he would have had to sit in the Krauts' laps."

So, after depicting dozens of battles in six different wars and hundreds of sporting events, it can safely be said that John Groth has time and again been drawn by the heat of action—and has performed superlatively under both kinds of fire. So well, in fact, that he has received almost identical words of praise from two men high in their respective fields, neither of whom is known for his charity to fellow artists. Said Hemingway of Groth the combat artist: "He gets to the essence of war." Said Jimmy Cannon of Groth the sports artist: "He's the only artist I know who gets the truth of sports in his work."

Pat Smith

Contents

Buz Kashi

Two most important wings of my work have been sport and war. In the buz kashi *I found the perfect welding of both, and although I had to travel some 13,000 frustrating miles to record the sport it was worth the effort. The* buz kashi *experience has inspired me to do 100 paintings and drawings.*

It all began one winter night in 1954. John Groth was attending a dinner on Manhattan's Upper East Side and was seated next to the United Nations delegate from Afghanistan. Being a gentleman who has dealt on every level from kingdom to rumdom, Groth fell deep into a discussion with the delegate. After a while John mentioned that he had been to Afghanistan and asked the delegate about a game called *buz kashi.* "The guy nearly flipped," recalls John. "He was practically hugging me because I was the first American who had ever mentioned the game to him." For the rest of the evening, the delegate waxed eloquent on *buz kashi*—a coupling of spectacle and violence like nothing else in the world. *Buz kashi* is a monumental—if rather primitive—form of polo, played by as many as a thousand whip-wielding men on horseback using a headless goat carcass as the "ball." Knowing Groth to be a war correspondent and a sports enthusiast, the delegate pressed home the point that *buz kashi* is the ultimate combination of both subjects.

Before the night was over, the delegate had extracted a promise from Groth that he would go to Kabul, Afghanistan, the next August to record on parchment what the delegate called "the greatest *buz kashi* match in the history of Asia." What Groth did not know was that he was soon to embark on the longest—and most frustrating—assignment of his career, although, in the end, it was also to be one of the most rewarding.

It was a hot summer day when Groth lugged his leather satchels and drawing pads off the plane at Kabul. There was the usual flurry of activity for a few minutes and then suddenly John realized he was alone. "Even the little hole-in-the-wall office was closed," he recalls. "I waited an hour or so until this little guy with an ox cart came along and gave me a lift. When I got into town a couple of hours later, I went to the Hotel Kabul and discovered that no one had bothered to make a reservation for me. What could I do? The guy at the desk said a room was available, but there were six Japanese already sleeping in it. I said no thanks. More talk, cajoles, threats. Finally, I got a room to myself, where I parked my bags. Then I asked the guy at the desk about the *buz kashi.* No *buz kashi.* So I asked about the *seshan.* (That's the name of the festival held every year in celebration of the Afghans' two victories over the British during the nineteenth century.) 'At the stadium,' he said. Gee, I thought, that might be it."

But when John arrived at the stadium and shouldered his way to the field, he was met with a scene straight out of a New England girls school. At one end of the grounds a field hockey game was going full tilt; at the other end a badminton match was being held. Under the stands several ping pong conflicts were in process; a gang of tennis players waited in the wings. "I didn't know what the hell was going on," recalls Groth.

Still unconvinced, John battled his way to the announcers' booth at the top of the stands and demanded, "Where's the *buz kashi*?" "Well," said the announcer, "your country has been so kind and has given us so much money in the last few years that we decided to express our gratitude by holding only Western games. So this year there is no *buz kashi*."

After learning that all government offices were closed for the week of the games, John returned to the lobby of the Hotel Kabul, where he sat and wondered if he could sketch a sport he had never seen. Finally, someone from the American Embassy materialized and offered him a room back at the compound. John quickly accepted and spent the week telephoning everyone in the country in a vain effort to locate an upcoming *buz kashi* match. Finally someone from the bureau of tourism suggested that John come back November 25th, when he would see the "greatest *buz kashi* match in the history of Asia."

By now John didn't care if he saw the worst *buz kashi* in Asian history. "Can't you stage one for me now?" he pleaded. Not in Kabul, answered the tourist agent. But if John were that anxious he might try the next province—Baghlan—where the governor, a great enthusiast of *buz kashi*, might just put on a match if he were asked by a famous American journalist. There was one slight hitch. The trip was several hundred miles away along a camel track, and since there was no communication between points, John would have to gamble that the governor would reward such enterprise. Now, calling it quits has never been one of Groth's dominant characteristics, so he hired two trucks, an interpreter, a cook and two armed guards, and pushed off into the desert bound for Baghlan.

Along the way John met with still more frustration. The first eve-ning out the small safari pitched camp next to a clear, quick-running stream outside a small native village. Deeply afflicted with fishing fever, Groth broke out his Smuggler trout—a small fly rod that breaks down to fit into a suitcase—and, vested in an Abercrombie & Fitch special adorned with an exquisite array of dry flies, stepped into the stream. After several fly changes had produced not a nudge, John was about to quit when he noticed that the villagers had quietly lined the banks to watch the spectacle. Now he was too embarrassed to quit. Suddenly three or four of the villagers began panning for minnows, while another ran off, then returned with several tree branches, each of which had bailing wire wrapped around one end and a point on the other end. Impaling the minnows on the sharp, hook-edged wire, the villagers began fishing. They soon had caught some twenty-five nine-inch-or-so trout, while John continued to flail the water with his handsome Smuggler trout and his fancy flies. "I was ashamed to go up the bank and face these people," recalls John. "But when I finally did, their leader presented me with the fish and said, through my interpreter, that they hoped I would not be hungry any longer. So naturally, I gave them food from our commissary."

Two days later the safari rumbled into Baghlan, where the gover-nor turned out to greet Groth and invite him to dinner. After a feast of yogurt, covered with flies "like raisins," the governor listened to the *buz kashi* proposition and declined. Explaining that the horses and riders—the prime elements in *buz kashi*—were lodged in the north, in the mountains, the governor said he had no influence with the mountain leaders, the Khans. "The Khans," he said, "are like kings. Their answer will be no. It is much too hot here at this time of the year for *buz kashi*. The horses would lose too much weight and would not be strong enough for the next battle in the fall."

Next thing John knew he was in Kunduz, a northern village eight miles from the Oxus River separating Aghanistan from Siberia. At a meeting with a dozen of the Khans—who were dressed in turbans and turned-up slippers and armed with inlaid flintlocks—the answer re-mained an emphatic no, the heat would sap the horses' strength. But

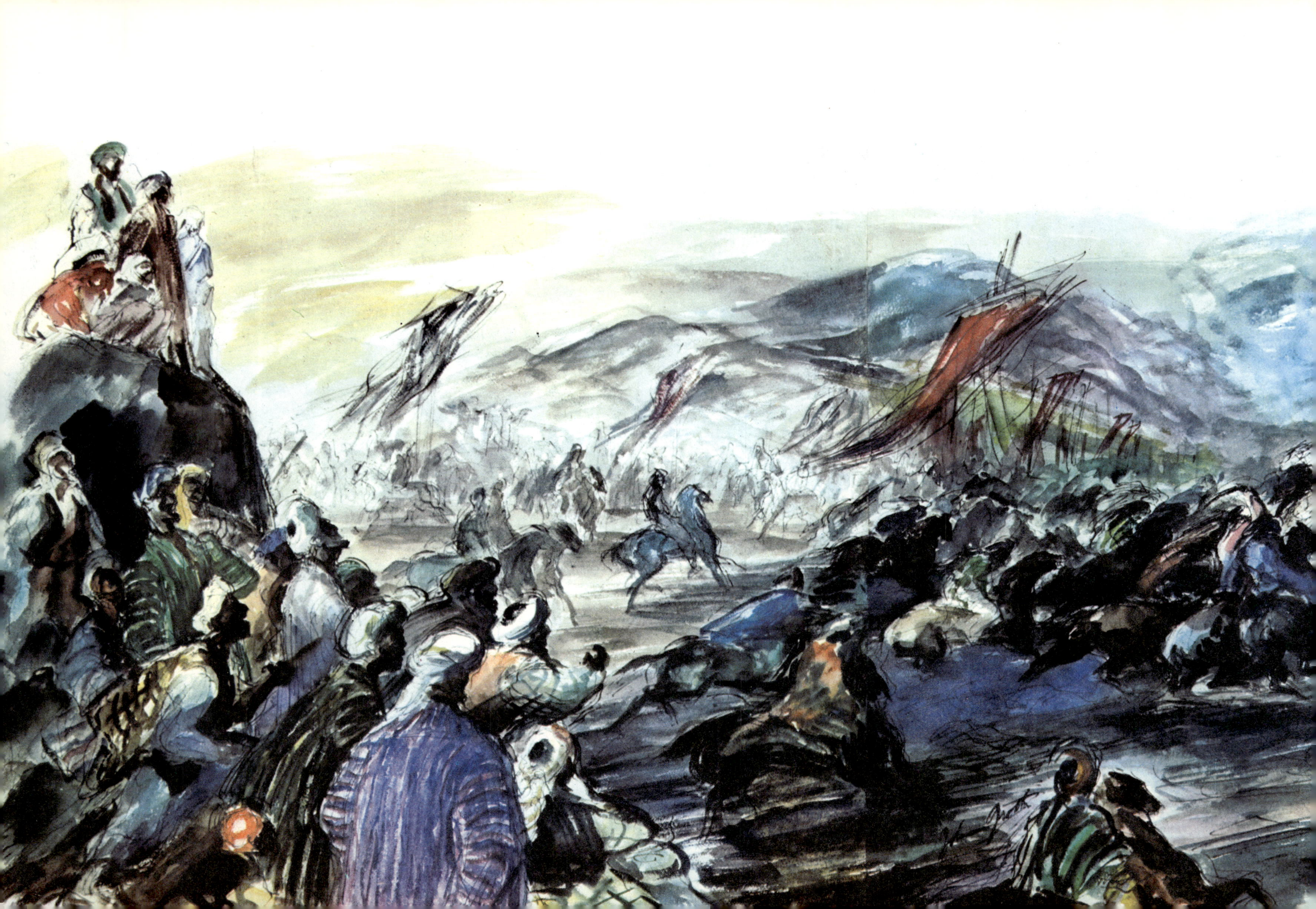

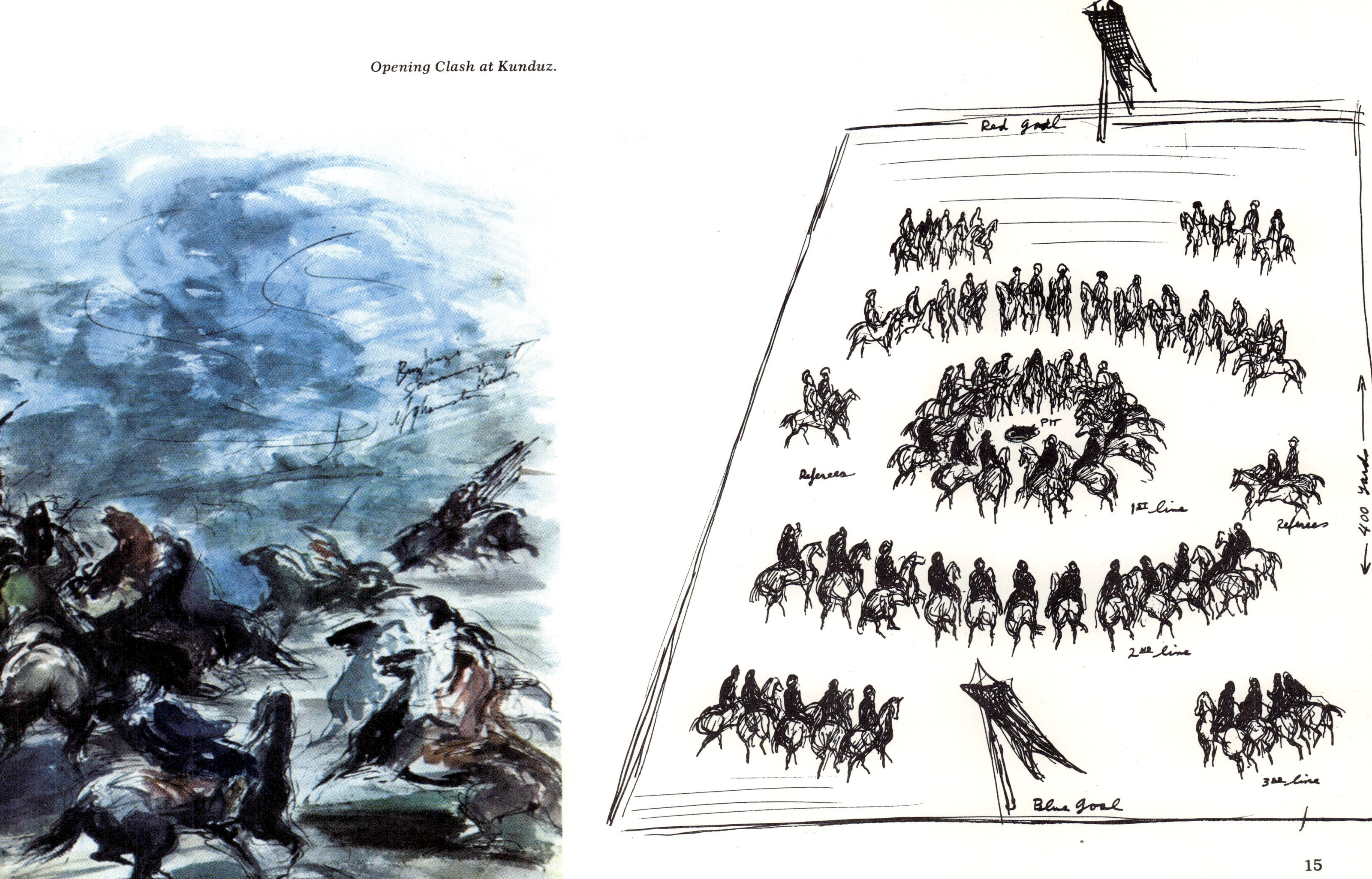

Opening Clash at Kunduz.

the interpreter made a last effort, pointing out that the U.S. had been very generous to the country—helping to build a highway and giving much technical aid—and that here was a journalist who had come some 17,000 miles especially to sketch *buz kashi*. It would be extremely bad form not to honor his efforts. This was it, the final plea. Here were the horses, the riders. Now everything rested on the next words.

They agreed to hold the match. But only twenty horses would be fielded instead of the usual total of some 400; and Mr. Groth would have to work fast because they would only perform for ten minutes. Furthermore, the Khans explained that they were competing for the national championship in two months. If they lost, Mr. Groth would have to assume some of the blame if their horses were too weak. John nodded solemnly.

So that afternoon the town criers strolled through the villages informing one and all that two days hence an impromptu *buz kashi* would be held outside the city. Soon the entire hill population within donkey and camel distance began flooding into Kunduz. Processions of champion riders accompanied by retinues of hawk-nosed, rifle-toting tribesmen arrived with whole villages in tow. Every inn was jammed to the roofs. Riders whose names are household terms everywhere in Afghanistan reared and wheeled their steeds to the delight of the turbaned fans thronging the melon bazaar and the Street of the Silversmiths.

Finally, the day of the John Groth *buz kashi* arrived. The playing field was a stretch of flat golden sand set in a natural arena of steep slopes. Bands of villagers planted their standards and ranged themselves around the valley. And while the premier riders changed into their cobalt blue uniforms and the horses were saddled, the crowd listened to a chorus of blind minstrels and bought sweetmeats from the hawkers. Meanwhile, the Khans reclined in the shade of a small concrete grandstand. Suddenly the crowd fell silent, the horses' flanks flexed for action and the riders became statues. "This was it," recalls Groth. "This was what I had waited for."

Not quite. The umpire, a red-cloaked gentleman on foot, emerged from the humping mass of horseflesh and asked, "Who's got the 'ball'?" Now the "ball" is not really a ball at all—it is a headless goat carcass that is dragged, thrown or carried by the *buz kashi* riders just as the pigskin is transported downfield by football players. To score a goal (two points) in *buz kashi*, one rider must seize the goat carcass, break into the clear and, with the assistance of a phalanx of interference riders, reach one end of the field, circle the flag, then gallop to the other end, swing around that flag and deposit the carcass back in the pit. In the good old days, when Genghis Khan's Golden Horde played the game, the "ball" was a live, bound, condemned prisoner. In fact, according to some reports, condemned prisoners are still used at occasional clandestine meets.

At any rate, the officials rushed back into Kunduz and returned with a goat carcass, which was placed in a shallow pit in the center of the field. At a signal the ring of *chapandas* plunged toward the goat. The game—or it might more appropriately be called a battle—began in a mad scramble. A massive quivering rosette of horseflesh rotated clockwise around the pit for what seemed several minutes. Suddenly, a rider squirted from the pack, followed by a stream of players. Hugging the goat and leaning half off his horse, he raced toward the goal line, as the opposing defensive line drove forward to block him—much as in a hockey game. They halted him momentarily as flanking riders whipped the ball-carrier furiously. Under the beating he dropped the goat.

Immediately the action shifted toward the other goal as an opposing player stole the carcass and plunged back through the charging riders. He, in turn, was bowled over. Horses hurdled him as he lay huddled on the baked sand. The action was lost to many of the spectators for some minutes in the dust clouds at the far end of the course. Then came the roar of the crowd again as the horde materialized and came streaming toward the other end of the field.

Two rival riders were pulling the carcass almost apart—each holding a foreleg. Others, wielding their whips, flailed at them. They both

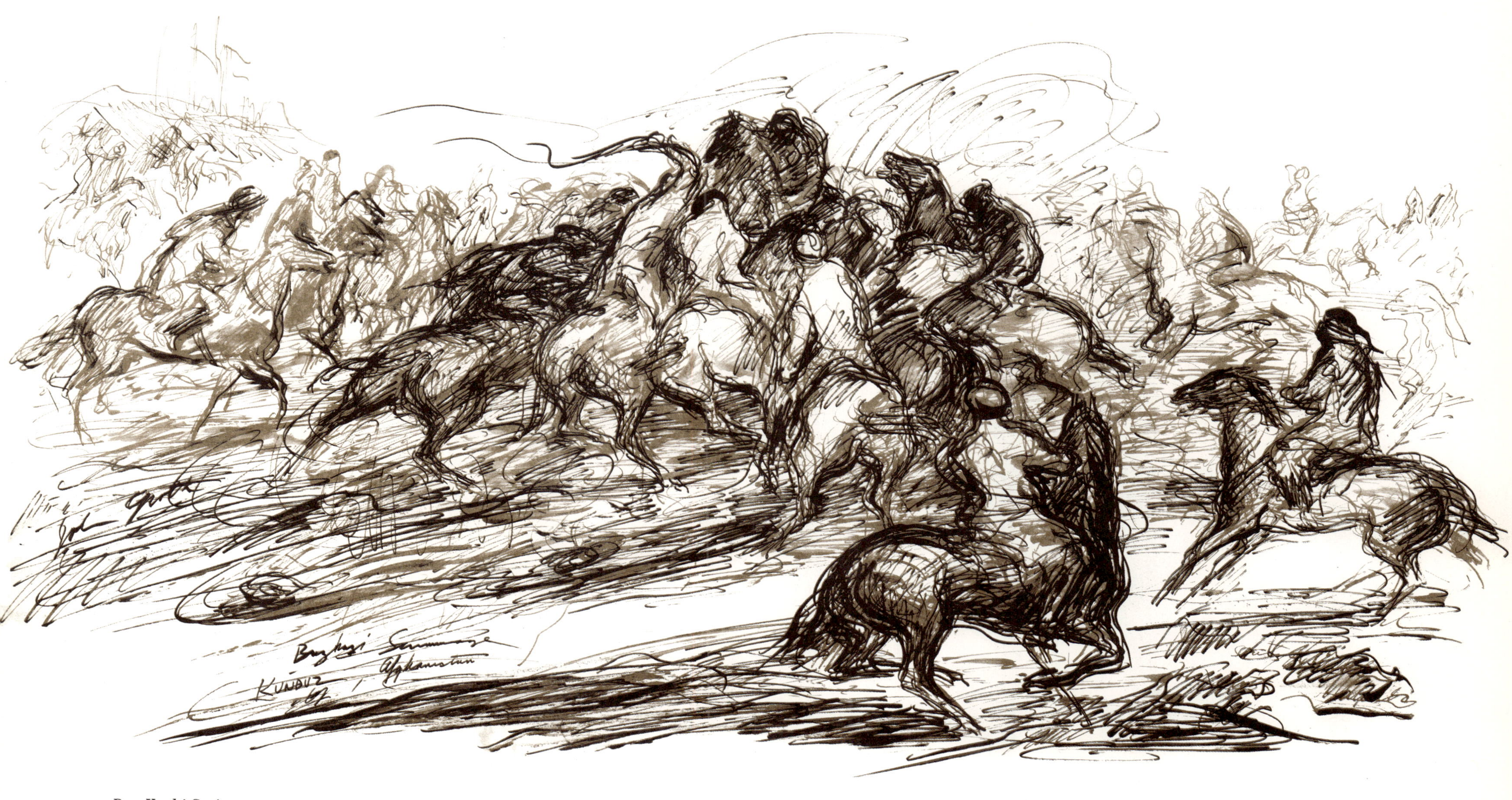

Buz Kashi Scrimmage.

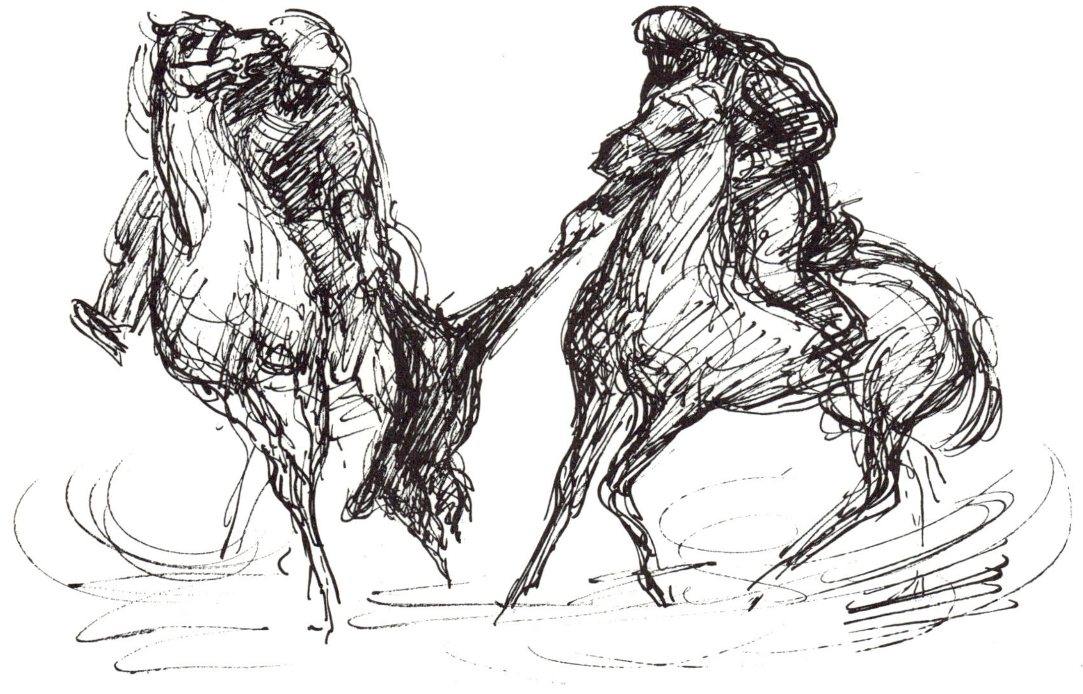

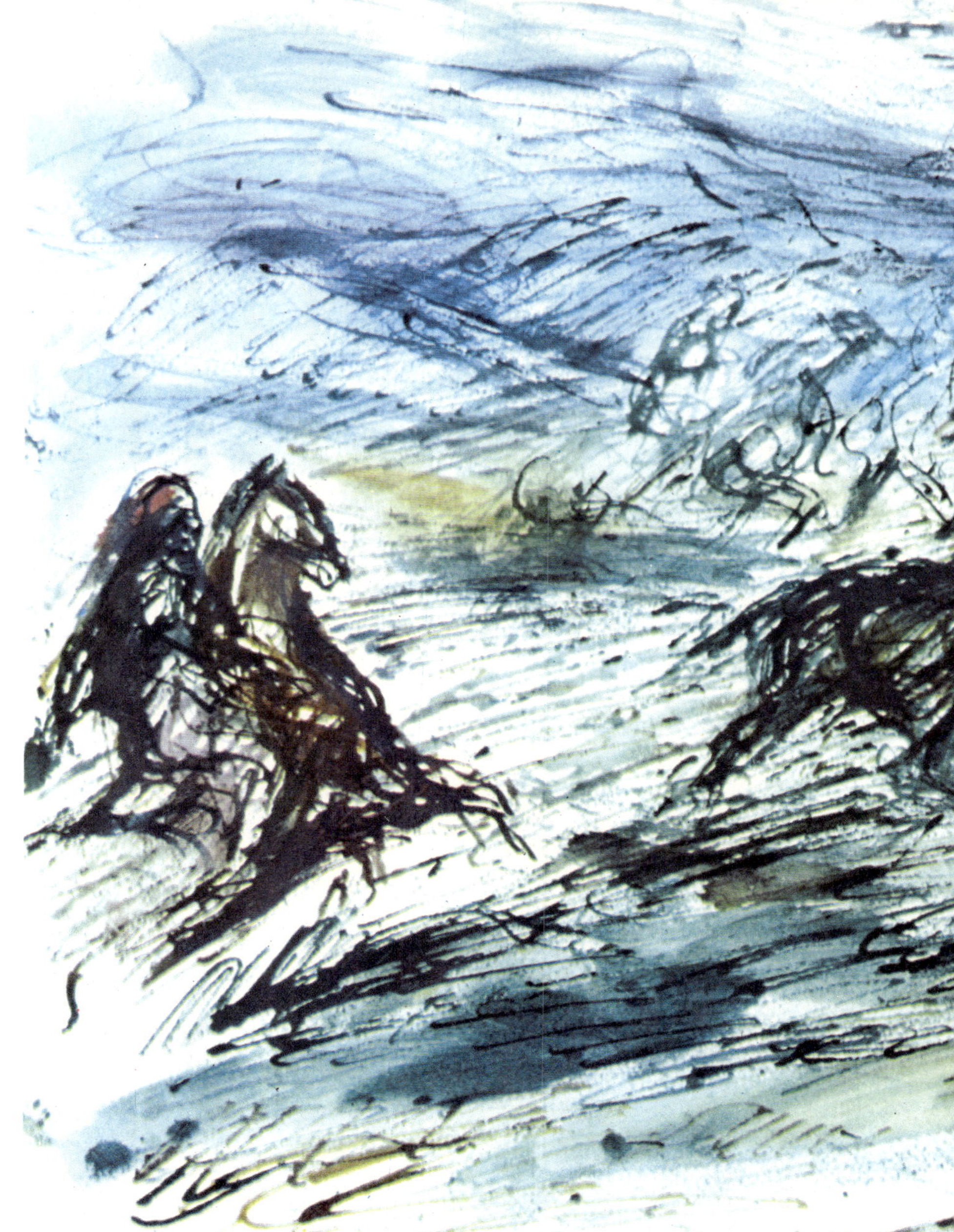

Battle for the Carcass.

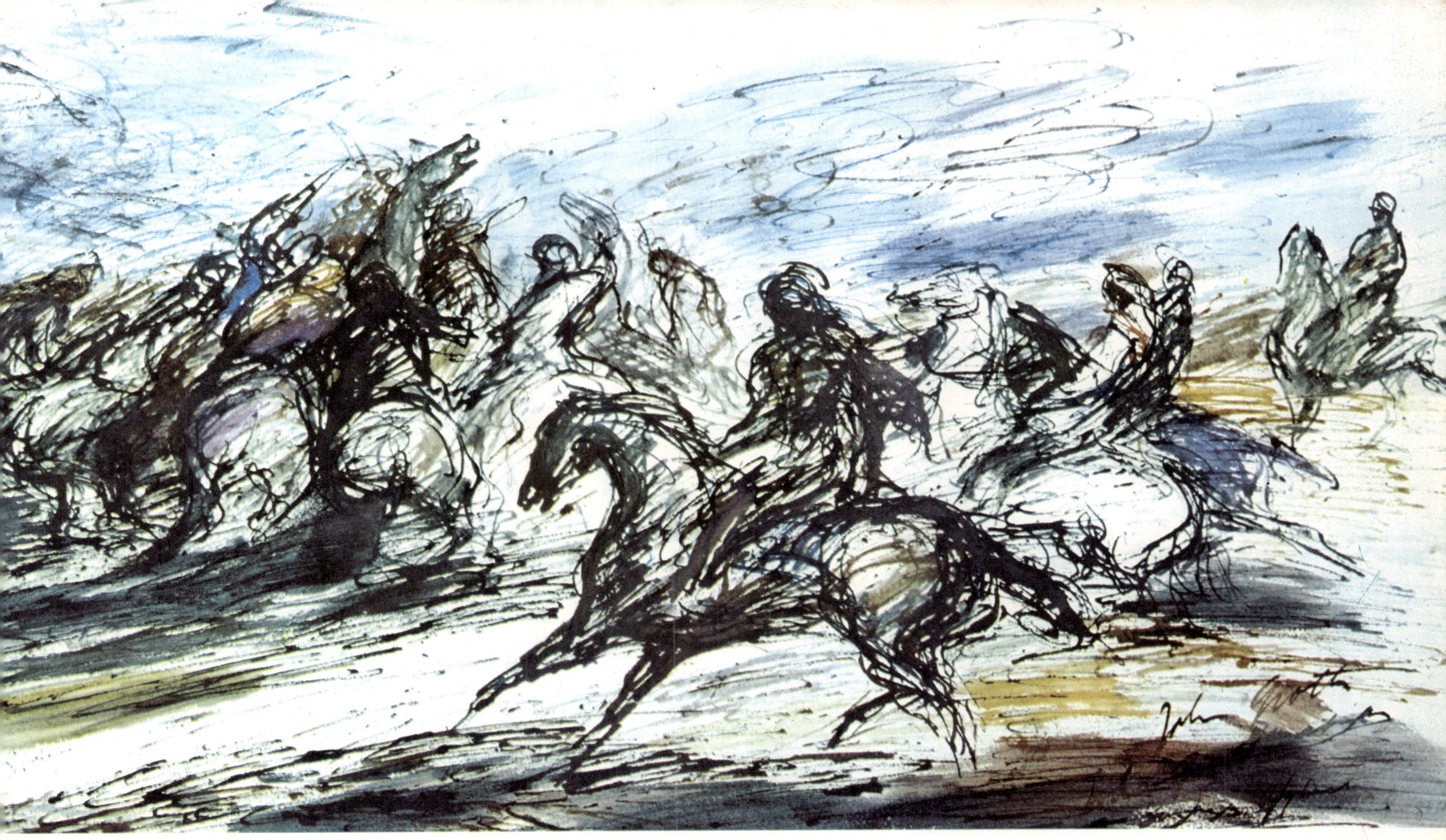

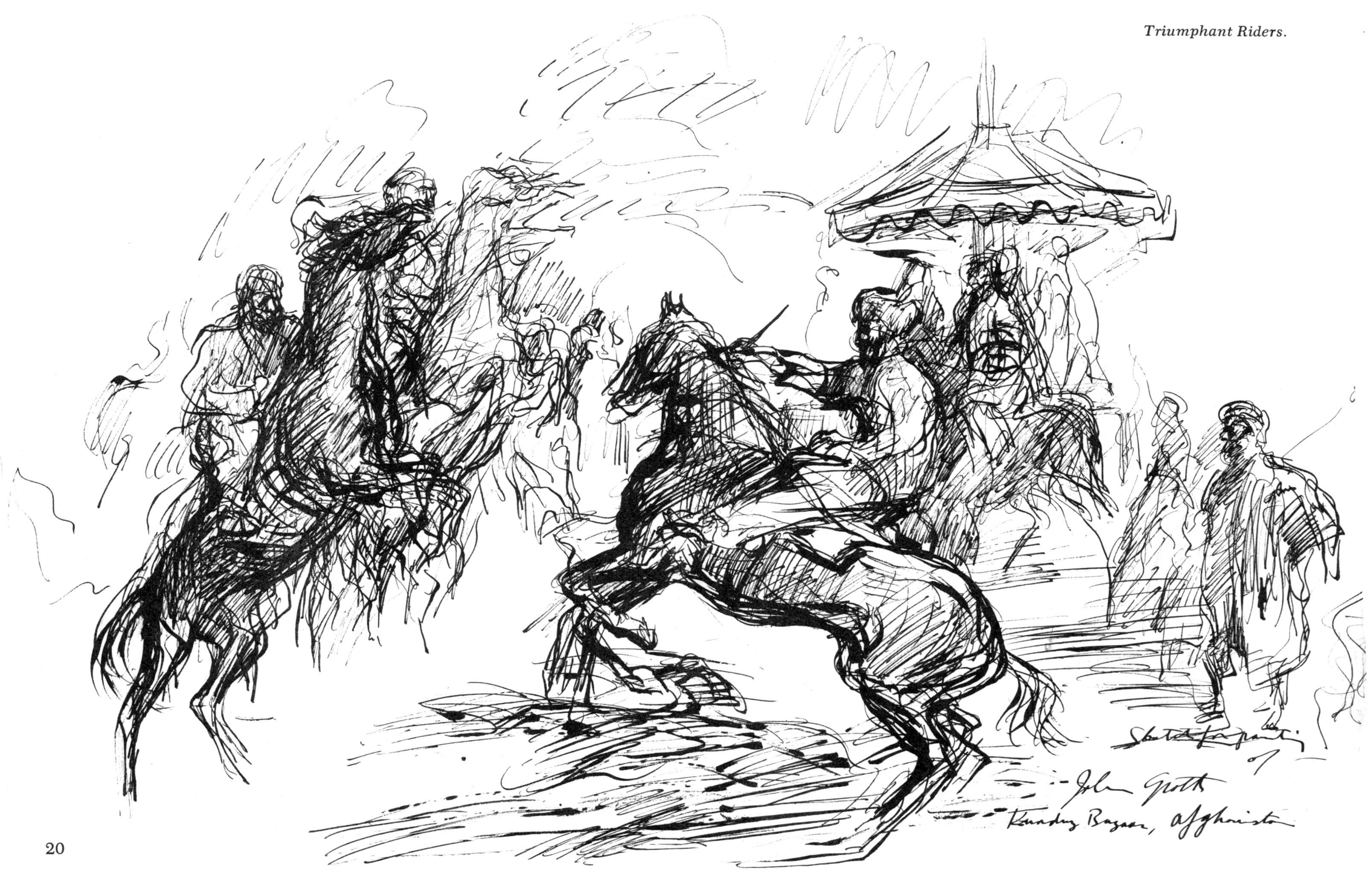

John Groth
Kunduz Bazaar, Afghanistan

gave up simultaneously, and again the goat was dropped. Then the main body raced back up the valley, as horsemen who had been torn from their mounts lay in their wake and the riderless horses galloped aimlessly about.

The judges called a rest period after an hour had passed. Clearly, once the Afghans got started on a *buz kashi* match, they were slow to quit. The players lined up once more, as they had at the beginning of the match, and the play was resumed. This time the action was even more furious. Tidal waves of fighting Afghans surged up and down the field. Several times swirling knots of riders and horses mounted the embankment, scattering the crowd. (One particularly violent collision produced the game's first serious injury.) After another full hour a red-bearded Afghan—hunching over the tattered carcass, his unraveled turban streaming behind him, his face bloody—made the circuit around both goal posts and, well ahead of the entire company, dashed down the center of the field and flung the headless goat into the pit.

The *buz kashi* was over.

Kunduz was jubilant that night. Gallons of tea and tons of pilau and sherbet were consumed; and while the victorious riders danced to booming drums and ringing tambours, drunken tribesmen rode madly through the streets firing their rifles into the night, making noise enough to keep the Siberian sentries across the river nervous until dawn.

After thanking one and all, John returned halfway around the world to his studio on 57th Street in Manhattan. Several months later he learned that the mountain men of Kunduz lost their bid for the national championship. "I'm sure that the tribesmen on the Oxus Plain would like to see me," says John. "Perhaps they'd like to show me the game again—this time in its purest form, with a bound prisoner—me—as the goat."

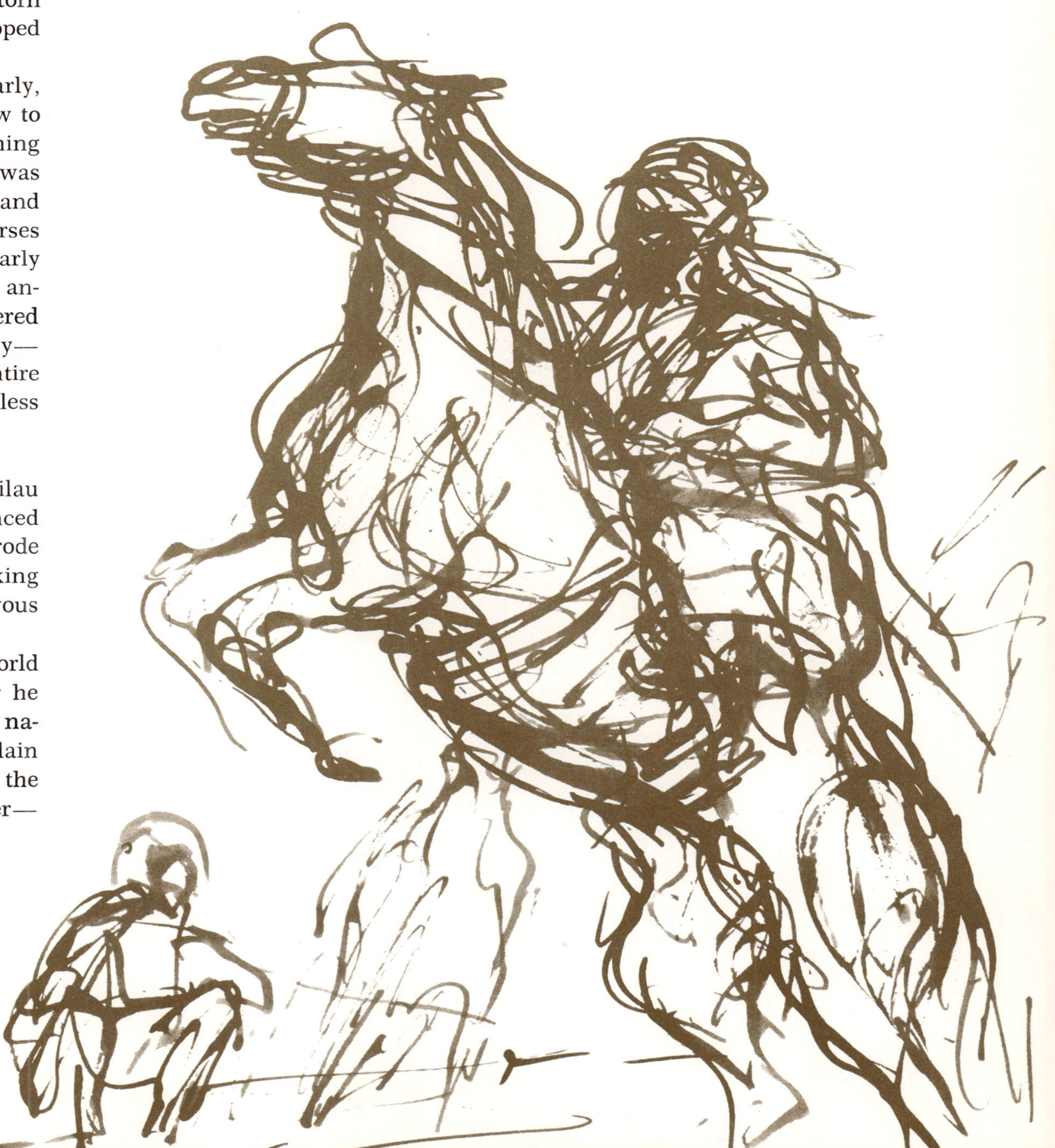

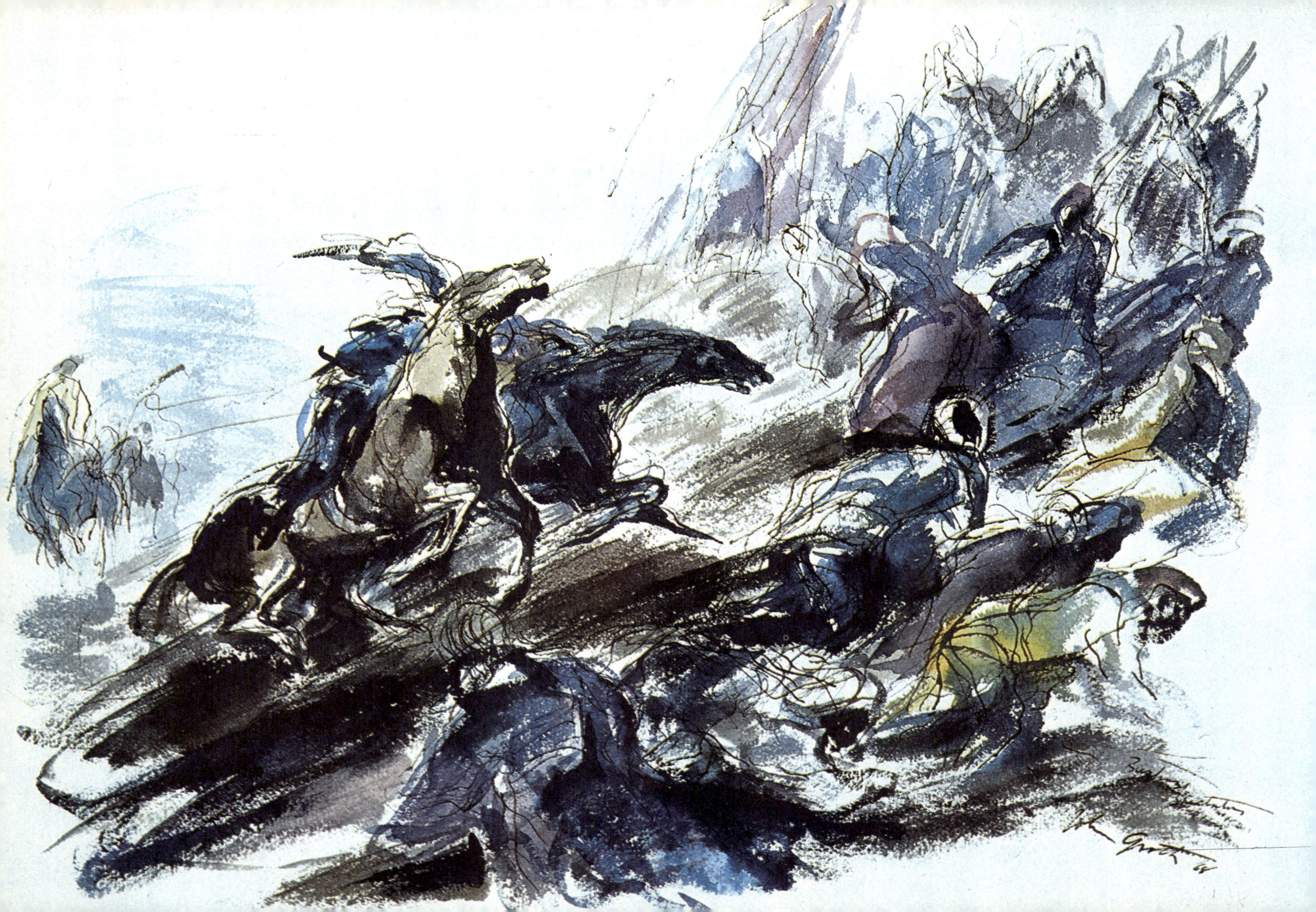

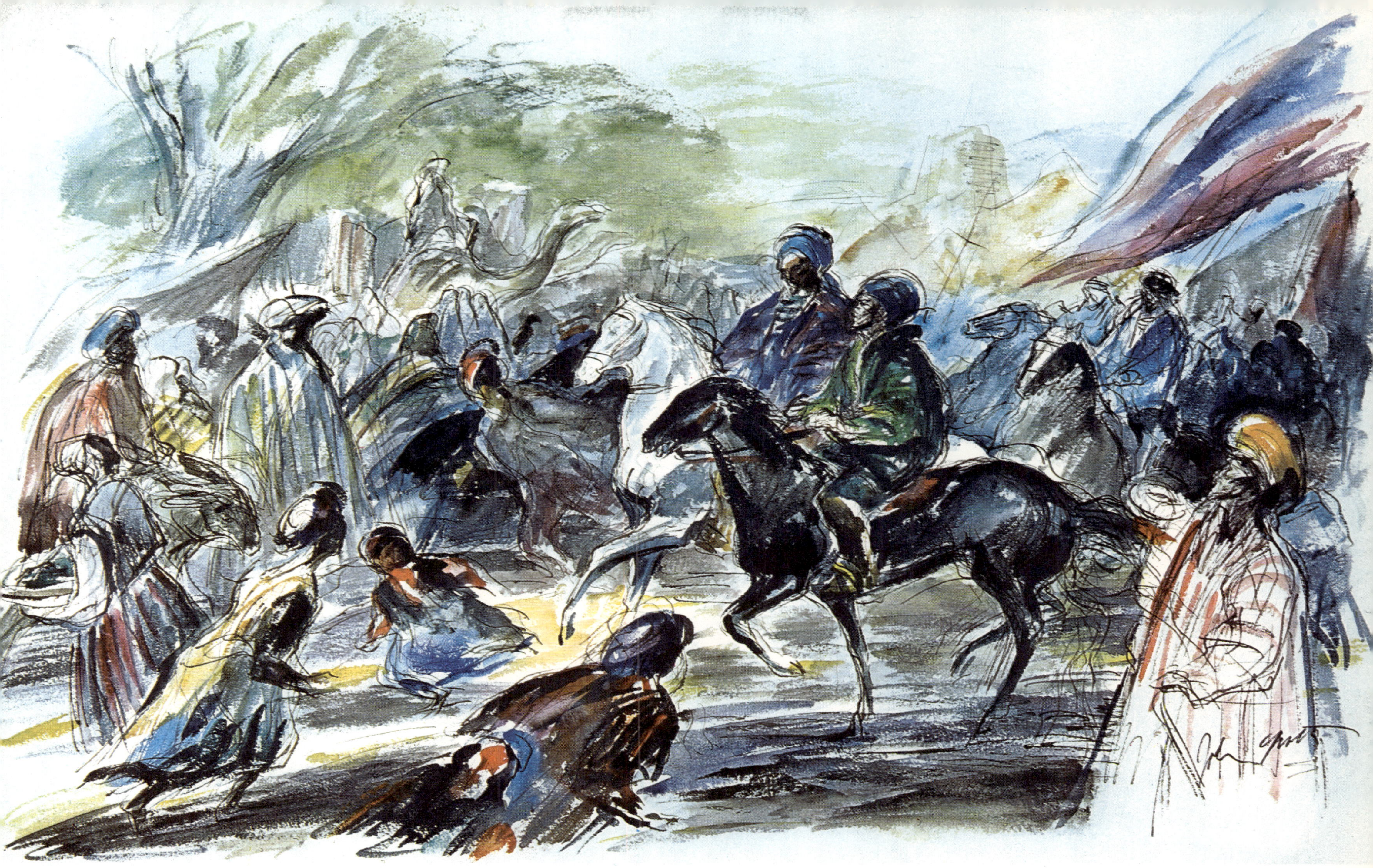

Parade of the Champions.

Scattering the Crowd.

Cockfighting

To be truthful, I am not the most avid cockfighting enthusiast. My interest lay in the excitement of the betting and the tension of the crowd.

We deal here with a particular·breed of bird watcher. Like his counterparts in the Audubon Society, this usually gentle, mild-mannered man seeks his esthetic rewards while observing the habits of birds. There is, however, one monumental difference between him and the rest of the bird-watching fraternity. What intrigues this gentleman most is a species possessed of an extremely pugnacious nature that compels it toward a singular objective: to tear asunder all other birds within its reach. "It's just natural for them to fight," explains one aficionado. "They'd rather fight than eat."

But despite the native ferocity of the gamecock, his handler claims to be among the most humane of men. Listen to one old cocker's theory: "The truly peaceful nations on earth are devoted to cockfighting—and those that aren't are warmongers. Russia wouldn't know a fighting cock from a leghorn; and there is no cockfighting in Germany. Now take England. At one time cockfighting pushed horse racing back into second place as the national favorite. But since 1849 cockfighting there has been virtually dead, and look what's happened to England!"

So much for philosophy. What about the gritty old battler himself? Be he a "gray" or a "claret" the gamecock has blood running through him that flows back to ancient times. Descended from "gallus gallus" —a breed of Asian jungle fowl transported to Greece specifically for the off-hour entertainment of the Spartan legions—the gamecock has evolved into as pure an aristocrat as any three-year-old that ever ran at Churchill Downs on Derby Day. And although he is legally unwelcome in all states except New Mexico, Florida and Kansas, the gamecock is alive and well and fighting throughout the U.S. for the enjoyment of some 100,000 underground patrons. At an average match the cockers' occupations will often run the gamut from gas station attendant to company president. Social background is of little consequence, so long as the handler's feathered charge breathes sufficient fire in the "pit."

Nevertheless, the high cost of raising a stout-fighting cock would seem somewhat prohibitive to all but the well-fixed. A cocker often spends thousands of dollars mixing bloods in the hope that he'll produce a champion. As often as not, however, the cocker ends up with a "dunghill"—the rather unsavory term for a cock that is truly chicken. Despite the expensive procedure, fighting cock raising can be profitable. In the U.S. alone, for example, professional breeders export some 14,000 birds to the West Indies, the Philippines and throughout Latin America. One of the lustiest leagues of cockfighting buffs is in Haiti—

where every Sunday afternoon, matches are held in Port-au-Prince and are attended by hundreds of heavy bettors.

Whatever the location, whomever the handlers, all cock matches follow an ancient ritual somewhat similar to a prize fight. As the crowd settles around the pit, the announcer signals the first match by calling out two numbers. (The cocks are assigned numbers to insure against any favoritism). As the handlers enter the pit holding their squawking charges, the crowd comes to life: "100 and 80" shouts one gambler, meaning he'll give $100 to $80, and upon acceptance he'll then pick the cock he wishes to back. Meanwhile the plungers—who may bet heavily—talk quietly to one another.

After meeting with the referee in the center of the pit, the handlers hold their birds beak-to-beak at arm's length and allow them to peck at each other—a warm-up technique called "billing." Back at the score-lines, the handlers await the referee's go-ahead. "Pit," shouts the referee as the gallery erupts, and the birds are launched. Wings beating, feathers ruffling, the red-eyed, screeching cocks mix it up like a pair of drunken prostitutes. A good fight seldom lasts more than a minute or so, and when it is over the second fight is announced—fight rapidly follows fight until the day ends.

Seldom are the cocks allowed to battle to the death. As a winner becomes apparent, the referee—or one of the handlers—steps into the fray and separates the combatants. The winner returns home to his club in triumph, to be fought again—or to be bred so that his blood and bone will pass on to another bird of battle. As for the losers, there are two possible fates. If, for instance, the losing bird showed promise in his defeat, he may also be allowed to go home under the theory that he incurred bad luck and that things will break better for him during his next battle. But more often, a loser is quickly dispatched into eternity by way of a clean, swift stroke of a sharp knife—and his carcass is left beside the barn for the garbage man to take away on one of his special calls during the cockfighting matches. Occasionally a fly-tier will pluck a few of the fallen warrior's rusty hackles so that at least a small part of him will see battle once again.

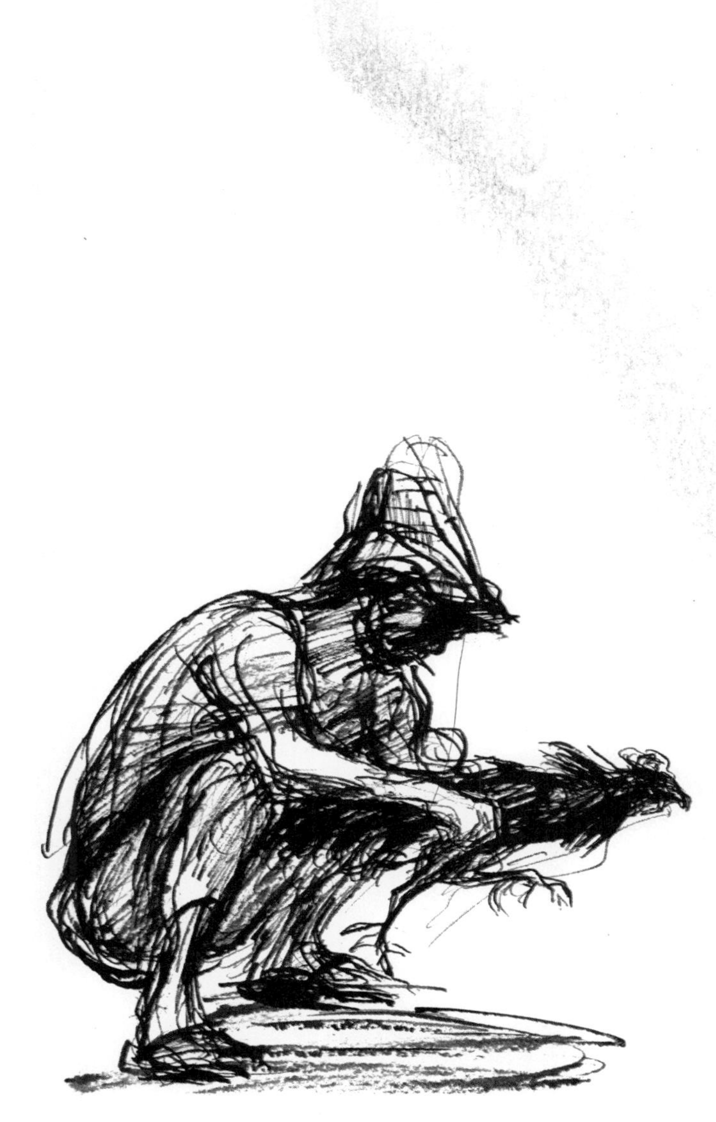

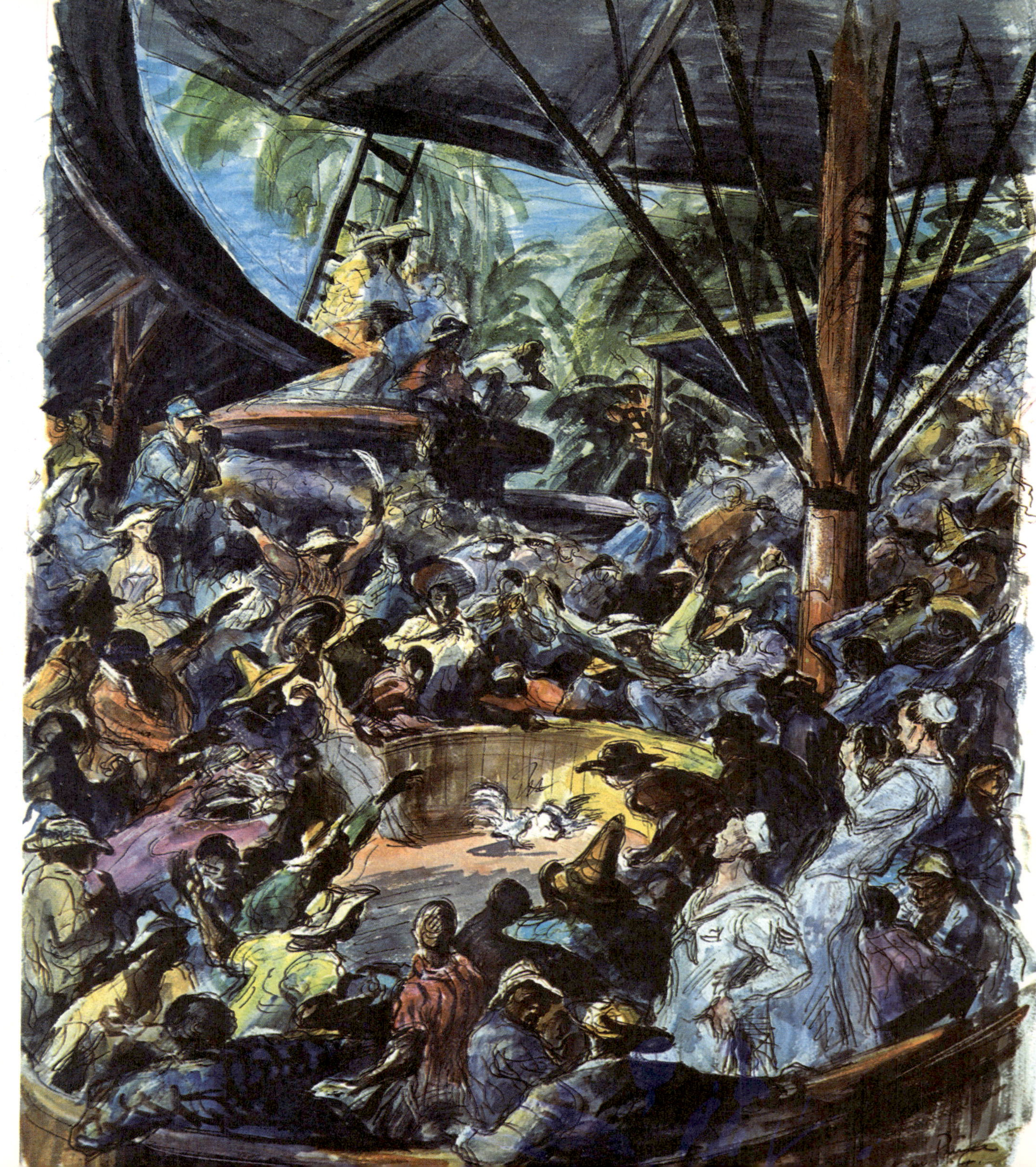

Sunday Afternoon, Port-au-Prince.

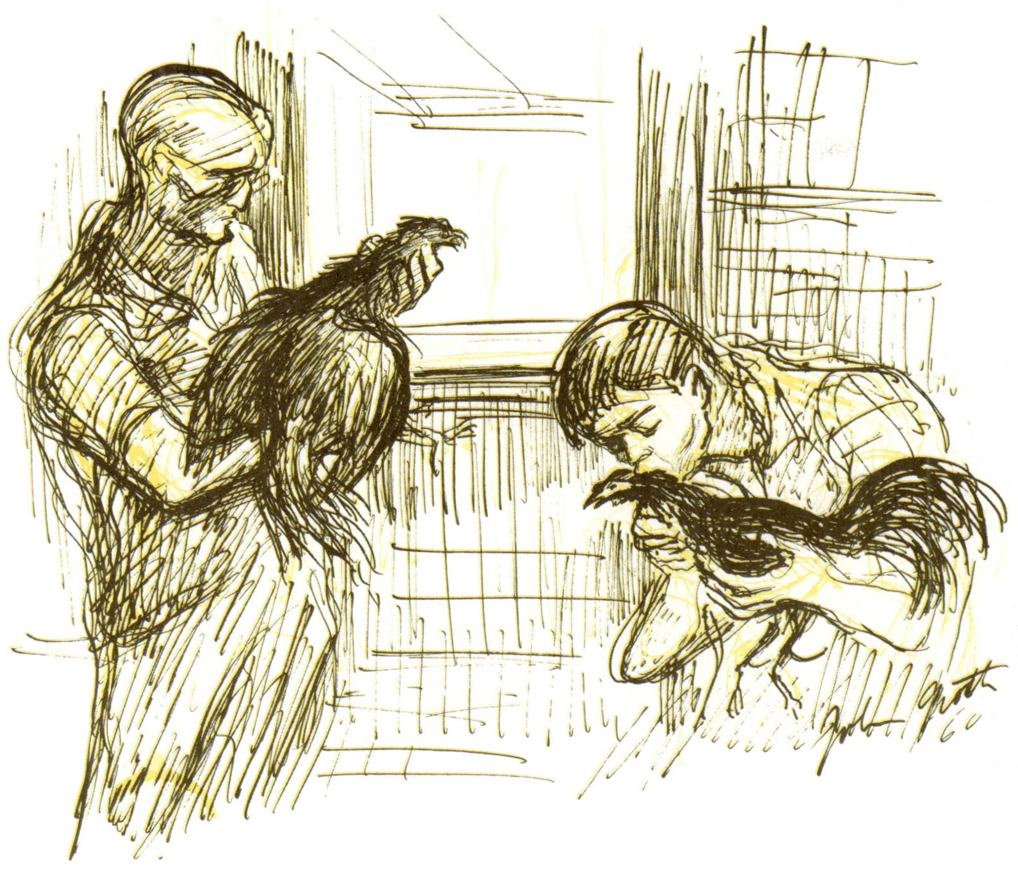

Reviving Birds.

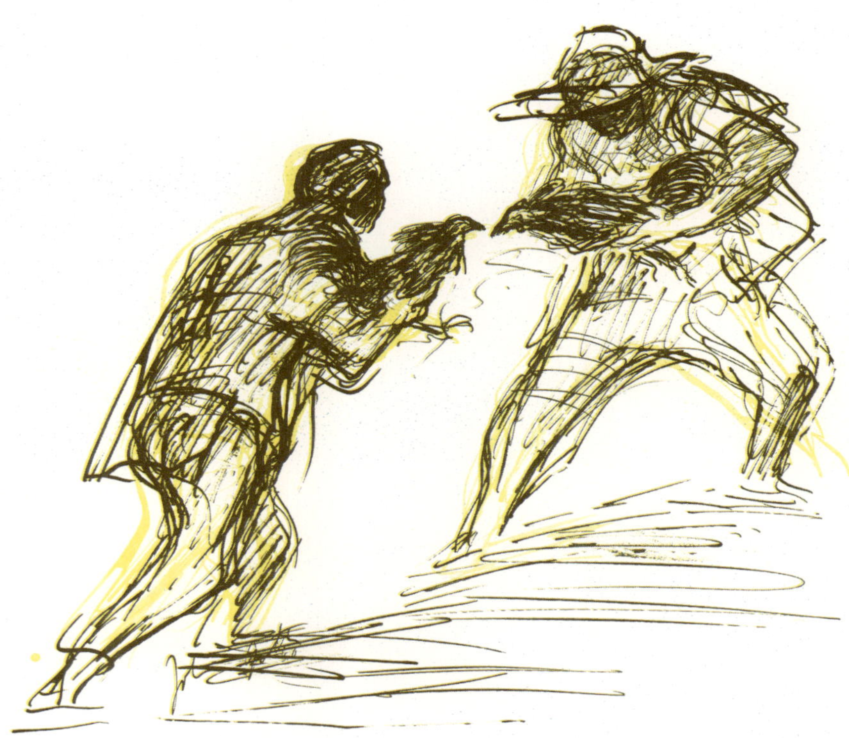

"Billing."

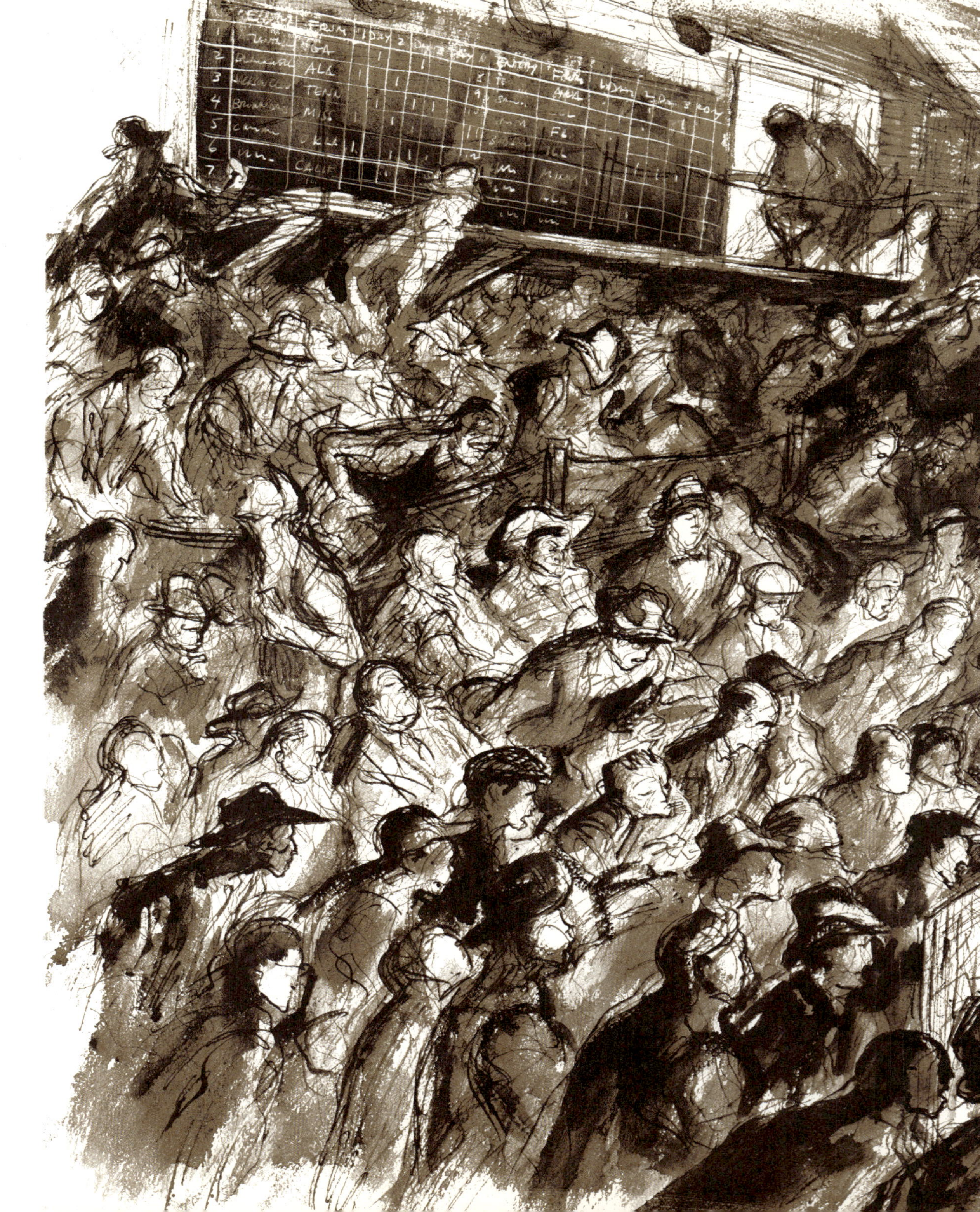

Pit Action, Hot Springs.

28

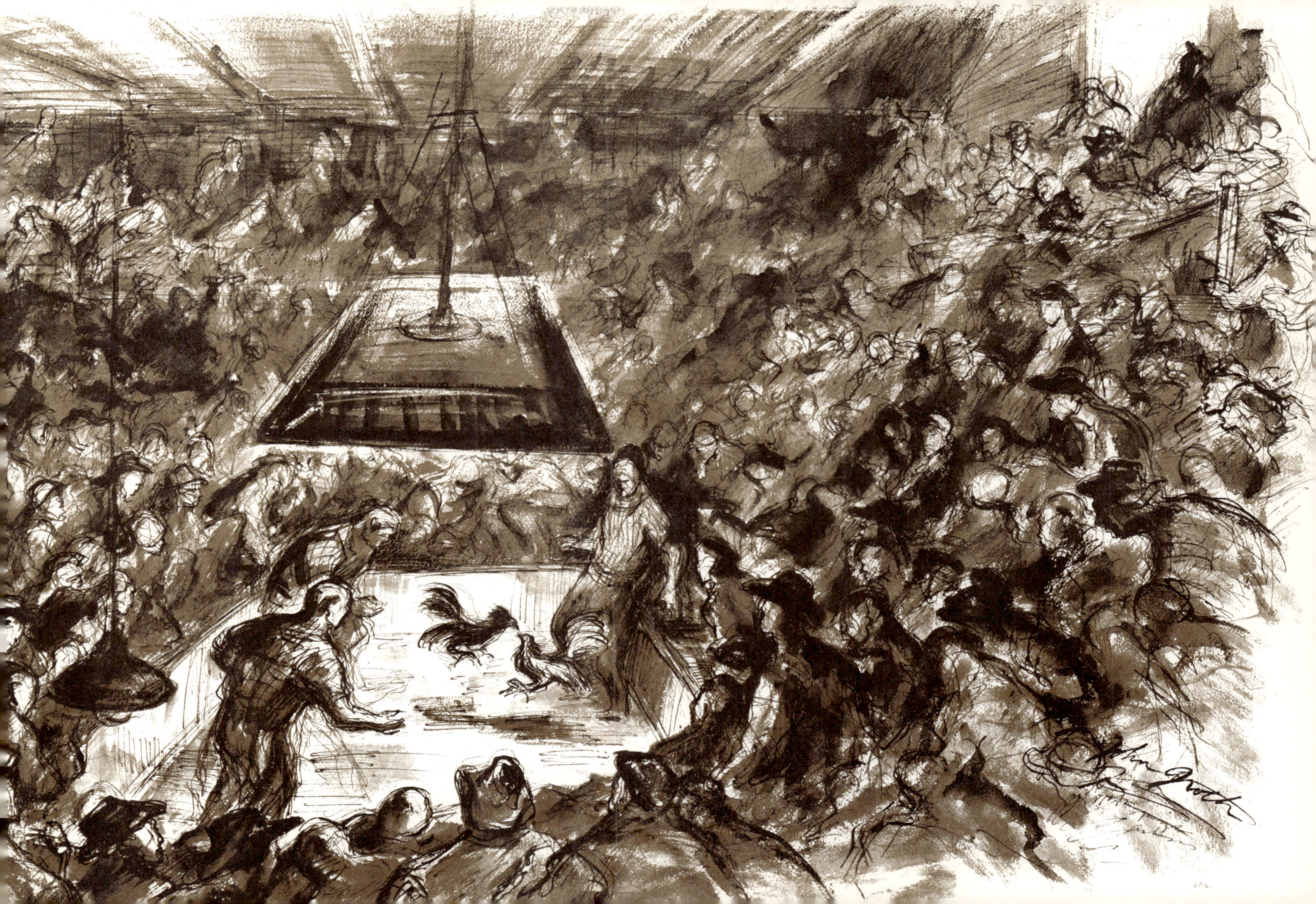

Indian Army Games

Among all the sports played by the Indian Army, the kabaddi *interested me the most. As played by the Sikhs, it is certainly the most graceful, fluid form of tag I've ever seen.*

Kabaddi is a popular game played in every village of India that is also used by the Indian Army in some training programs. School teams compete in meets, and well-paid professional teams travel throughout India. Battling in a small 11-by-14-yard area—divided in the center by a line—the seven-man teams compete for two fifteen-minute periods with a five-minute rest at halftime. The teams alternately send a raider into the enemy's area. The raiders are required to repeat "*Kabaddi*" or "*Hu-tu-tu*" over and over, then touch an opponent and return to home base across the line without losing breath to score a point—reminding one of a Neapolitan game called "Ring-O-Livio." Opponents are allowed to bring down the raider by tackling and wrestling him, but are restricted. The Groth picture here reproduced is of Sikh troops playing in a regimental match at their New Delhi encampment. The game is used in training because it requires healthy portions of endurance, running and dodging ability.

Tent peg sticking is a highly difficult sport that goes back well beyond the arrival of the British Army in India. Originally, it was developed as a technique of war rather than of sport—and was used widely throughout Asia. Enemy tribesmen would storm a camp before dawn and, pounding at full gallop, would spear the tent pegs, thus

Kabaddi Match, Delhi.

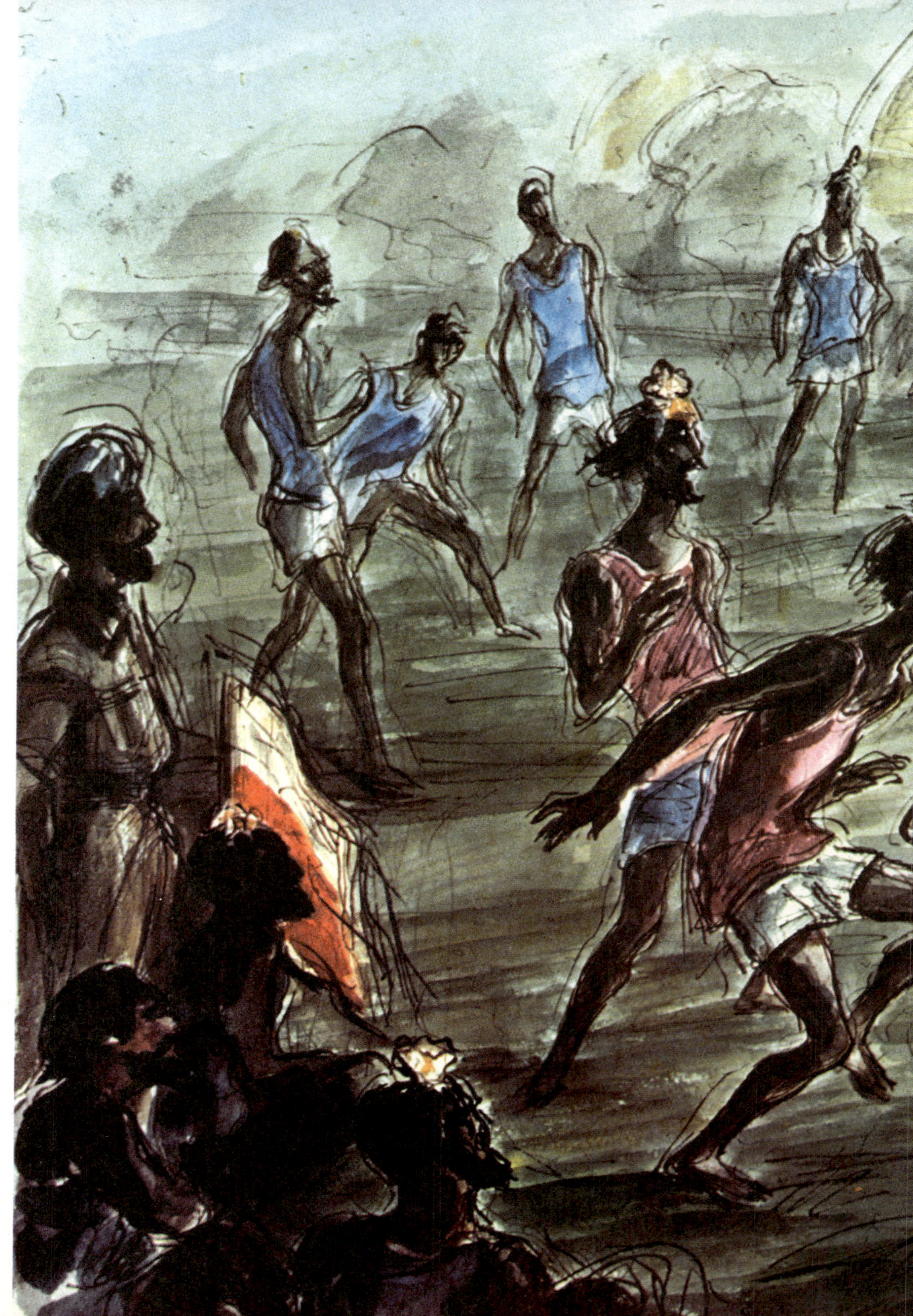

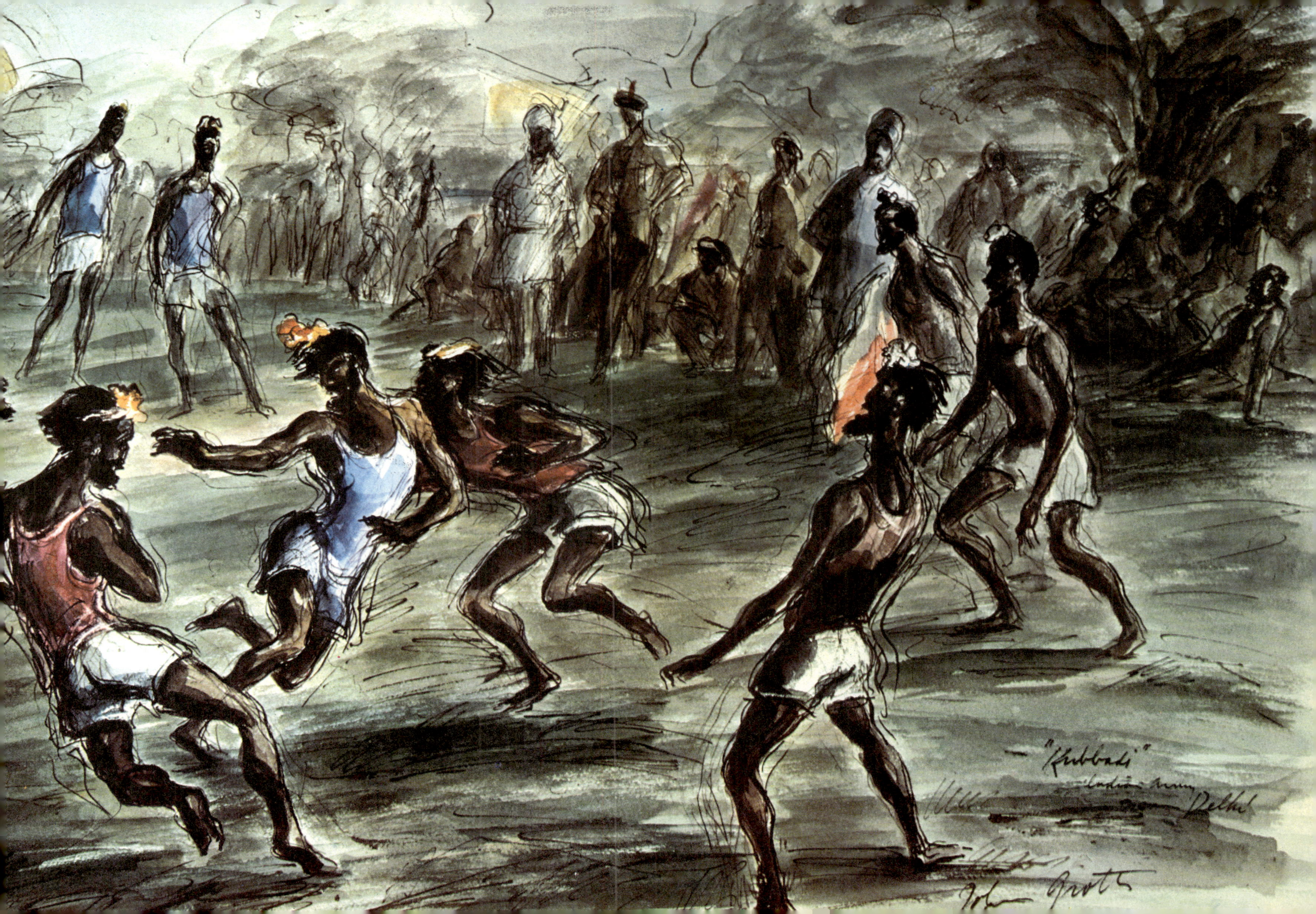

"Kubbadi"
Indian Army
Delhi
John Groth

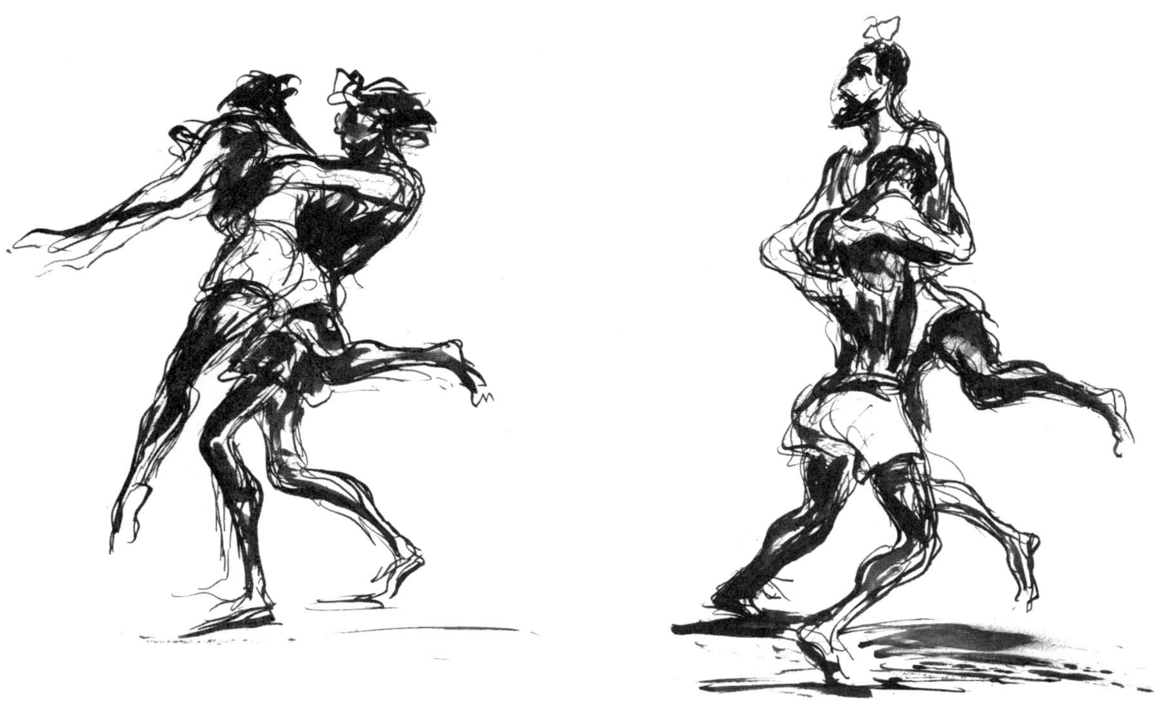

collapsing the heavy tents on the sleeping defenders and immediately gaining the upper hand. Today tent peg sticking is played on the fields of sport and, quite naturally, has its most accomplished participants in the Indian Army. The players, armed with 10-foot-long lances, take turns charging a set of wooden tent pegs hammered into the baked earth of the parade grounds and attempt to impale them on their needle sharp spears.

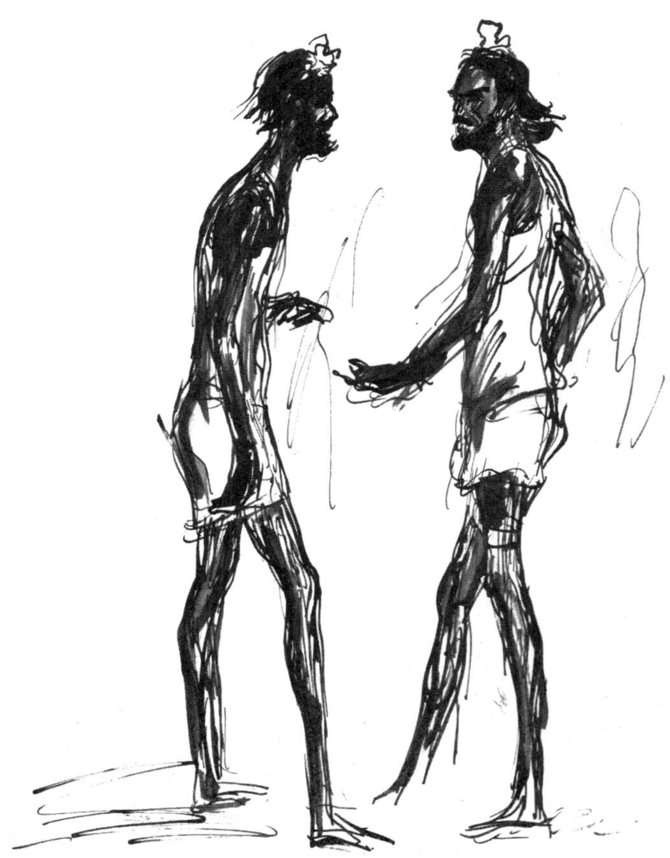

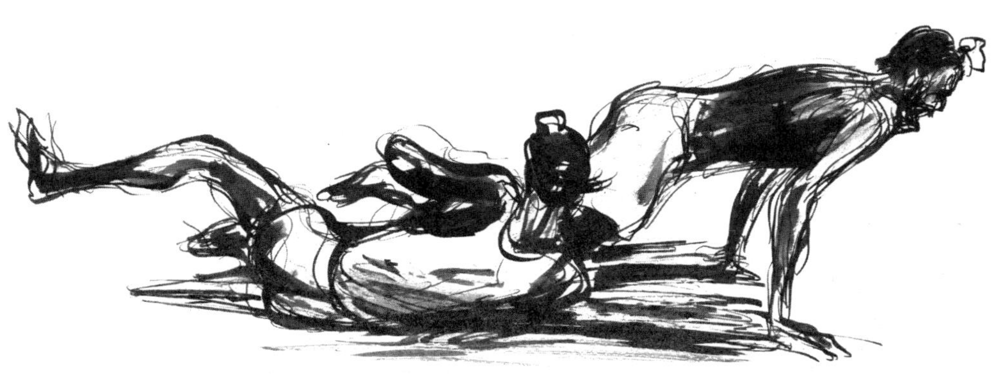

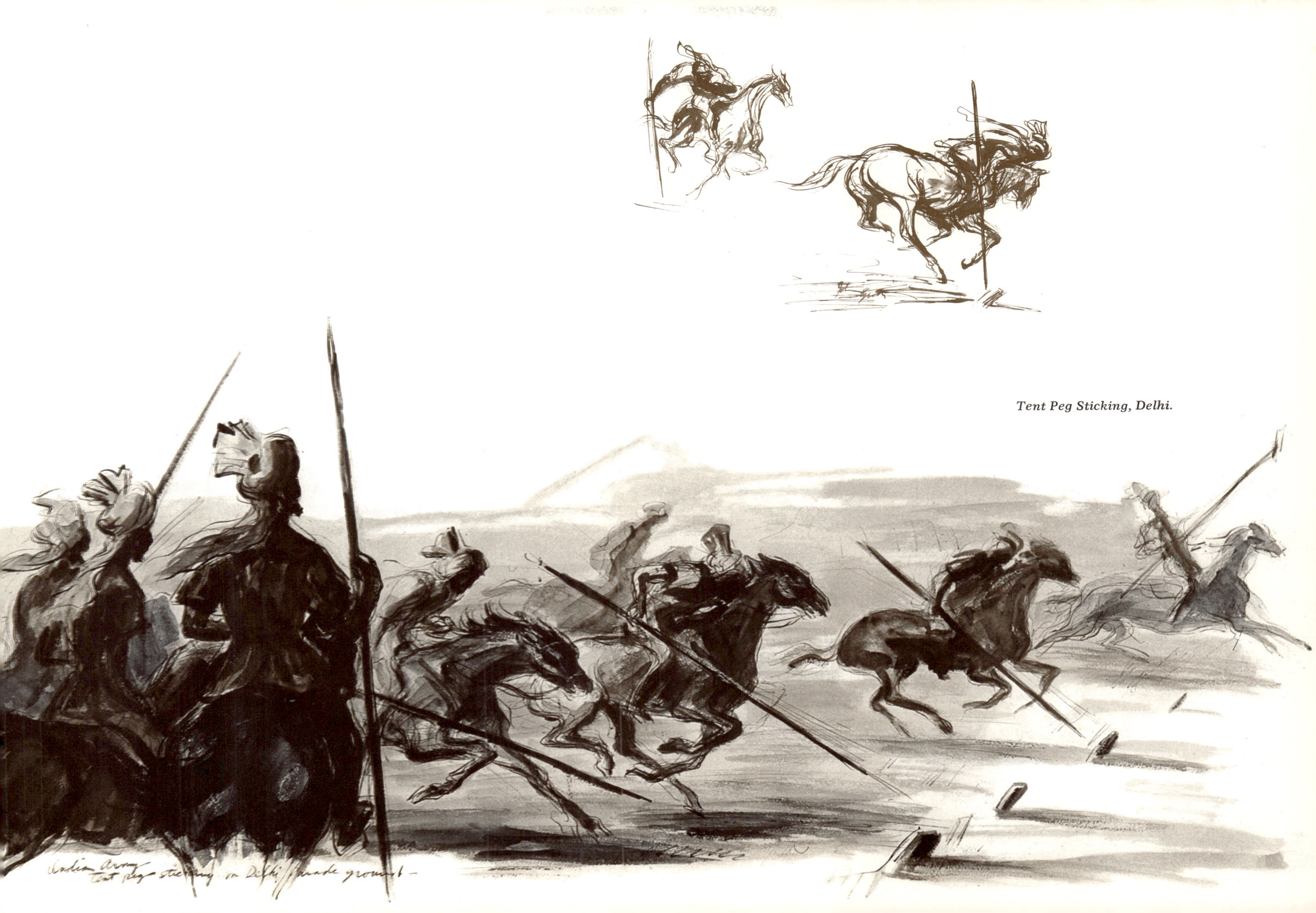

Tent Peg Sticking, Delhi.

Kite Fighting

The kite-fighting picture painted itself. The soaring shapes and colors composed themselves.

Perhaps it's because we have misplaced our sense of the sublime that in our heady race for the moon and beyond, Americans no longer are gratified at the sight of a kite dipping and dodging against a deep blue spring day. Certainly this loss of innocence is a fairly recent symptom. There was Benjamin Franklin with his handkerchief, his key and his lightning bolt—and Orville and Wilbur Wright were notable and inveterate kite buffs. But today adults who have a yen to fly a kite often cover themselves by bringing along a passel of kids, thus avoiding the chance that their sanity will be questioned.

If kite flying is a dying art in the Western world, however, such is not the case everywhere. Going back as far as the written record allows, there are accounts of sparkling, soaring kites—fashioned of rice paper and bamboo in the forms of butterflies, birds, fish and dragons with serpentine tails dancing in the sweet, soft-blown skies.

Nowhere is kiting pursued with greater passion than in Thailand— where legend has it that a love-struck lad met his maiden fair while chasing the string of a runaway kite. Beginning in February, when the brisk Lom Ta-Phao winds blow in from the south, a mad party of color and motion begins in the skies over Bangkok. The season ends in May, when the Lom Ta-Phao discreetly slips off into the north.

In Thailand young boys receive their first kites at about the same age Americans get their first baseball gloves. Thai kites come in some bizarre shapes: cobras, peacocks, bats, owls, hawks, tigers. But whatever kind he learns to fly, the young boy of Thailand dreams of growing up to become another Poon Uyvanyom—the Willie Mays, Babe Ruth and Ty Cobb of kite fighting wrapped up in one 5-foot, 2-inch, 110-pound, 55-year-old package.

The sport could be described as simply another version of the battle of the sexes. The kites come in two styles: The star-shaped mail (*chula*) and the smaller, diamond-shaped female (*pakpao*). The male sports five razor-sharp bamboo talons called *champas* (literally, fruit pickers), and the female is armed with a long lethal noose known as a *nhiang*. Each kite costs about $18 and is operated by a team that can range from four to twenty men, depending on the size of the kite. While the male kite attempts to capture the female with his talons, she in turn tries to snare him with her noose.

The rules of kite-fighting heavily favor the male. Only half the size of her opponent (85 sq. in.), the *pakpaos* must rely on much speed and a little guile. In some battles two females will swoop down on the big male much in the manner of fighter planes pecking away at a big bomber. Even if she catches her man, the female must then struggle to bring him to the ground on her side of a fence separating the two teams. Champion Poon is strictly a *chula* flyer. "I am a man, am I not?" he frequently explains. "And I like male kites."

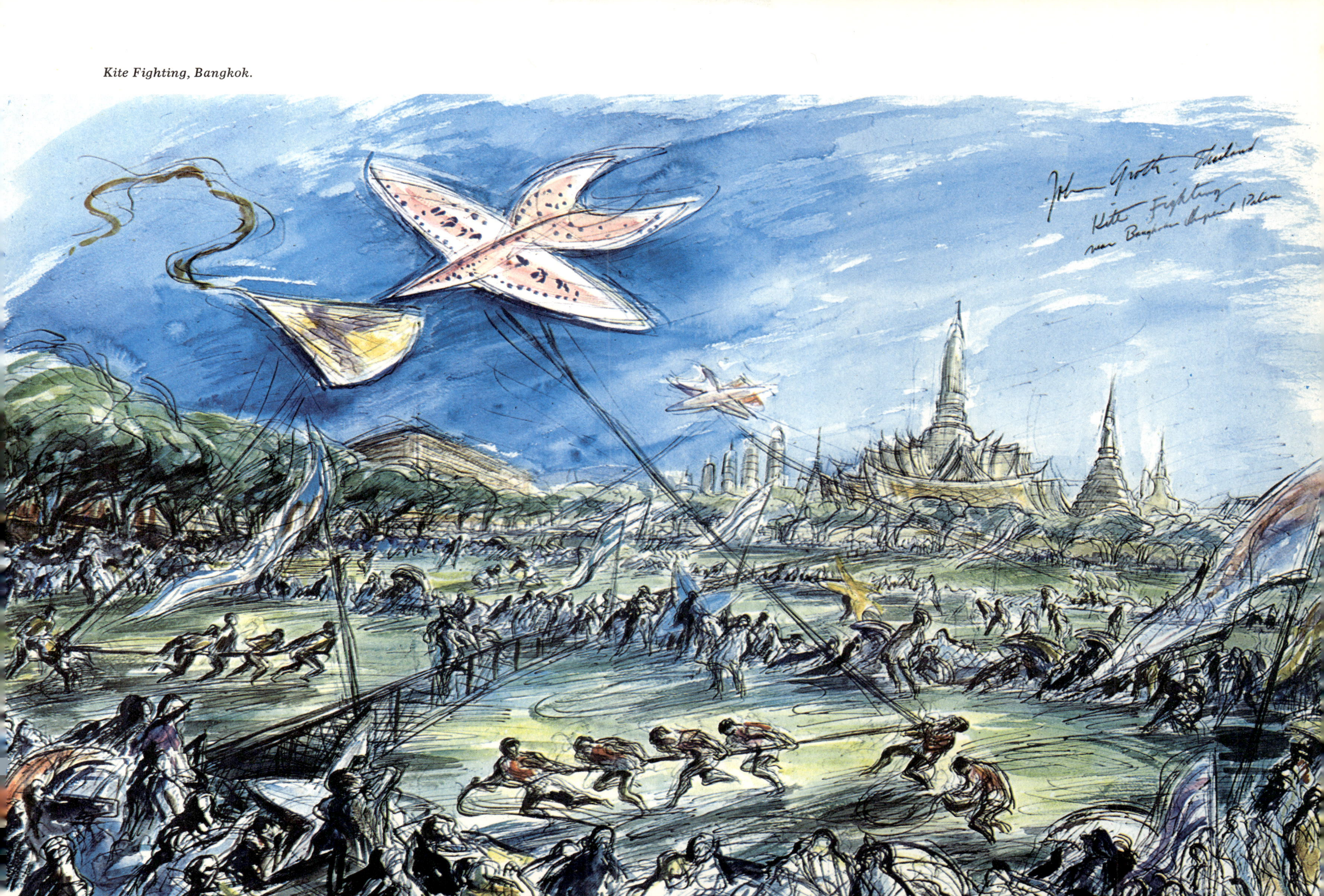

Kite Fighting, Bangkok.

Basque Games

Basques are a rugged people and their sports reflect their closeness to the soil and the traditions that they have kept alive despite an encroaching world.

The Basques are a people apart. Although the 6,000-square-mile region they inhabit straddles the Pyrenees between Spain and France, the 1.6 million inhabitants display an almost uncompromising ethnic solidarity. In their estimation they are neither French nor Spanish, they are Basques. With only the slightest encouragement the most uneducated among them will relate a detailed history of his people: how they withstood constant attacks from the Visigoths, Franks, Normans and even the feared Moors; how it was the Basques—and not the Moors, as credited by most historians—who slashed the rear guard of Charlemagne's army to pieces at Roncesvalles in 778 A.D. Even though the Basques have long been folded into either Spain or France, they still maintain a "national government" in Paris—a symbol of their fierce territorial and cultural pride.

So it is with their sports—almost all of which reflect their deep attachment to soil and sea. During the Basque Games, held annually in Bilbao, the major competitions are Stone Pulling, Scything, Log Splitting, Wood Chopping and Ox Pulling. But many of the Basques are townspeople, too, and several sports have grown out of the streets. For example, the ball-and-pin game of *boules* was literally born in an alleyway in Navarre several centuries ago and has since spread to

Italy in the form of *bocci* and to the United States, where it is called bowling.

Another Basque sport, a court game known in its homeland as *pelota,* was created in the small towns of the region and played against church walls. Devised some 300 years ago, *pelota* has since been highly refined and is among the most popular of international spectator and wagering sports. It is called Jai Alai.

Pelota remains a game of the people, a street game that requires only a small rubber ball and the side of a building. In the summer, when Spain's fierce sun blasts the villages, Catholic priests wrapped in their heavy cassocks can often be seen catching the hard little ball against the wall of the local church with a leather glove similar to a first baseman's mitt. Certainly they play for enjoyment and for exercise, but they also play to seem less remote to the young men of their parishes.

There is, however, a classic *pelota*. It is played in a *cancha* (a court 11 meters wide and 60 to 80 meters long), and the participants are divided into two teams of three, consisting of one forward and two backs. Each team plays with twelve balls, the first of which is flung against the wall by the *delatero*—forward—and must, in return, bounce beyond the section of the court so marked before the opposing side catches it and returns it to the wall. Each miss counts as a point for the opponents.

Exciting to observe, the game invariably involves heavy betting; prices constantly change according to the progress of the game. The betting is handled by bookmakers who stand in the front of the crowds, shouting the prices so rapidly that one would almost think he were at the New York Stock Exchange. The bets are placed by means of a small hollow wooden ball split into hemispheres. The money is deposited by the bettor, the top is screwed on and thrown down to the bookmaker. Payoffs are made the same way.

Although there are variations to the games, they are so esoteric that the average spectator would not detect them. Often the game is played inside—in a hall known as a *fronton*.

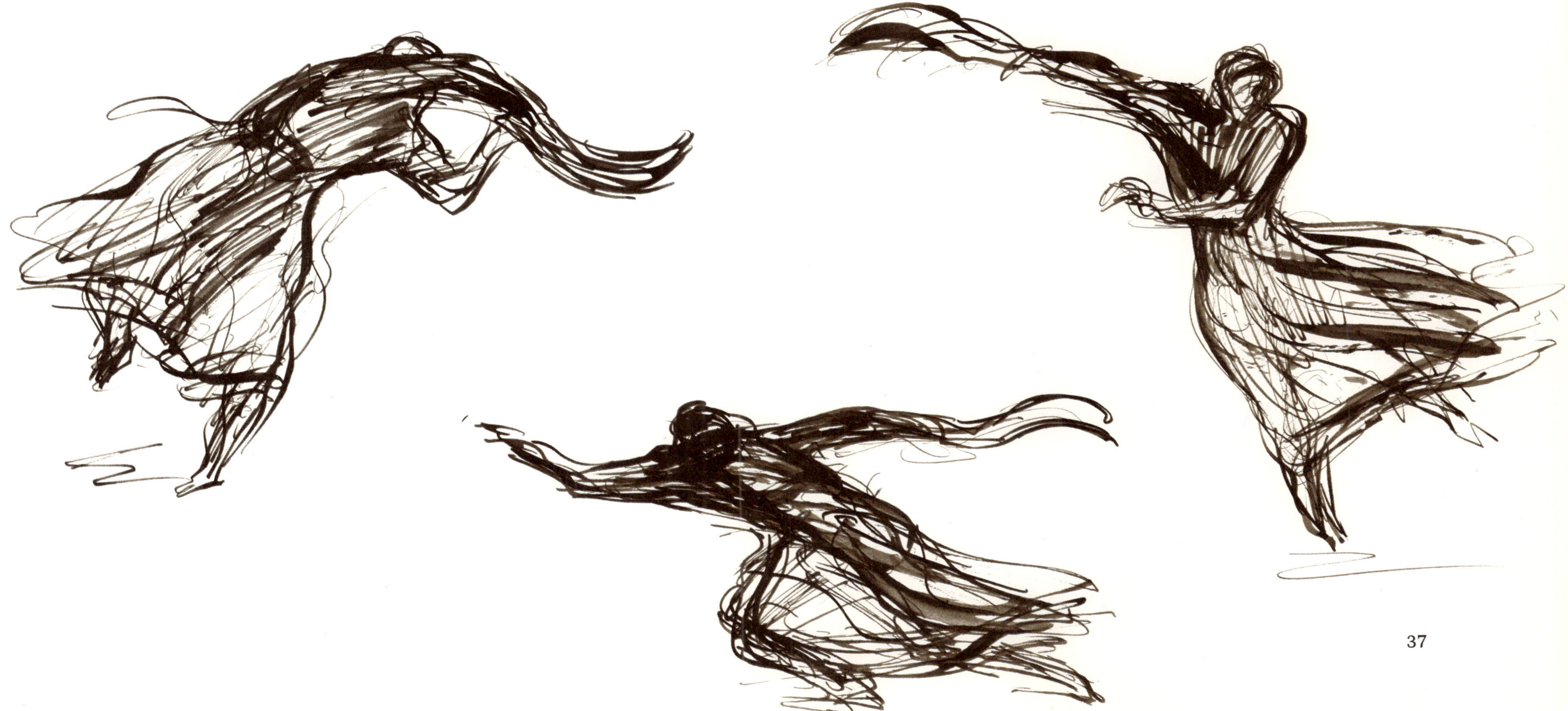

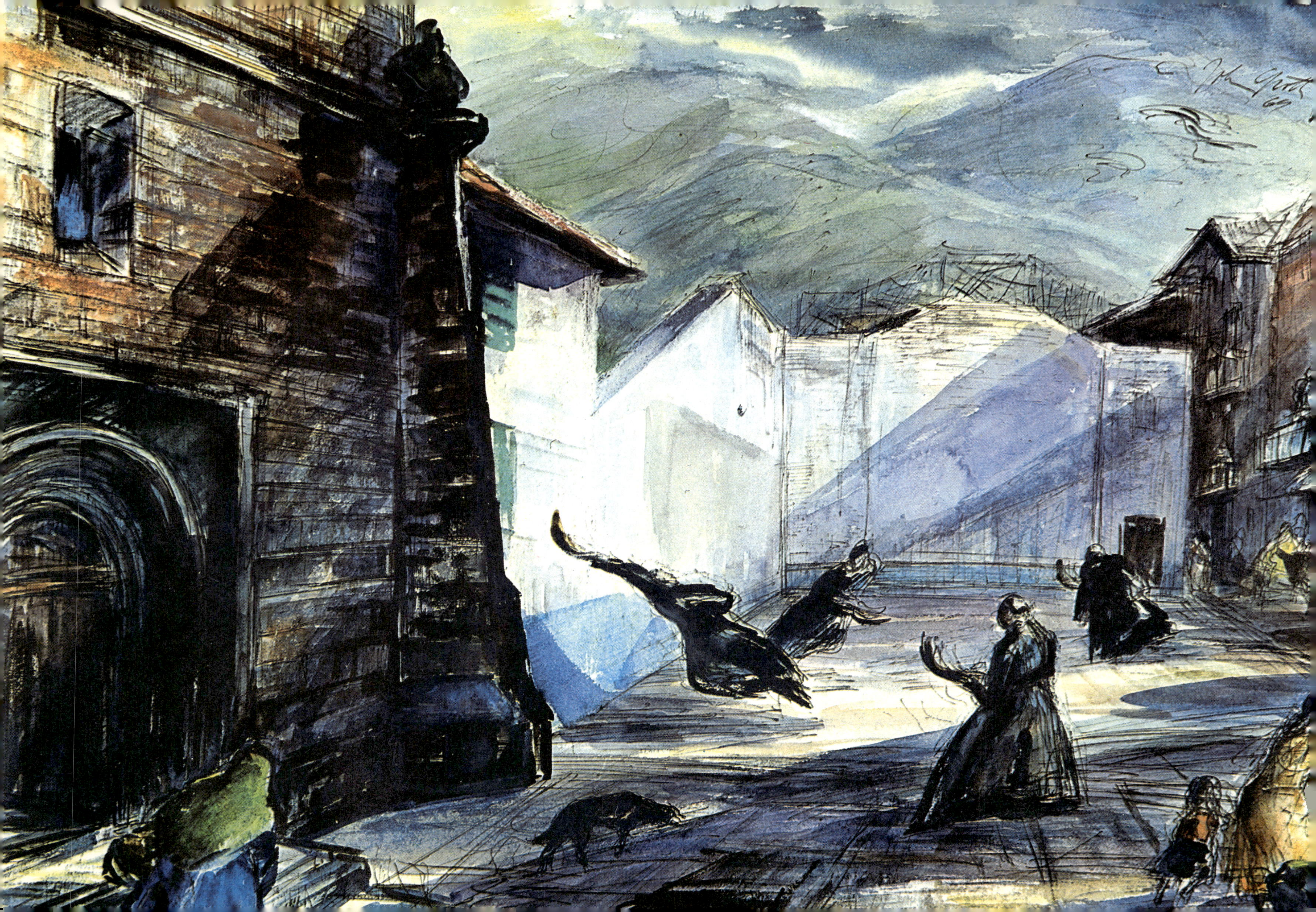

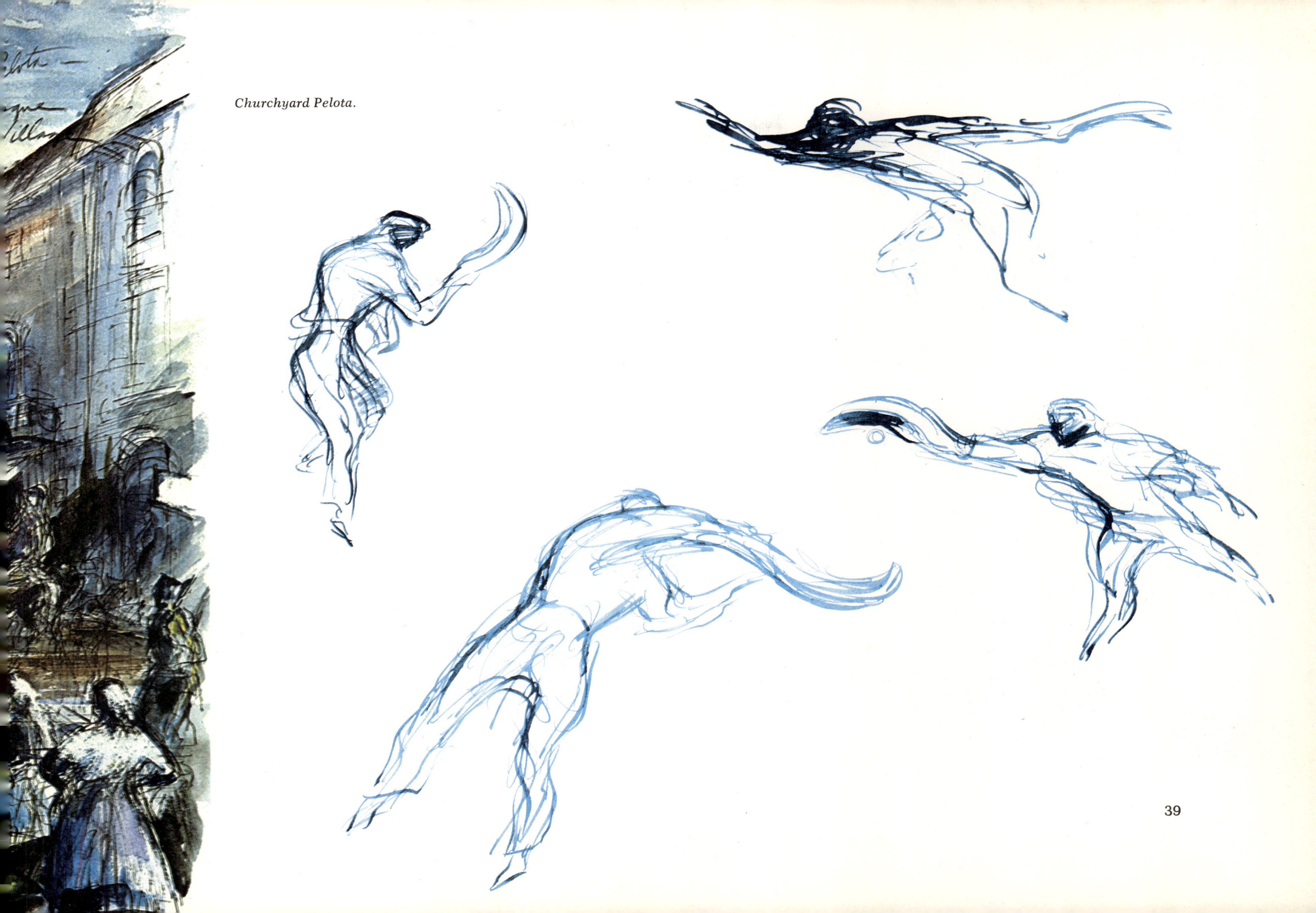

Churchyard Pelota.

39

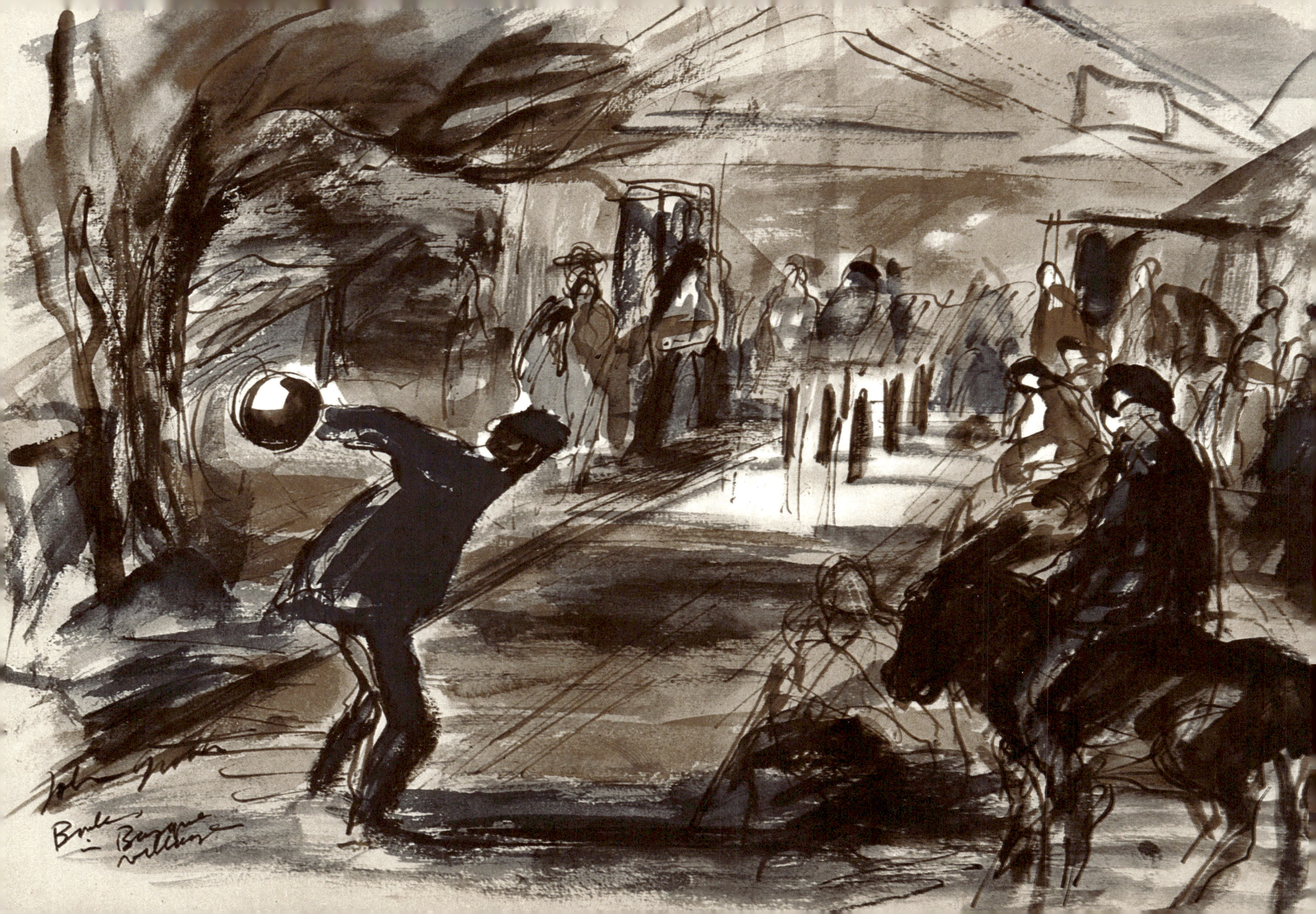

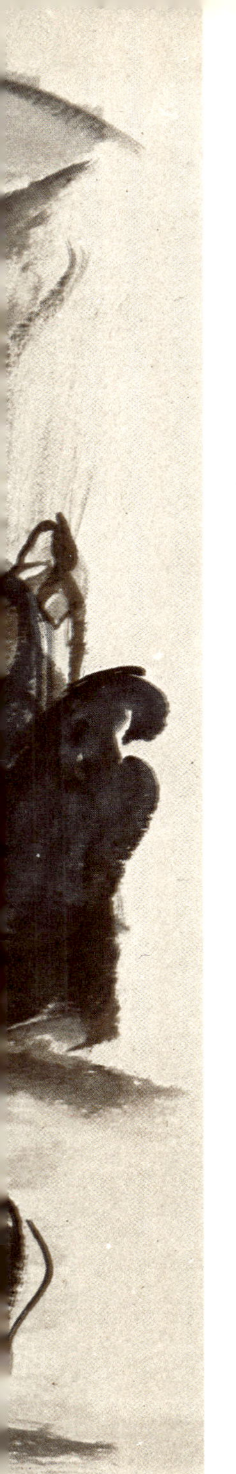

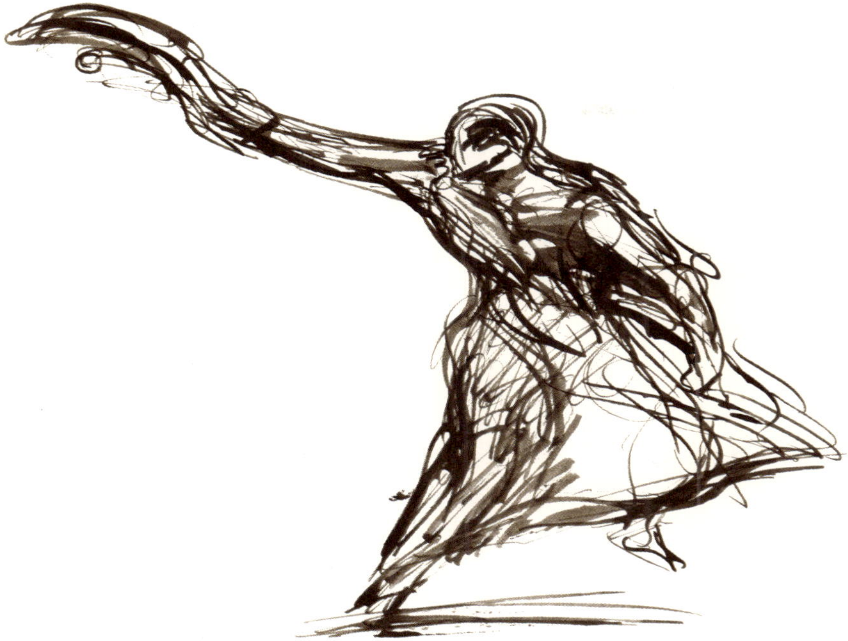

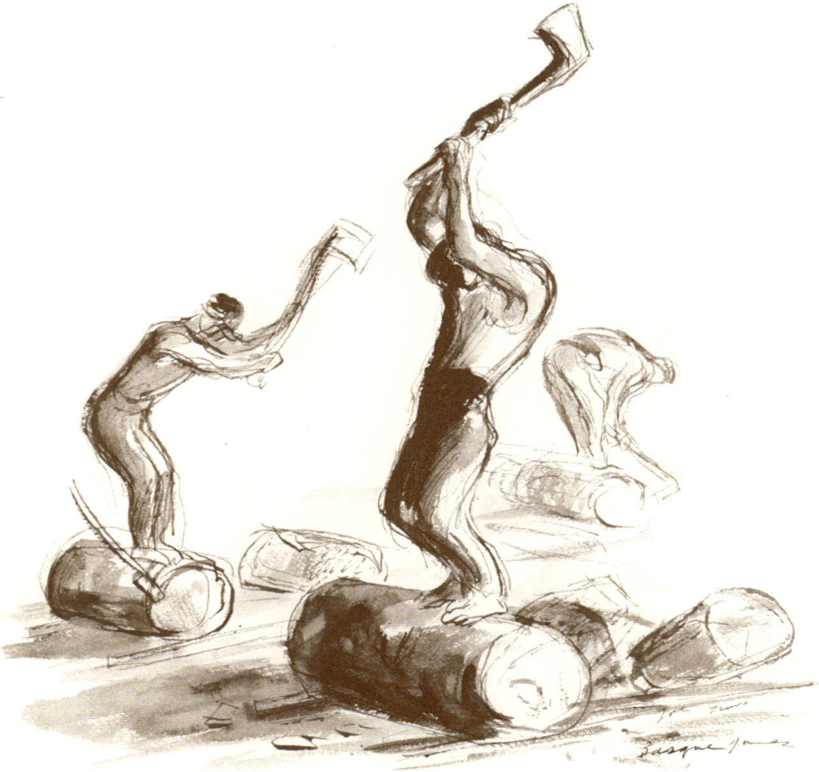

Basque Woodchopping Contest.

Boules—A Game of the Streets.

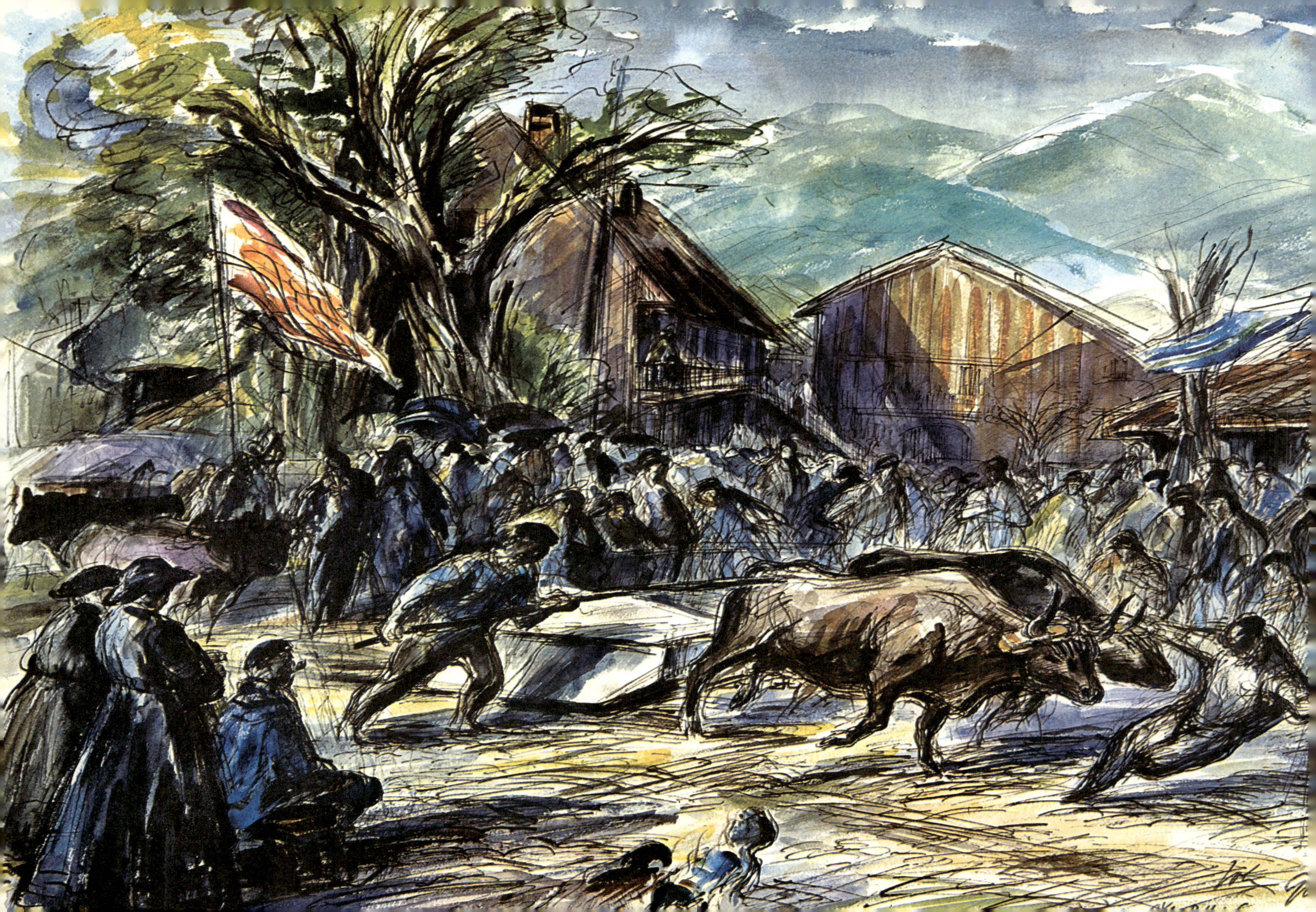

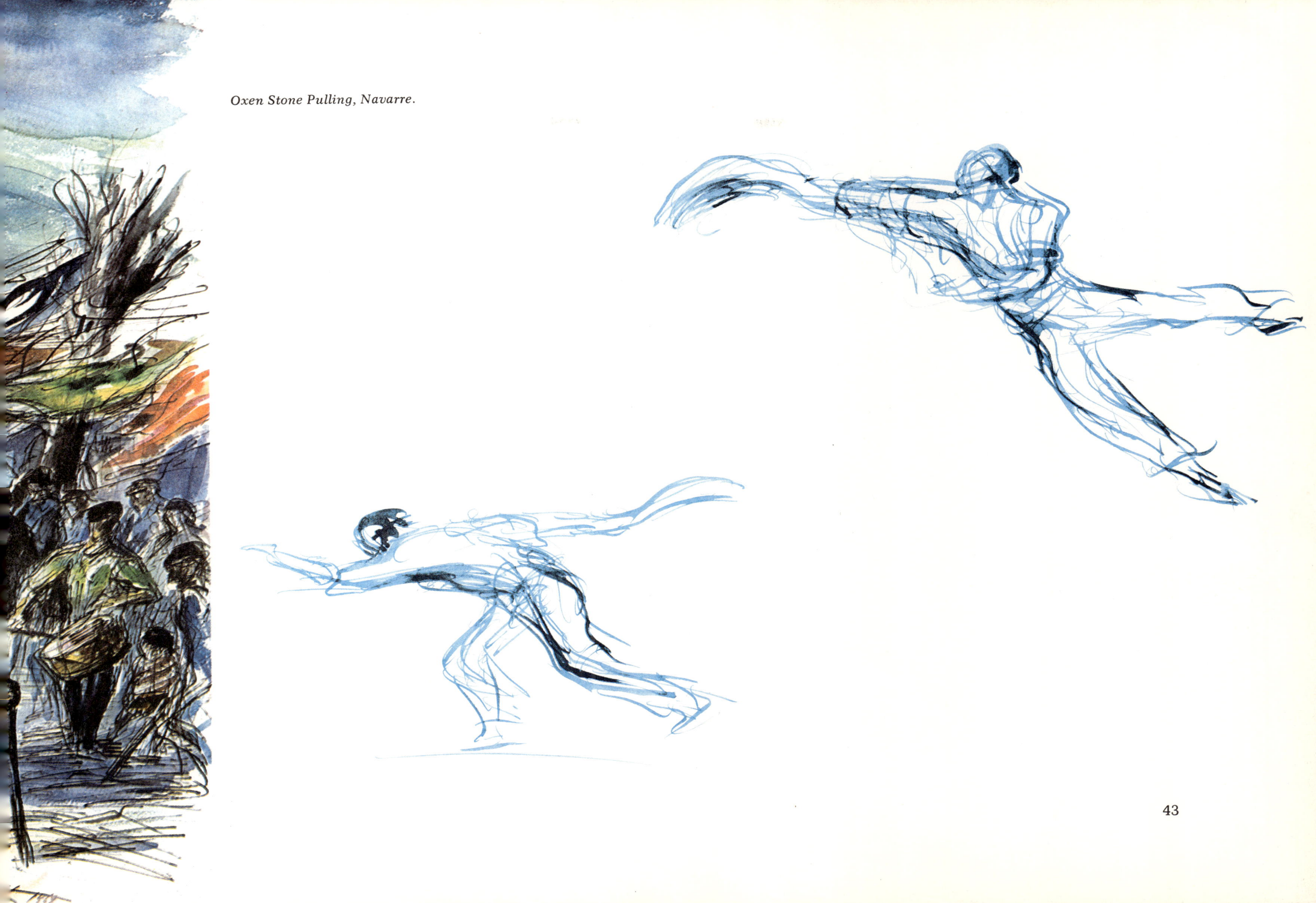
Oxen Stone Pulling, Navarre.

Highland Games

To me, the games were perfect material—the moors, the mountains, the sports and most of all the athletes, cool and loose in their kilts and undershirts, enjoying being Scots.

The exact year of their birth has never been determined but the Highland Games of Scotland certainly go back well over 500 years. Originally, the games—mainly athletic competitions stressing feats of strength and speed afoot—were held during the hunts, military exercises and general gatherings of the clans of the Scottish Highlands.

The games were largely confined to what moderns call track and field events—flat and hurdle races, long and high jumps, the pole vault, hammerthrowing and putting the weight (or shot). But an exclusively Highland event, without which no program was complete, was tossing the caber, an awesome contest in which athletes hoist a fir pole 17 feet long and weighing about 90 pounds, run with it and hurl it for distance.

The games were interrupted in Scotland by the Jacobite uprising in 1745, which broke up the clans. They were resumed about 1835, with the famed Lonach gathering at Braemar and Strathdon. Lonach was followed between 1864 and 1871 by resumption of the meetings at Balater and Aboyne, two lovely Scottish villages deep in the Aberdeenshire Highlands, in the valley of the famed salmon stream, the River Dee, and hard by Balmoral, summer castle of the British royal family. Around the same time the Argyll gathering was reestablished at

Oban and the Cowal gathering at Dunoon. New gatherings came into being in other Highland regions, and today there are forty major meetings in Scotland and many others elsewhere in the world, usually sponsored by local Caledonian societies. Their character is essentially the same as the original meetings in the Highlands, but there now are competitions in bagpipe music and in such native highland dances as the reel, the fling, the sword dance and the Seann Triubhas. Although these dances had always been considered male dances, early in the twentieth century the Scots removed the ban on women competitors provided they not wear the kilt—which was and is strictly male garb.

However much the individual program of events may be expanded, it is a safe to assume that tossing the caber will always be a part of the Highland Games, wherever staged. When John Groth attended the meeeting at Aboyne, he executed a powerful watercolor of the caber event. He was fascinated by the central figure, a burly Scotsman with heavy shoulders bent forward under the weight of the fir tree trunk, forearms gripping the caber, muscular legs churning the turf to get up speed. Groth's enjoyment of the Highland Games very nearly gave him a chance to test the efficiency of Scottish hospitals.

"My wife had suggested," John said, "that I would be able to cover more events by using a movie camera. I decided to try it out on the hammer-thrower. I focused on the man as he began to whirl, arms extended and hands gripping the wood shaft of the hammer—the head of which is really an iron ball. I started the camera rolling and was peering through the finder to keep it true on the thrower as he spun faster and faster. Suddenly I realized that the hammer was getting larger and larger. Instinctively, I ducked just as that damned cannonball went over my head with inches to spare. I had seen the man whirling to build up his leverage but I had not seen him let go of the handle. That ball nearly put a new part in my hair."

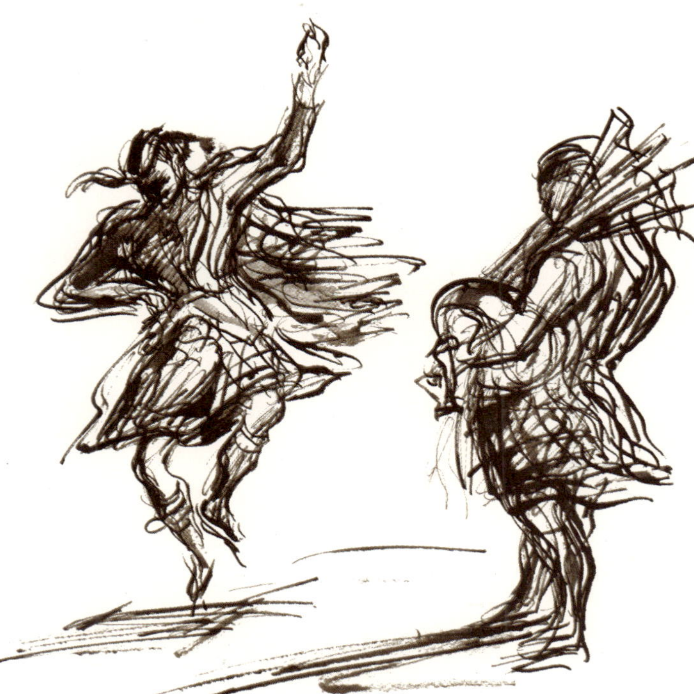

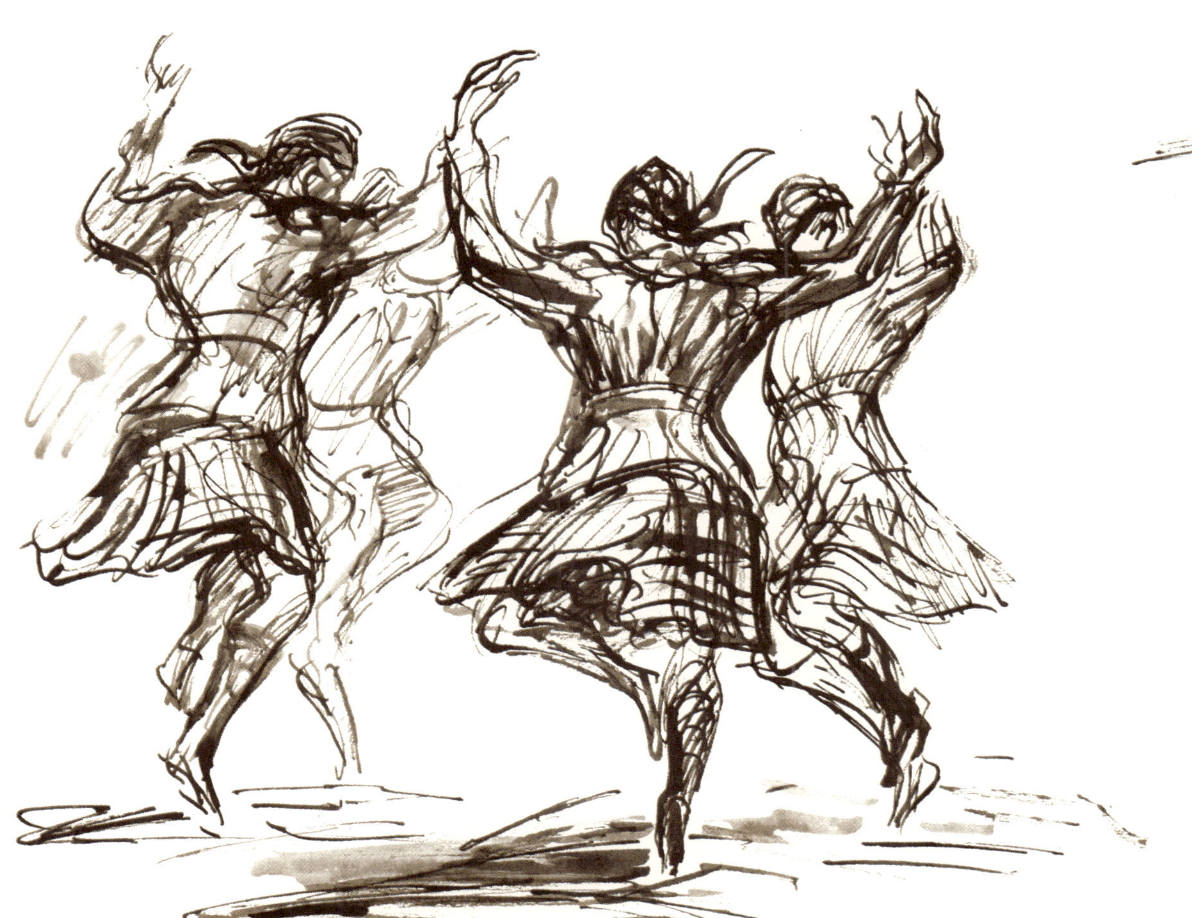

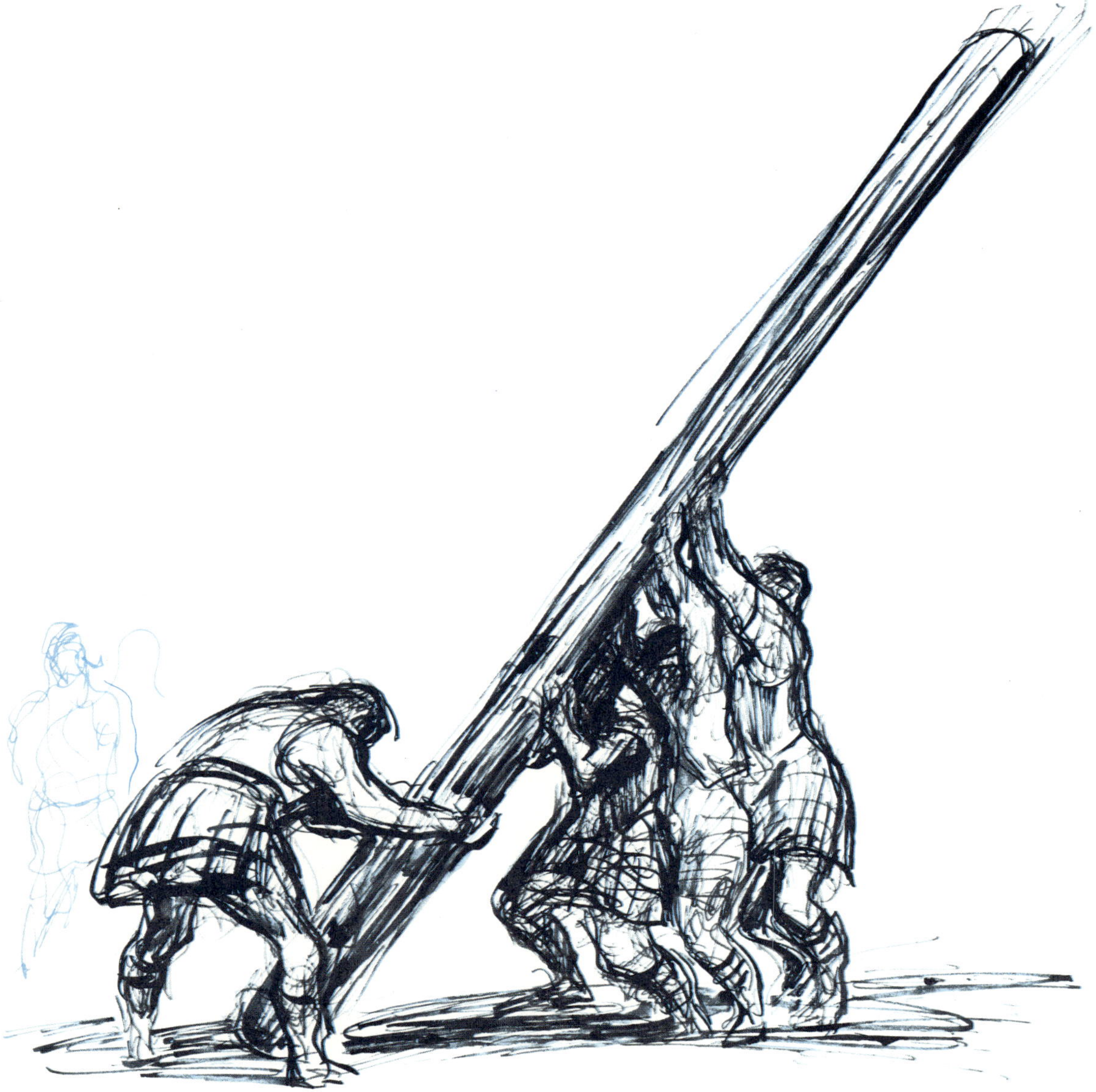

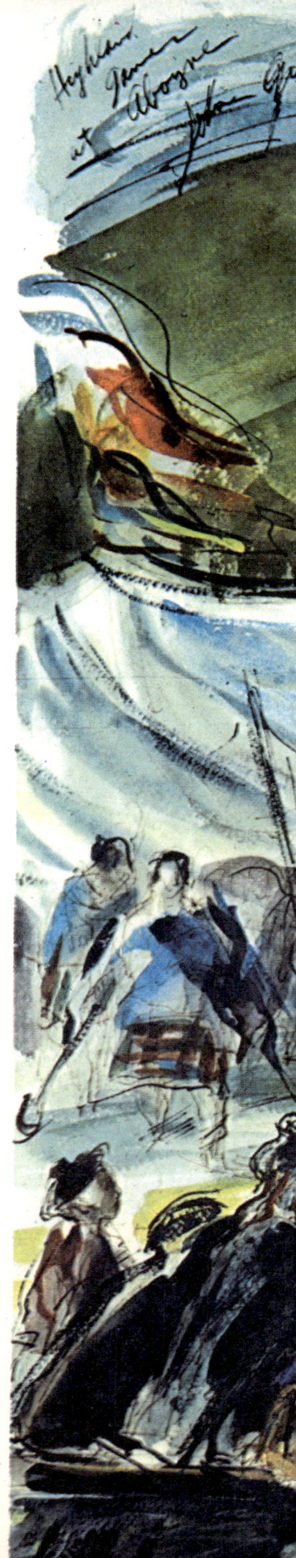

Tossing the Caber at Aboyne.

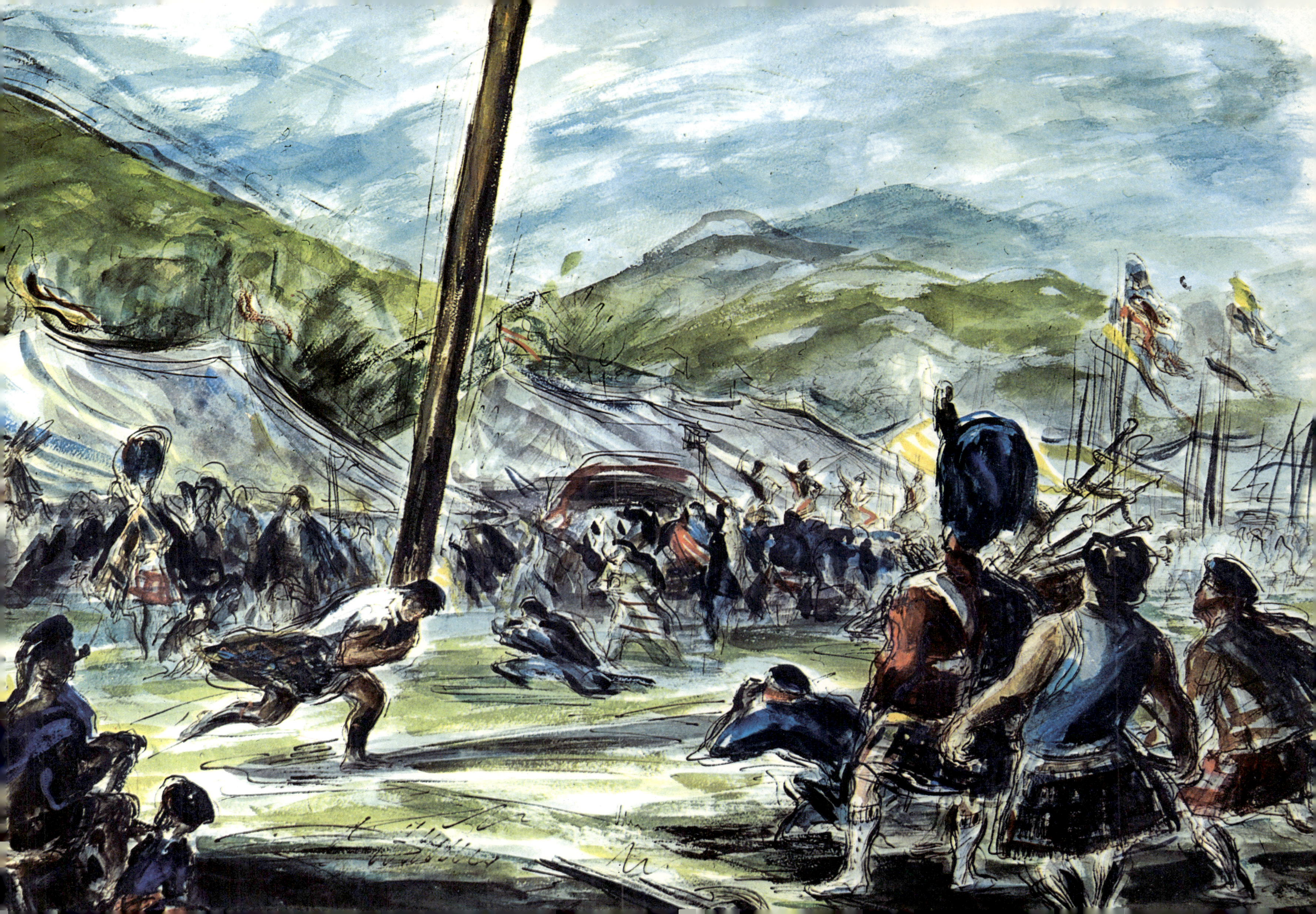

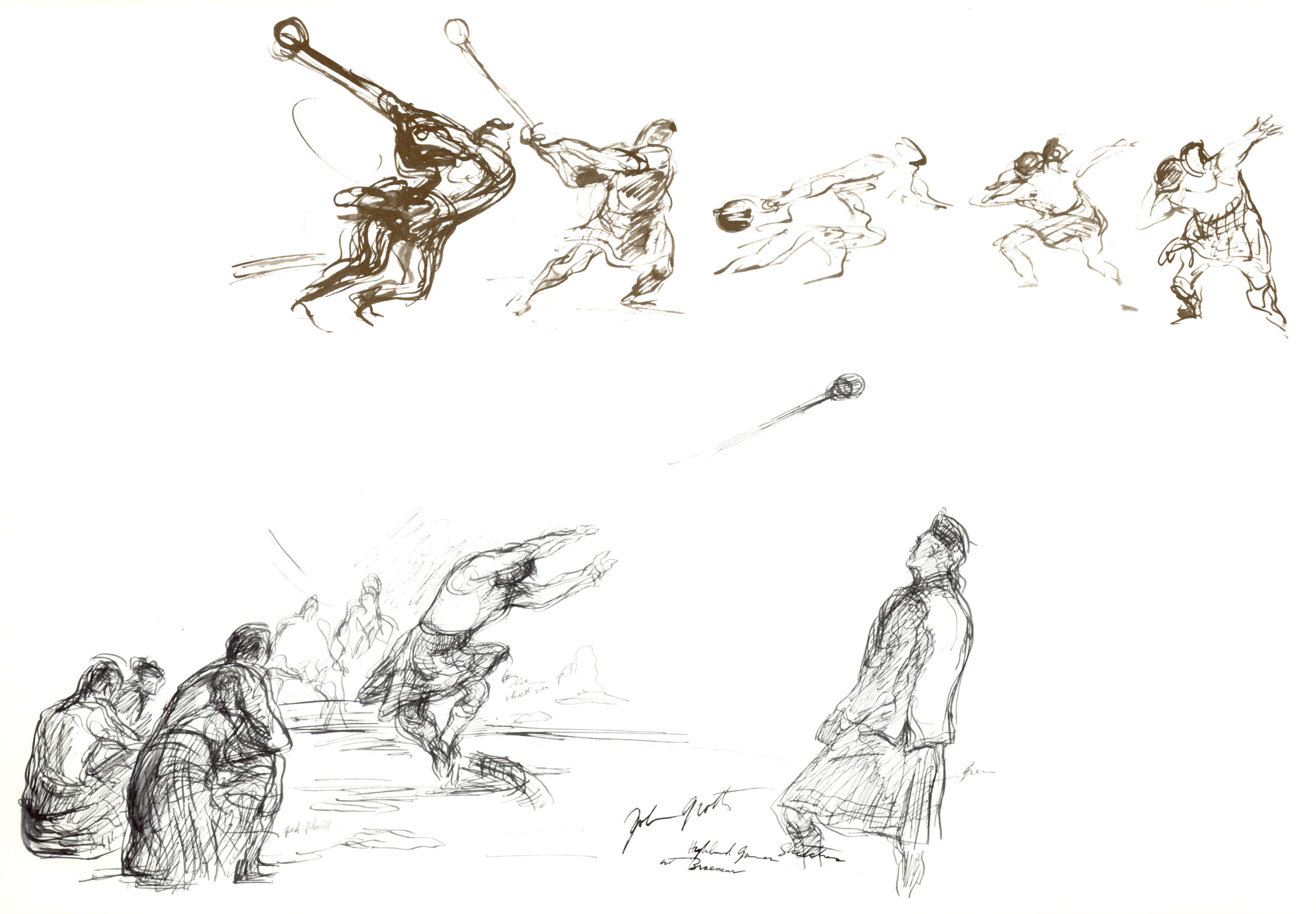

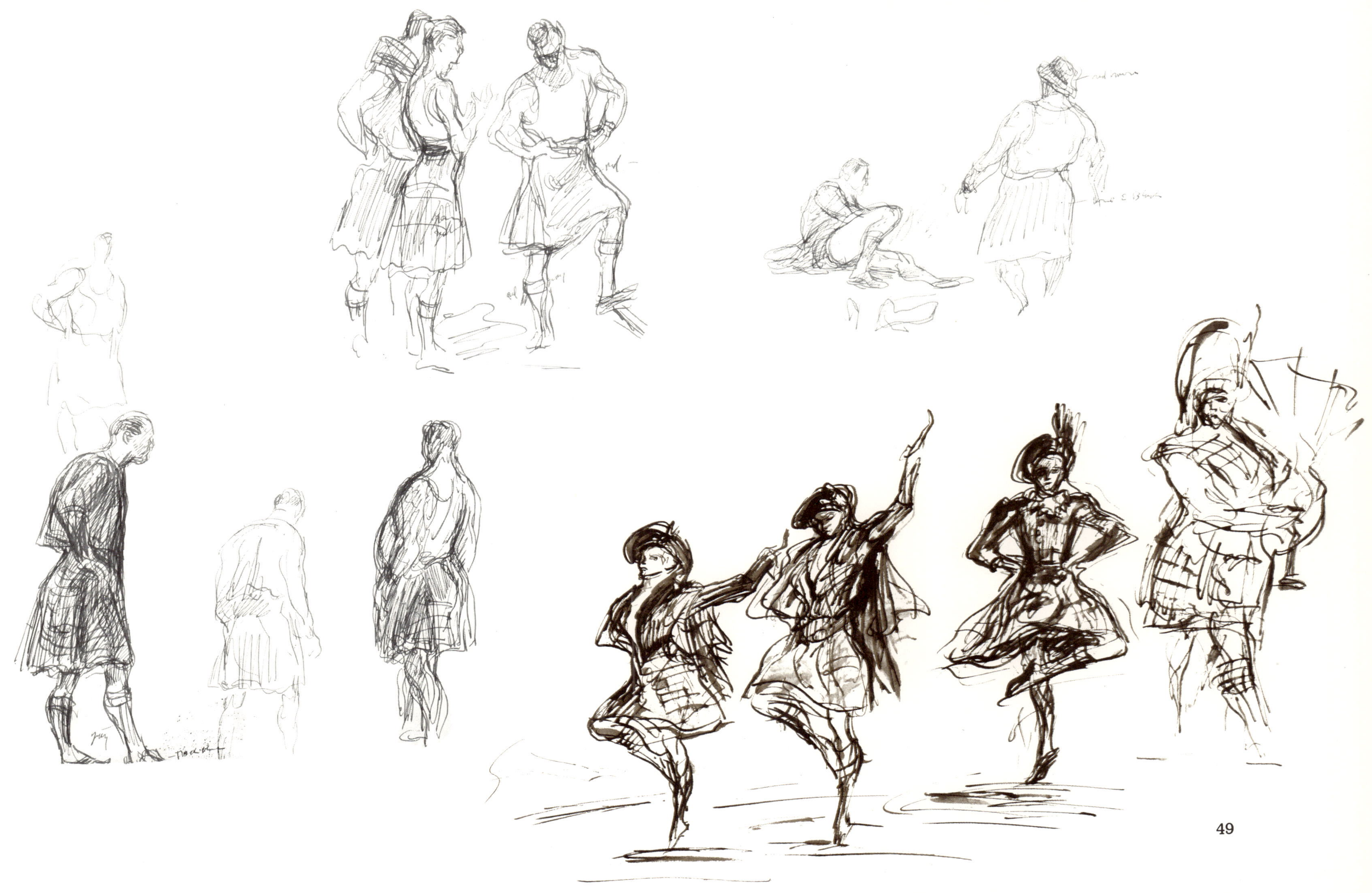

Traditional Football

While working in the twin shadow of Michelangelo's David and Cellini's Perseus, I felt almost as though they were looking over my shoulder.

As its name would imply, traditional football is one of the earliest forms of a sport that has taken on a number of different techniques—including soccer, U.S. football, rugby, hurley, International Association football and others. The original game was called *harpastum*, a rugged competition played widely by the Romans . . . who are believed to have adopted the sport from the Greeks.

Traditional football, which is played annually in the Partito al Calcio of Florence, seems a combination of all of the various forms—including wrestling. Played with a round ball much like that used in soccer, traditional football is certainly one of the most primitive forms, since its practitioners are restrained by the sparest set of rules. For example, the ball may be thrown, kicked, butted; and the defensemen may use virtually any tactic to stem the advance—tackling, tripping, kicking, etc. So rough was the sport that when the English adopted their own version after the Roman invasion, the game was soon outlawed. The reason: Too many of the young men preferred it to archery, and it was thought the game would indirectly detract from England's military effectiveness.

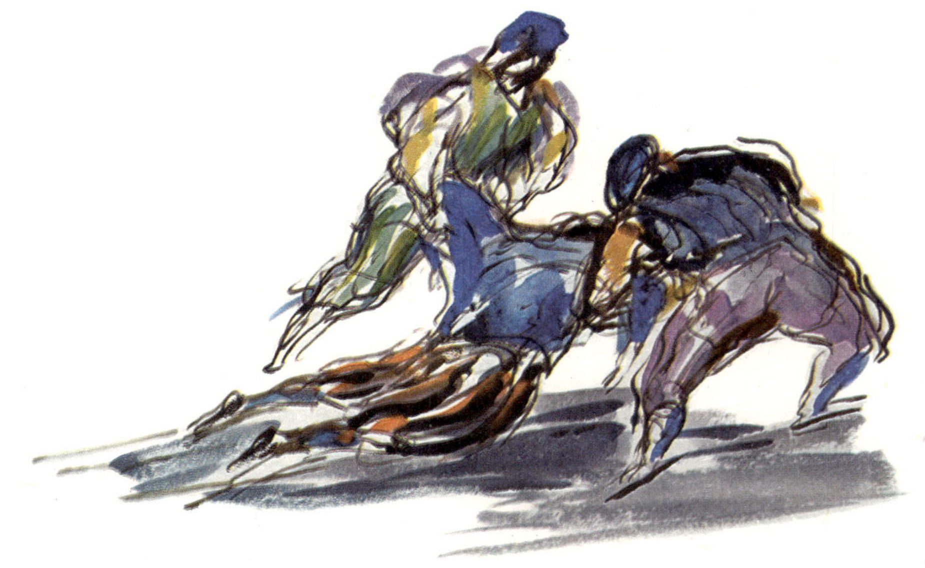

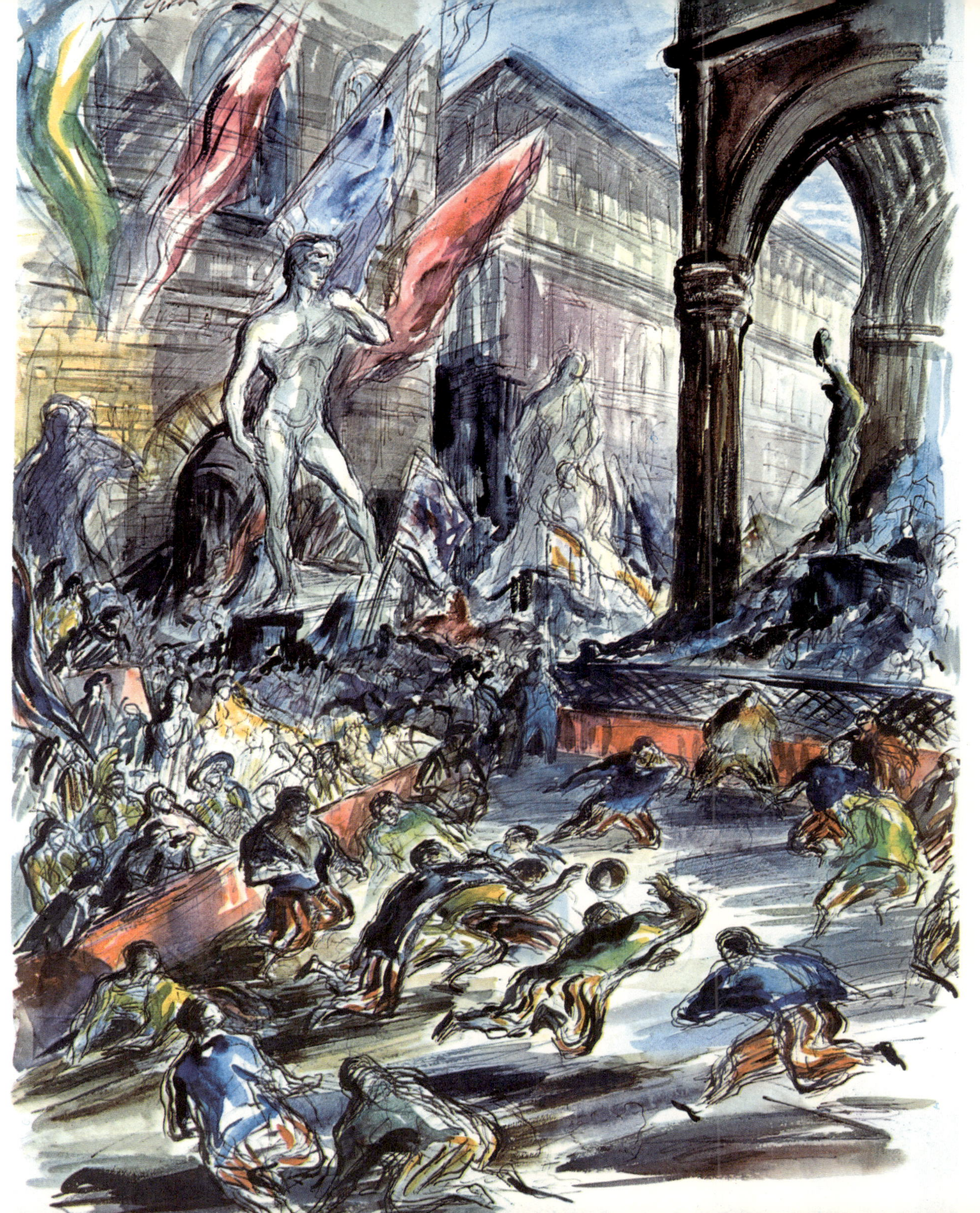

Traditional Football, Florence.

Elephant and Camel Racing

The elephant race is literally an earth-shaking event—like a huge gray mass pounding down the stretch. The camel race stirs a sandstorm with a medley of flailing legs and swaying humps in the dash for the finish.

Perhaps the most closely followed events in any Asian festival are the animal competitions. Often grueling, quite savage encounters, the competitions vary widely from country to country. In Thailand tiny fighting fish duel to the death in large glass tanks at an annual festival held outside Bangkok, while in Kabul Afghans bet heavily on the bloody outcome of a battle between pocket-sized partridges. In India cheetahs are set loose to capture and slaughter sambhar deer, and in Arabia falconers unleash their feathered charges against gazelles and bustards.

Then there are the races. Every four-legged animal that can possibly be kept on a course is raced in Asia: Bedouins ride swift Arabian horses across the desert plains; Afghans compete aboard stumpy Mongol ponies; and in Ceylon miniature bullocks pull high-wheeled carts around small half-mile tracks.

Perhaps the most ceremonious competition of all is the elephant race. To record the action Groth arrived in Kandy, Ceylon, where, he had been informed, elephant racing is held periodically. Shortly after his arrival he learned that "periodically" means approximately once every century. The last time they raced elephants in Kandy was when Queen Elizabeth II visited Ceylon on a world tour in the twenties.

Convinced that elephant racing was indeed one of the world's rarest sports, John decided to arrange the twentieth century's second elephant race. After leasing fifteen elephants and as many riders (mahouts), he convinced the local school superintendent to give his kids a holiday so that he would have a decent-sized crowd for the race. The holiday, however, was not necessary. On the day of the John Groth Elephant Stakes, the entire town was in attendance.

Using a field about 200 yards long and half as wide, the elephants lined up at the post each carrying a turbaned, tawny jockey wielding a steel-tipped prodder. "I was amazed at how fast they ran," says Groth. "As I watched them gallop, I realized how much like horses elephants are." The race lasted exactly an hour. The winner was Rajah—by a trunk. Following his well-earned victory, Rajah was led to a nearby river where he cooled off with a four-hour bath.

On the other side of the Suez Canal, camels race one another across the Jordanian desert. Rolling and rocking like ships in a storm the stilt-legged, gangling beasts display surprisingly fluid form, as evidenced in Groth's renderings. "The race absolutely fascinated me," says Groth. "The camels moved with an incredible grace, giving one the illusion that they travel in slow motion." Not quite. In peak condition a camel can hit speeds of 30 miles per hour and may sustain the pace for two or three miles—more than enough to cover the Trans-Jordan race of just under a mile-and-a-half in surprisingly quick time.

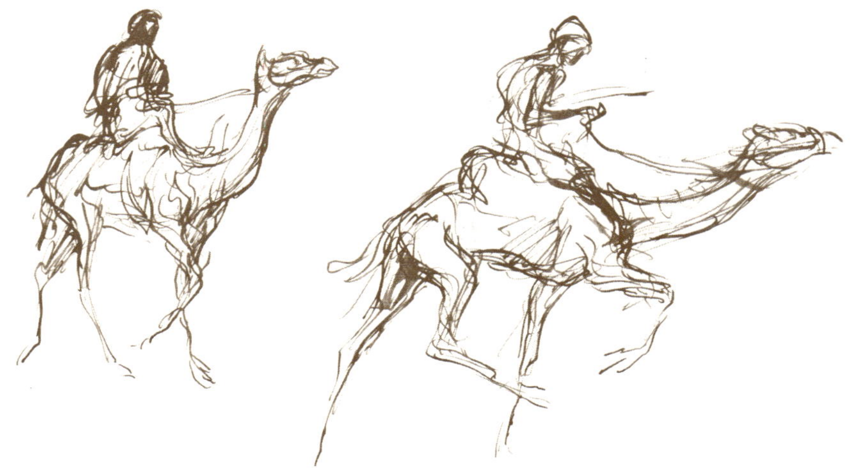

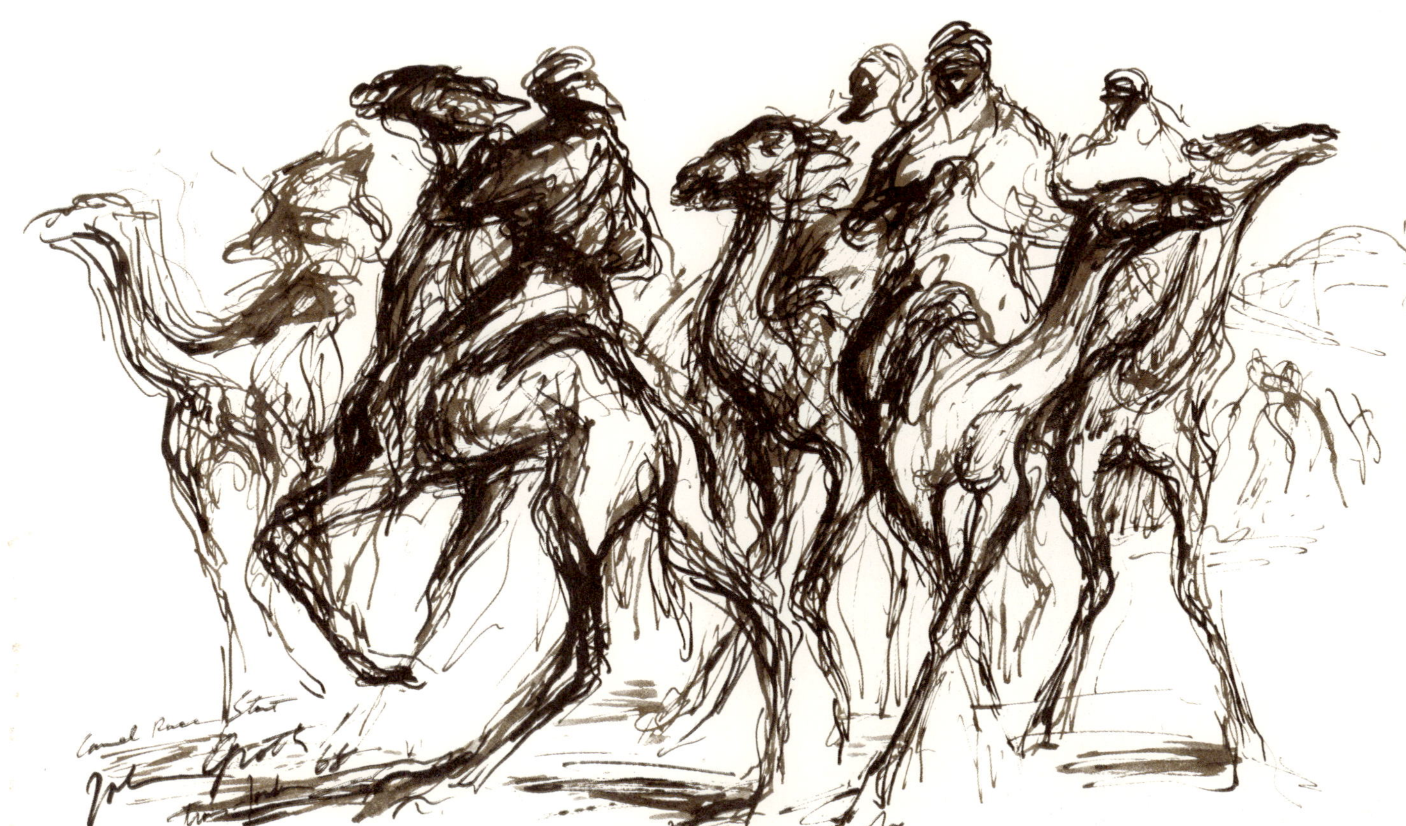

Milling Around at the Start.

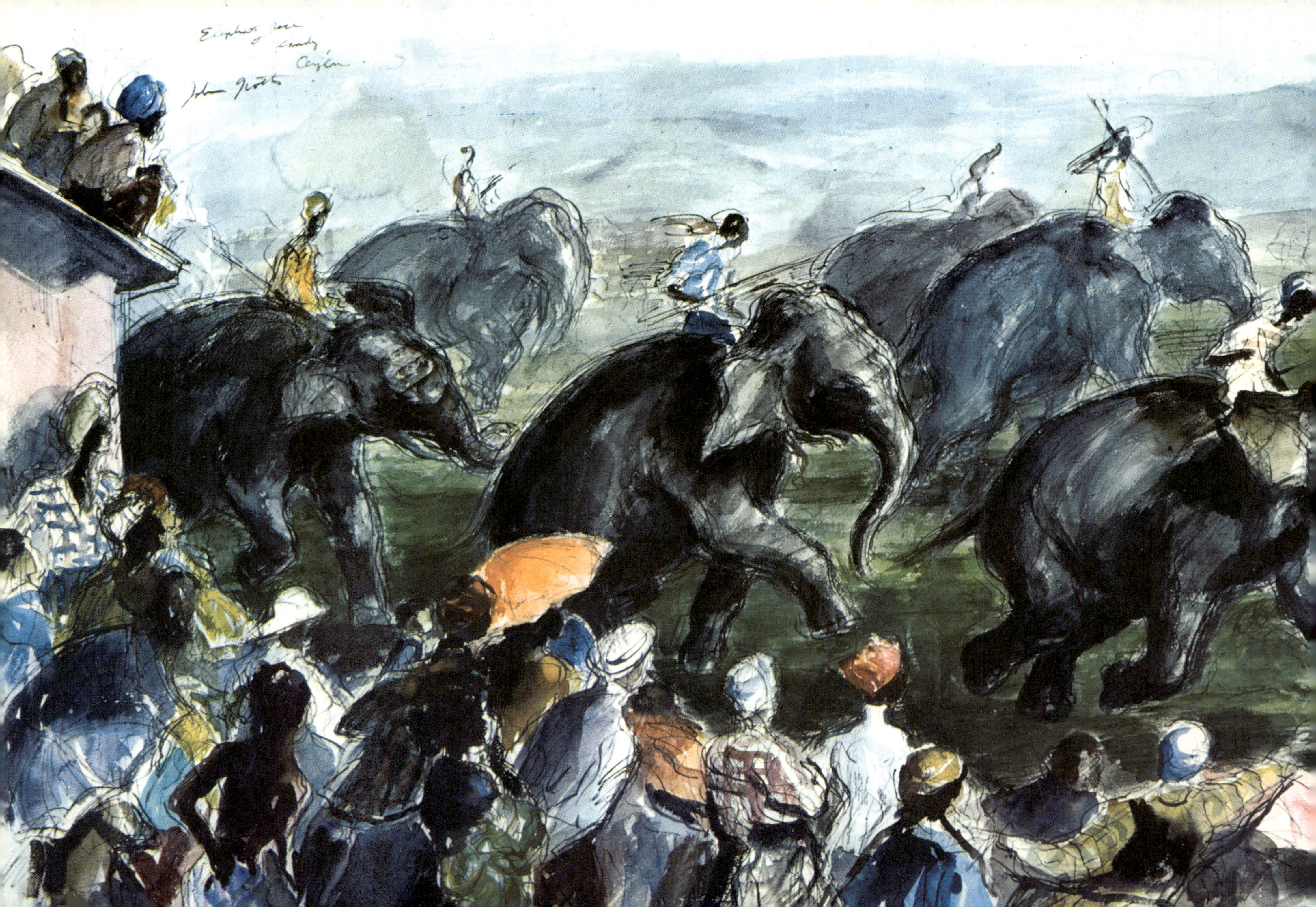

Elephant race
Kandy
Ceylon
John Scott

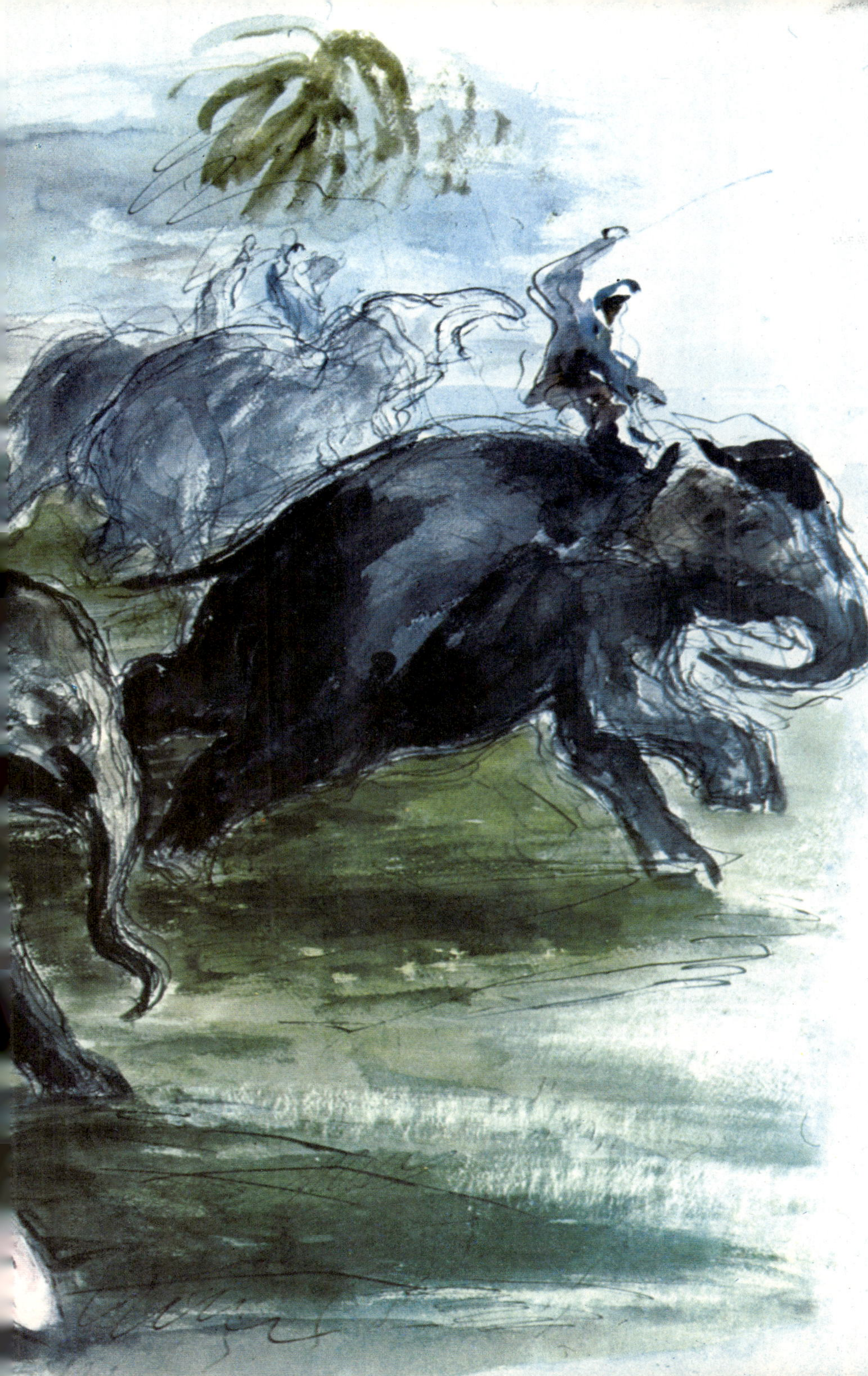

Race of the Elephants, Kandy.

Camel Racing, Amman.

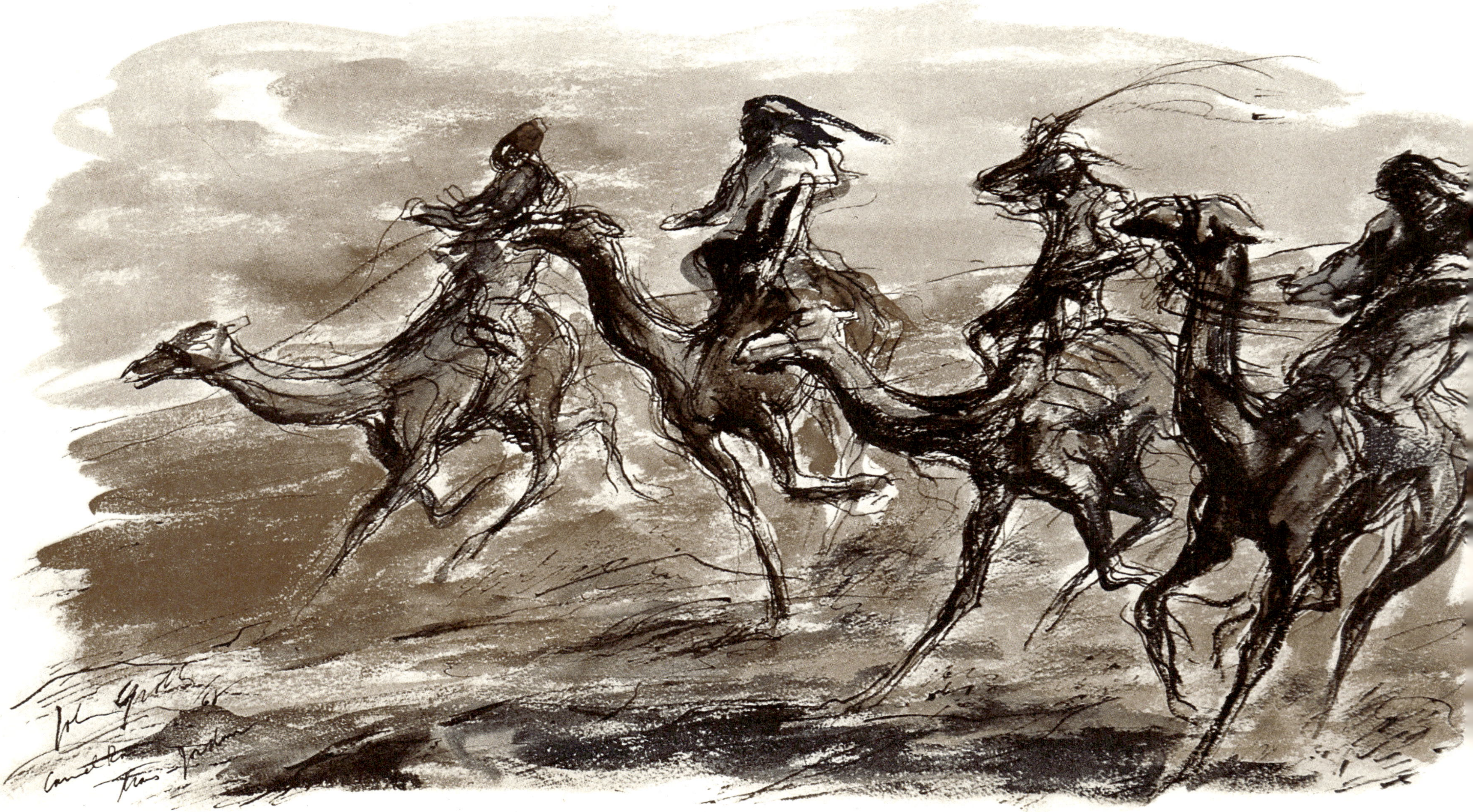

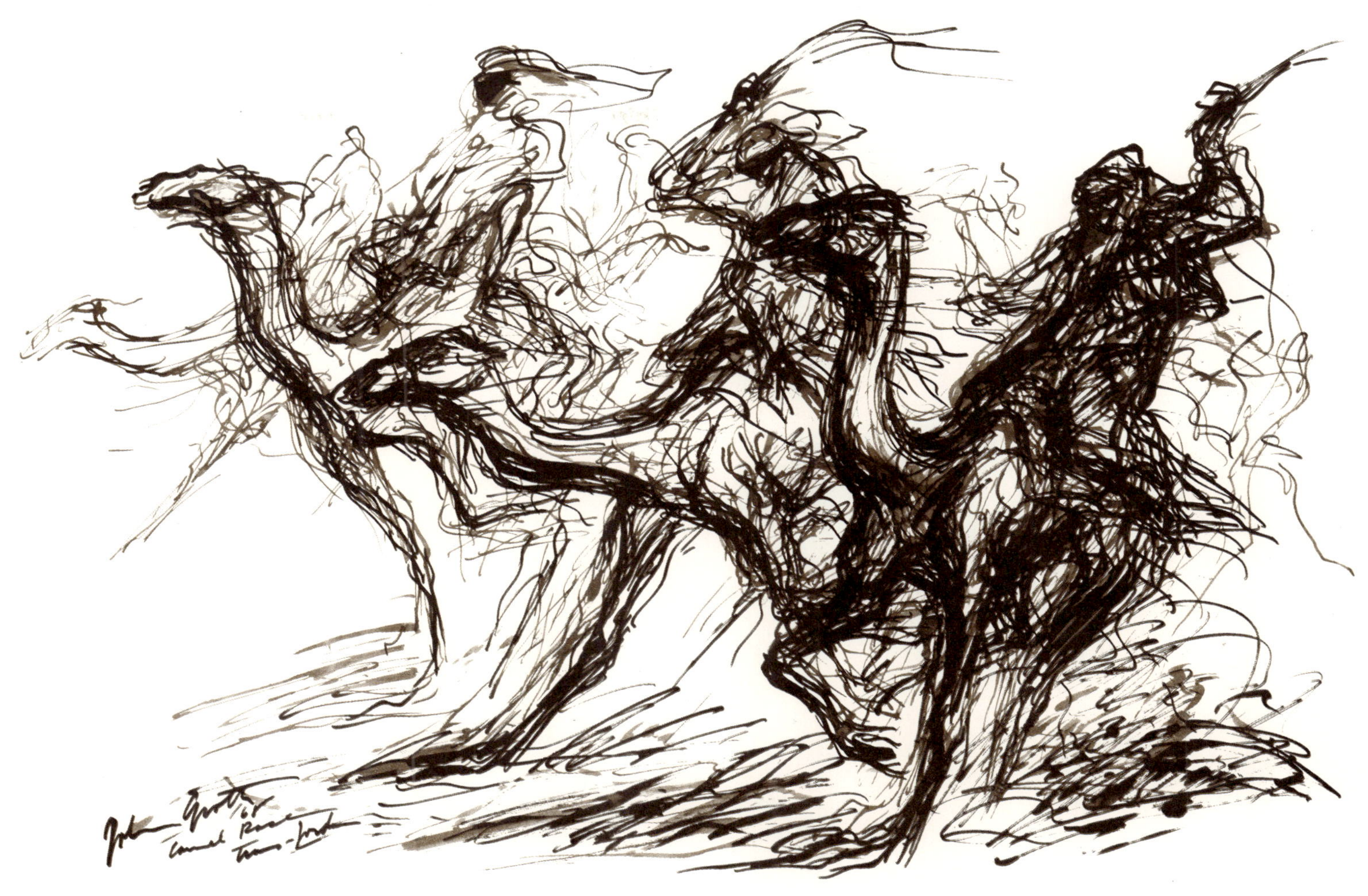

Tilting the Ring

Aside from windmills, the tilting of the ring competition provided the only visual excitement in my trip through the flat, ordered land of Rembrandt.

The midday sun smacks the flat, hard fair grounds in Walcheren, Holland, and several thousand spectators—seemingly unmindful of the heat in their sixteenth-century costumes—begin to stir. The colorful man on the hulking farm horse reaches the end of the dirt track and turns his steed, like a big jet poised for takeoff. In a single motion the rider lowers his lance and digs his spurred heels into the bareback steed's mammoth flanks. Slowly, horse and rider gain momentum. The crowd begins rumbling, its volume swelling as the big animal picks up speed and closes on the small ring suspended by a wire between two 15-foot-high poles. Now the horse is going his best and the crowd noise has scaled its highest decibel, men shouting encouragement, maidens—in their puffed-up short-sleeved blouses under brilliant pinafores—screeching. The lance goes up, hits the edge of the suspended ring and sets it to spinning and sparkling in the sun.

Although a far cry from its ancestral beginnings, which involved shining knights astride sleek steeds, their helmet plumes streaming behind in the charge, the modern version of Tilting the Ring is no less chivalric an attraction in the eyes of the contemporary farm maidens. Like so many rustic sports, the event affords the district's young men to display talents other than pitching hay, cultivating fields and milking the cows. For the Dutch farming community tilting the ring is also a kind of "coming-out" ritual; according to tradition the winner of the event has his pick of the available maidens.

Scoring a Point, Walcheren Fair.

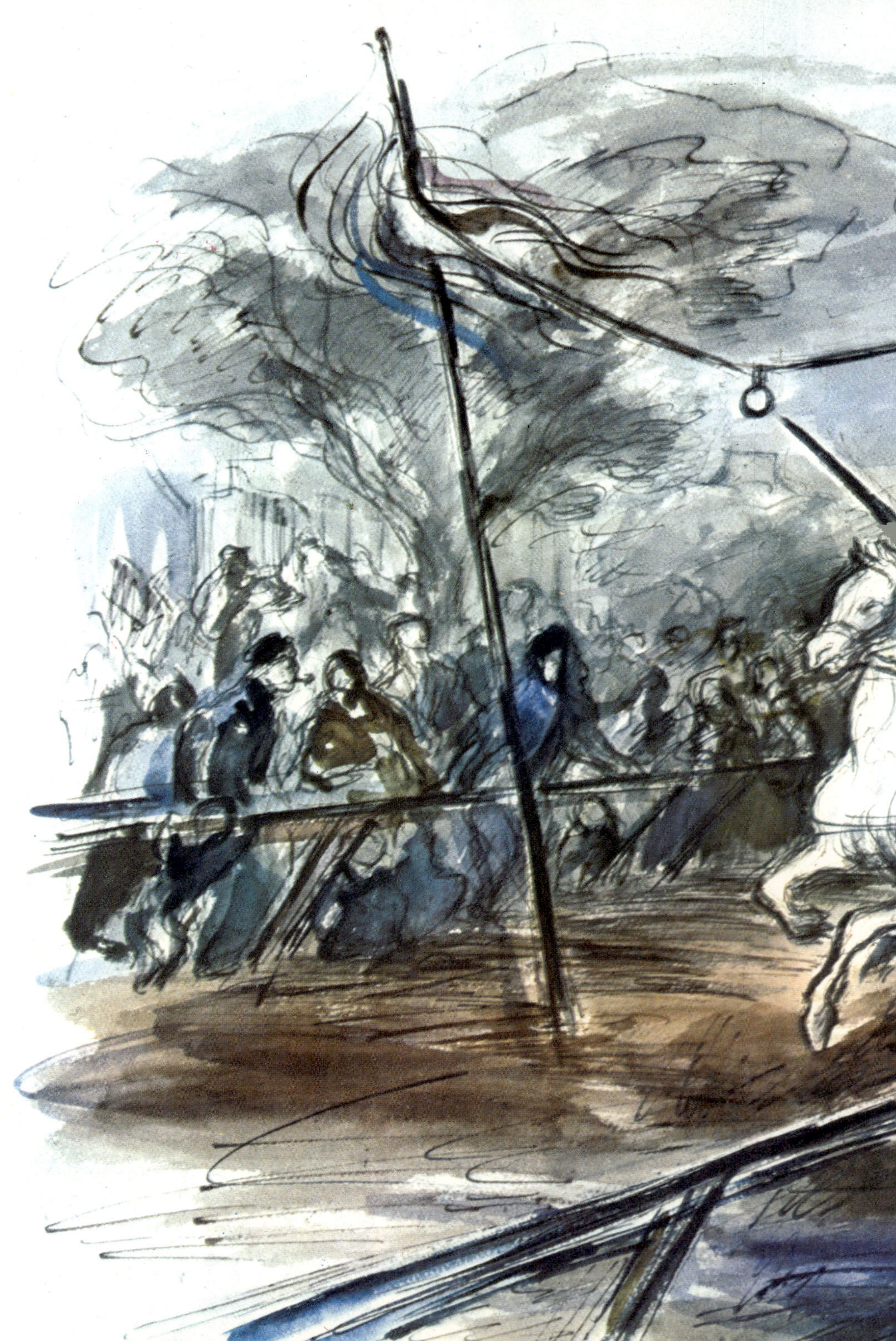

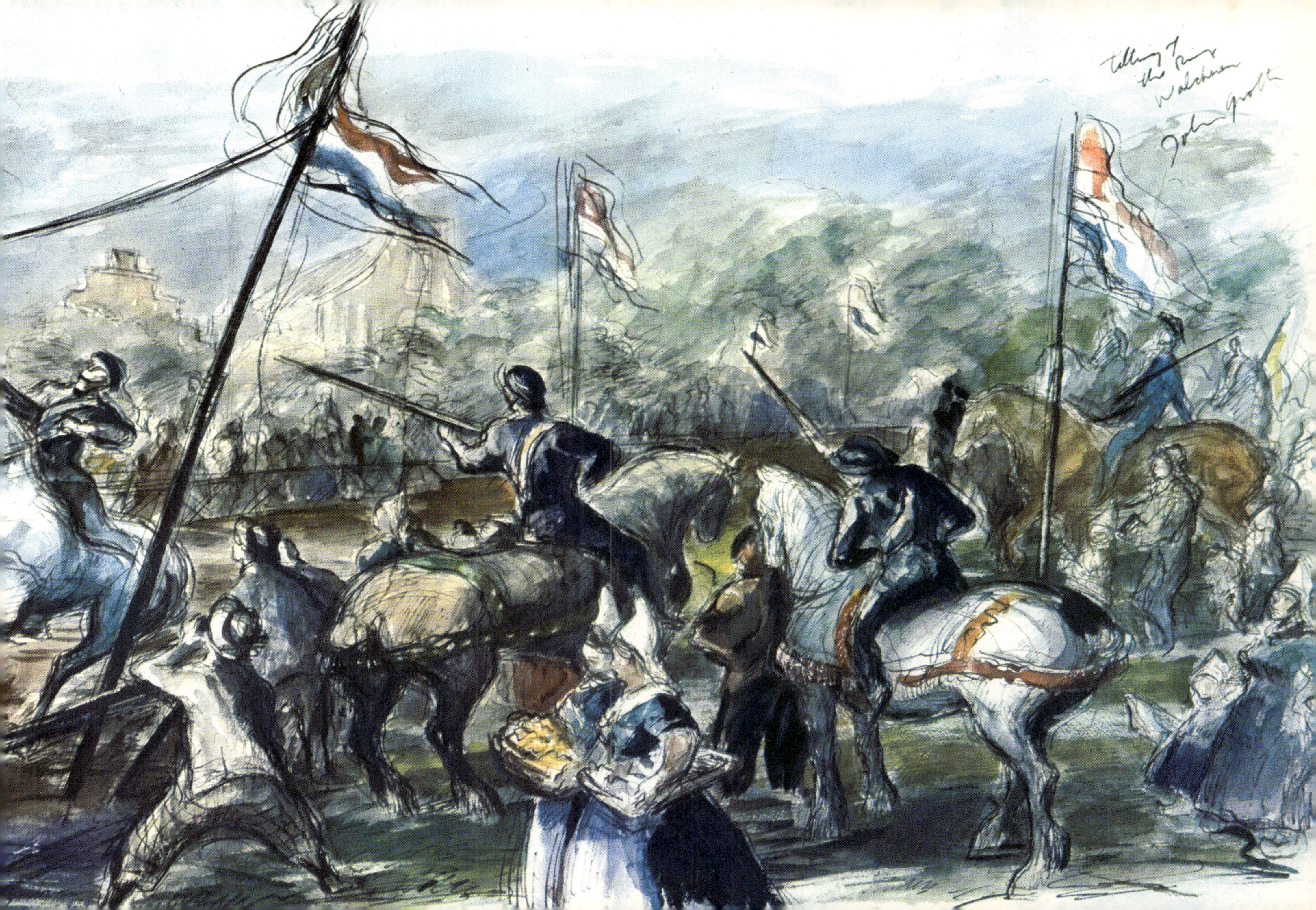
telling of
the Fair
Walcheren
John Groth

Road Bowling

Irish Road bowling involves the spectator more than any sport I know. For the tourist it provides a pleasant afternoon of hiking, drinking and friendly interchange.

This nonviolent, convivial pastime played along dusty, twisting roads is particularly suited to the Irish, since the only timeouts are signaled by the arrival at a pub. Played mostly in Antrim and Cork, the activity is often referred to as "bowels" with the sort of Johnsonian forthrightness typical of its brawny practitioners. A complete bout of bowels—or road bowling—is also known as a "bowl of odds". But by whatever name the game is invariably played the same way.

The bowl is actually a ball of iron about the size of a baseball, and the idea is that the bowlers (usually four men on a side) hurl it in competition along a selected road, often at some danger to any unsuspecting man or beast unfortunate enough to be coming in the opposite direction. The team to reach a given point in the smallest number of "lofts" is proclaimed the winner, and being such can often be profitable since the betting on road bowling is spirited.

Most often the sport is an intertown affair—and the "alley" thus becomes the road connecting the two towns. Usually played on Sunday afternoon, a bowling match always attracts a heavy crowd to follow the two teams' progress, betting fiercely and drinking heavily during the timeouts. Since most of the roads in rural Ireland are irregular and twisting at best, the knack of the game is to put a sufficient spin on the ball—known outside of Ireland as "English"—so that it will travel around curves. Although each bowler has his own style, the most accepted method of delivery is a sidearm motion somewhat like that of a discus thrower. When the bowlers arrive at a particularly sharp curve, they attempt to hurl the iron ball over trees, hedgerows and even small buildings, just as professional golfers all over the world occasionally try to drive over the rough on a dog-legged fairway.

Such flamboyant flings have resulted in enough broken windows and even split skulls for the police departments in both counties to have officially outlawed the game. But despite several attempts to kill the sport altogether by bringing the practitioners to court, the stout-hearted game of bowels, bowl of odds or road bowling continues to roll along as one of the more popular pastimes in Ireland. As one old road bowler put it: "Let the bowl be lofted, and to devil with any consideration but who can loft the longest."

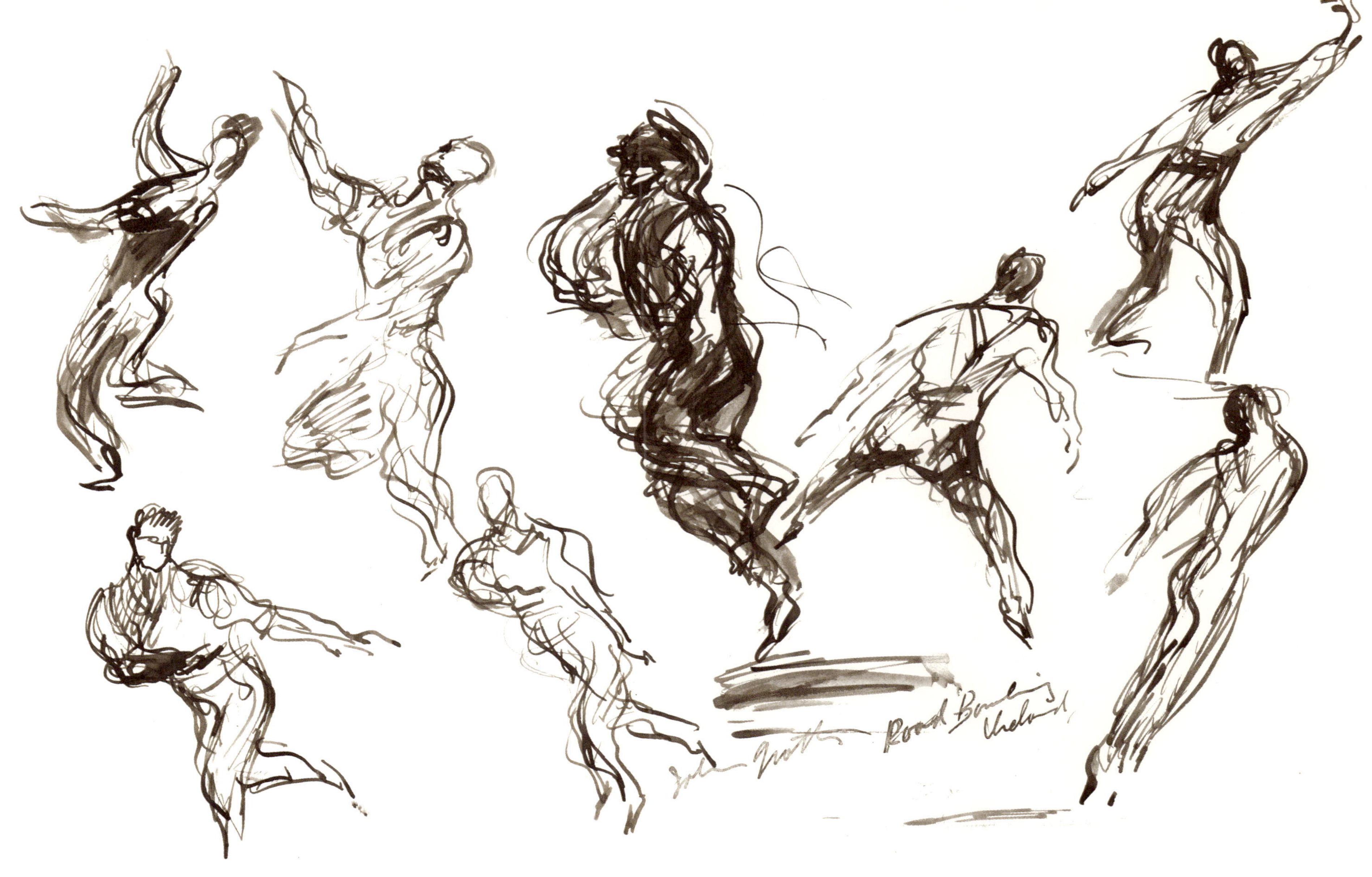

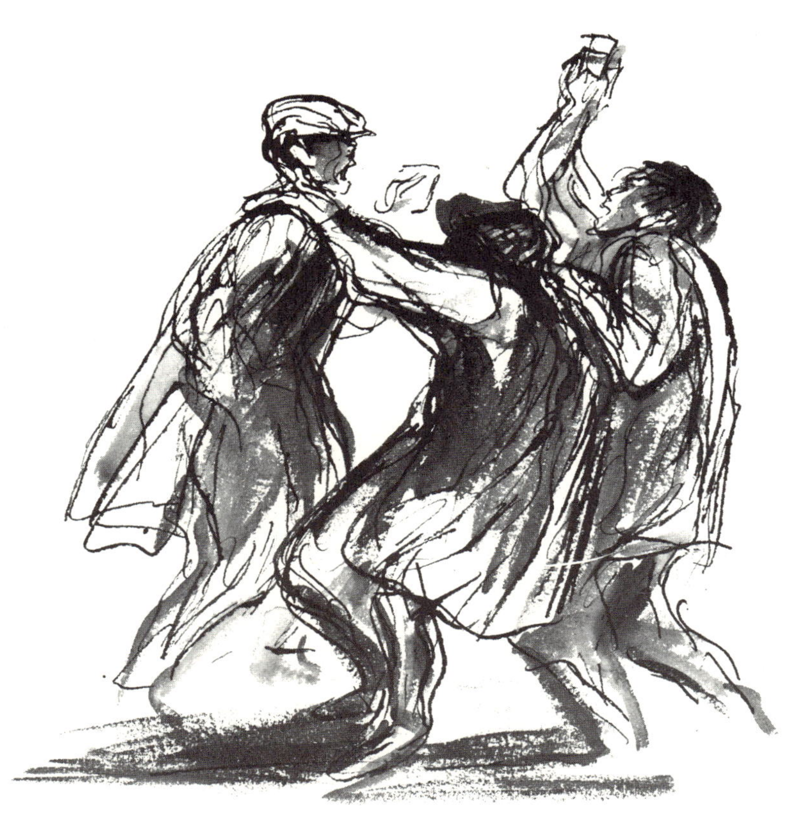

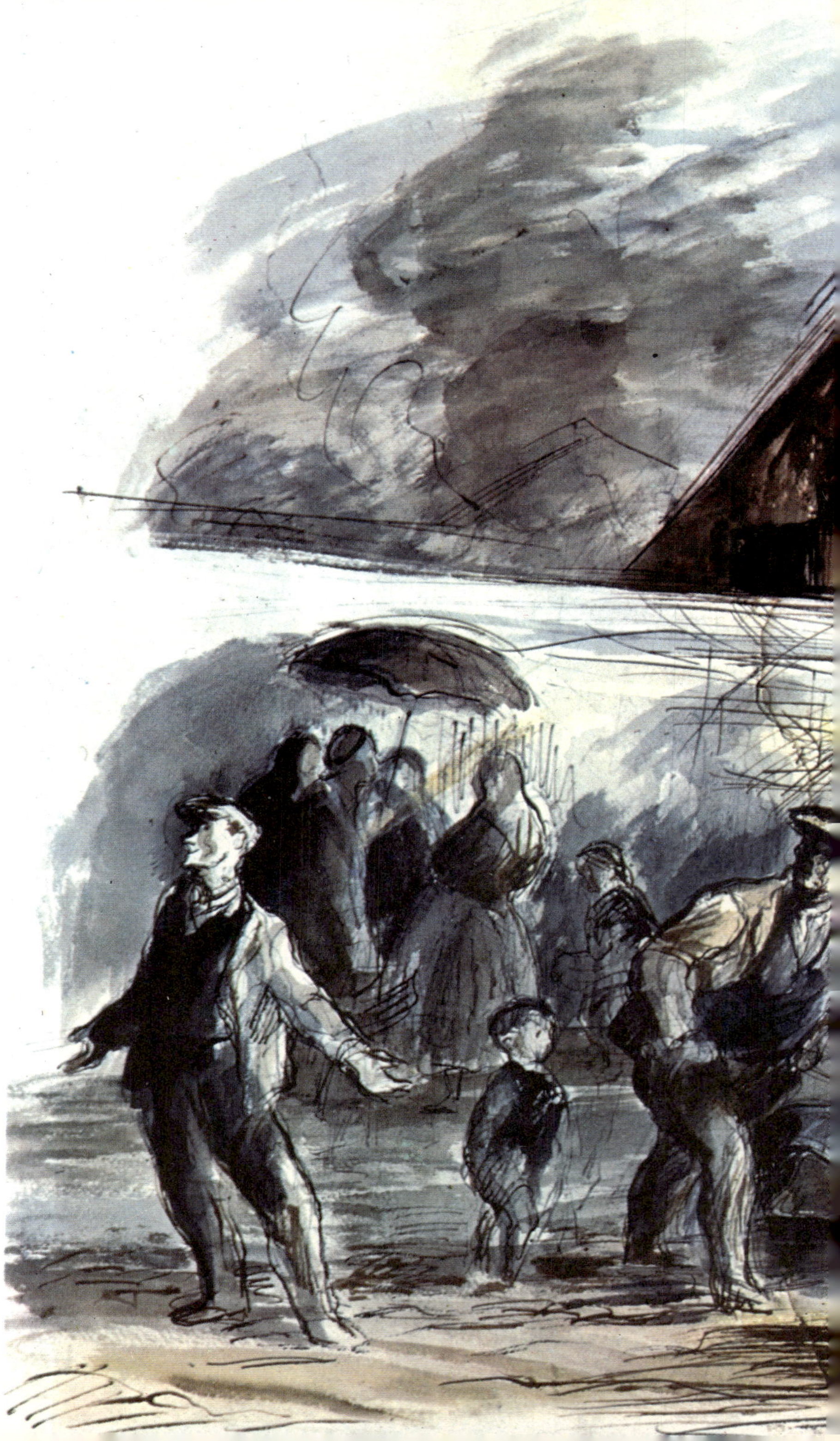

Lofting the Bowl, Near Cork.

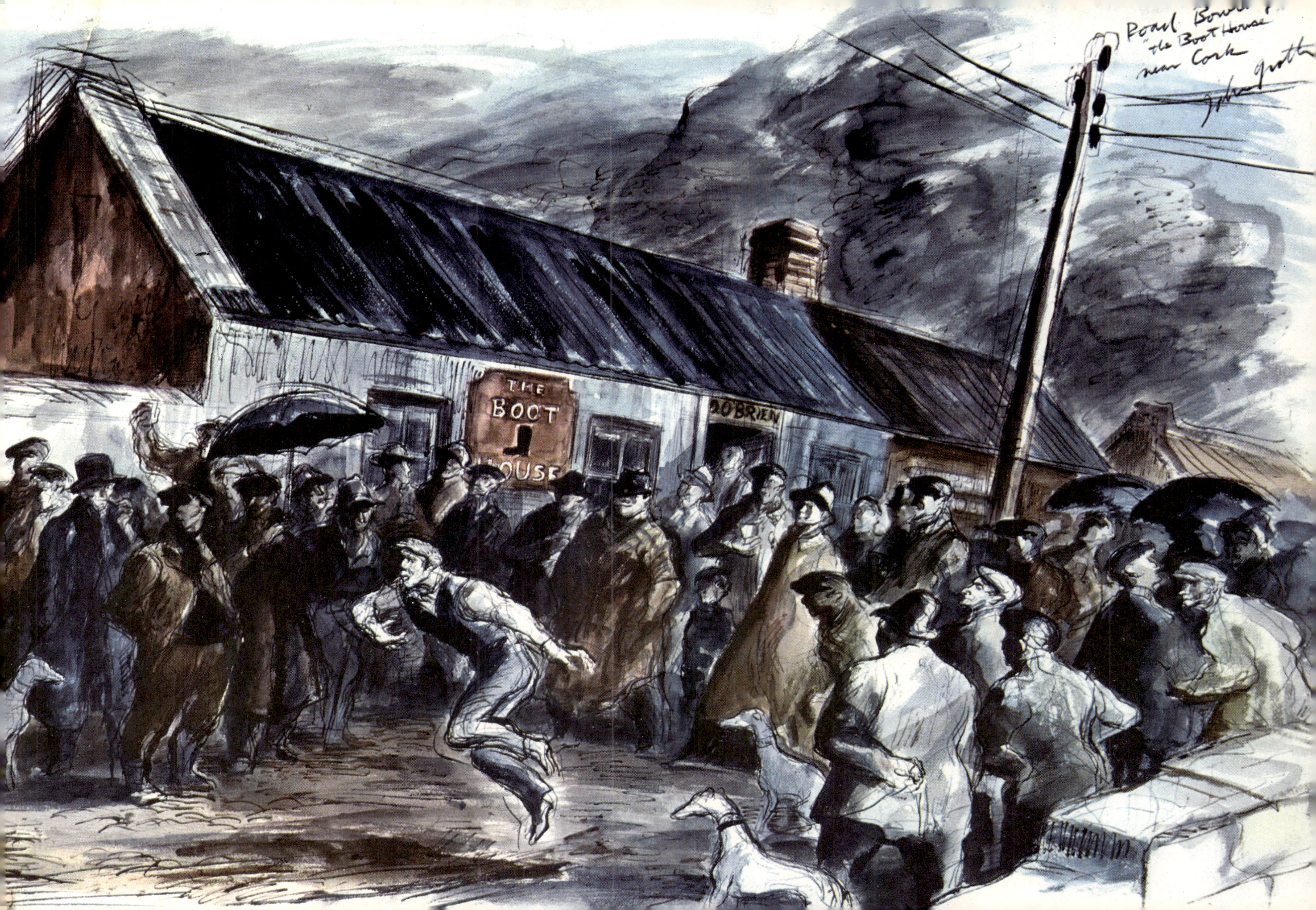

Road Bowl
"the Boot House"
near Cork
John Groth
THE
BOOT
HOUSE
O.O'BRIEN

Arctic Games

Most Eskimo games were played within the confined space of the igloo. Part of my problem was to keep well away from the action.

Winter in the Arctic is quite literally a long night's journey into day. Beginning in November the sun sets across this bleak region, and its inhabitants—mostly Eskimos—retire to their igloos and coastal shacks to wait for the coming of the dawn in April. During this period of confinement the Eskimos ply their various crafts—sewing their fur-lined parkas, executing their deft black-and-white engravings and carving miniatures out of the ivory they have collected in the summer from the mouths of seals, whales and sealions. To break the monotony the Eskimos over the centuries have developed a series of diversions, each as much a tribute to their genius for utility as are their home-made products.

Perhaps the most popular of these pastimes is *nuglugtaktok*—a rigid test of skill, nerve and reflex that only someone with a great deal of time on his hands could ever hope to master.

Although the game can be played outdoors, it is most often staged inside an igloo. Several Eskimos, clad in furs and wearing gauntlets, sit in a circle beneath a caribou antler, drilled full of tiny holes, suspended from the ceiling. Each Eskimo grips in his mittened hands a small harpoon. At a signal they start stabbing away at the caribou antler, seeking to impale it by spearing one of the drilled holes.

Each time someone strikes the antler it sways to the opposite side of the circle and is set to spinning madly, often perilously close to another head. Also, since a man's chances to win are enhanced if he stabs and jabs from close range, the safety of the other players is never out of doubt.

Interest in the game is heightened by that universal activity—betting. However, Eskimos do not generally carry a great deal of cash in their parkas, so payoffs are usually in furs or kayaks or other such Arctic equipment.

Another Eskimo game, whip ball, bears a loose relationship to ice hockey. A sealskin filled with moss is fashioned into a sphere roughly the size of a bowling ball, and the athletes (any number can play) set upon it with long-lashed whips, also made of sealskin, seeking to drive it by the opposing team. Since not every Eskimo possesses complete accuracy with a whip, eyes, ears and noses are frequently in jeopardy as the lashes sing through the air.

Whip ball is not the only Eskimo game where there's a danger of injury. In "parka hanging" a man is hung by his parka top from tent-pole nails. Under the victim's own weight the throat of the parka tightens—cutting off his air supply. The lack of air is the thing; it produces a kind of euphoria that lasts some time after the player is unhooked.

An outdoor game in which girls and women and even some small children participate is the Arctic version of trampoline acrobatics. A walrus skin (even in their games the Eskimos depend heavily on animal skins) is tautly stretched on stakes, providing a bouncy contrivance. All manner of stunts are attempted by the gymnasts, the girls using an exaggeratedly feminine flutter-kick to maintain balance. The Eskimos call this activity *nuglugtuk* (not to be confused with the riskier *nuglugtaktok,* previously described).

On John Groth's second trip to the Arctic, aboard the Hudson's Bay Company's supply ship, *Rupertsland,* he witnessed the annual Eskimo kayak race, which thrilled him more than the most harrowing Arctic games. As the ship hove to off Port Harrison, the Eskimos came surging out from shore—their one-man, closed-deck craft slicing through the icy waters of the bay, double-ender paddles spinning, in a mad race to be the first at the big ship's side. For the winners, the Hudson's Bay Company offered such prizes as sacks of flour, rifle ammunition, canned goods and, of all things, phonograph records.

Still another widely practiced game is called simply the ice-out game. It is the closest thing the Eskimos have to a sweepstakes. Just before the lakes and rivers freeze solid in late October, a log is suspended in a nearby stream and a wire is run from the log to an all-weather clock. When the ice breaks up in the spring, it releases the log which trips the wire which stops the clock, and whoever among the bettors guessed closest to the time registered on the stopped clock is declared the winner. It is undoubtedly the Eskimo's and the Arctic white man's most popular game. Not only can one win a sizable chunk of cash, but the ice-out game is pegged to the happiest time of year: The end of the long night's journey.

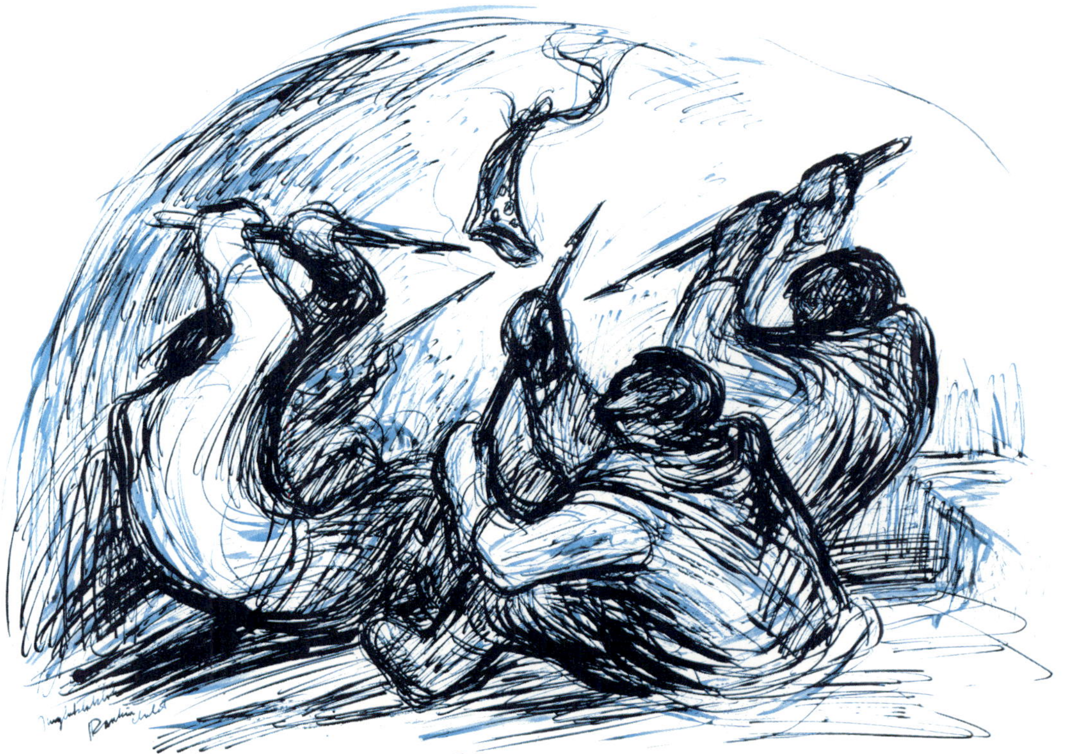

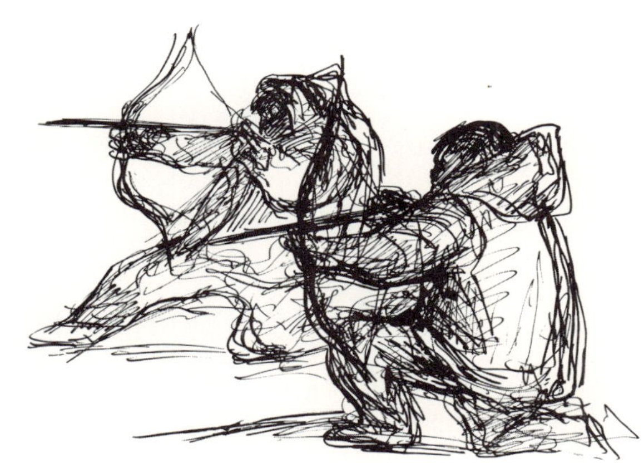

Nuglugtaktok.

65

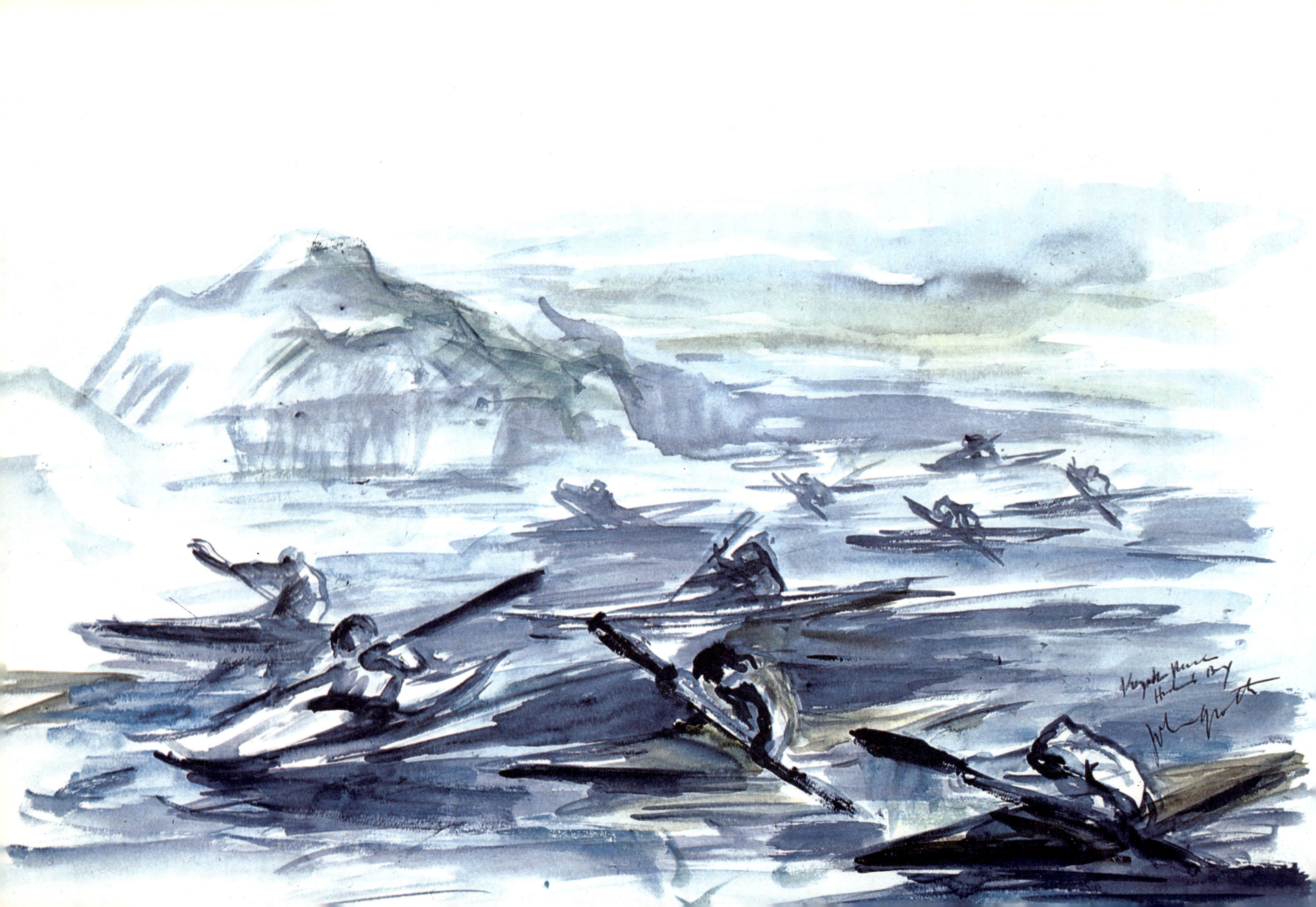

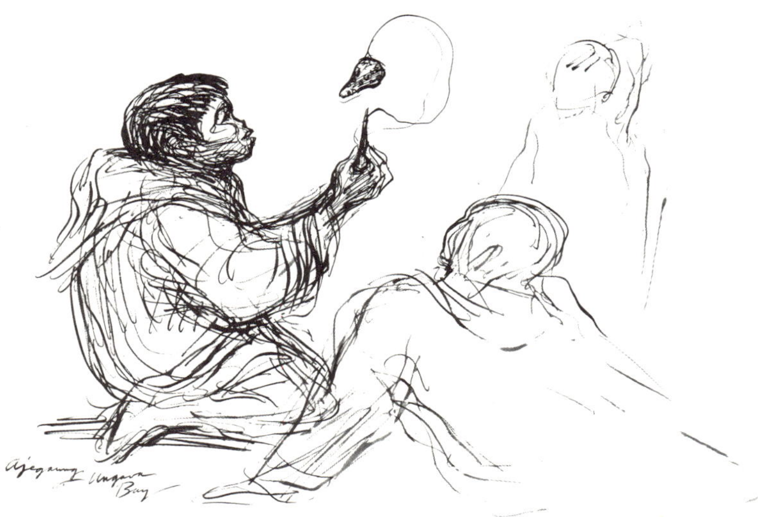

Ajgeung.

Kayak Race, Hudson's Bay.

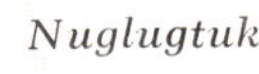

Nuglugtuk.

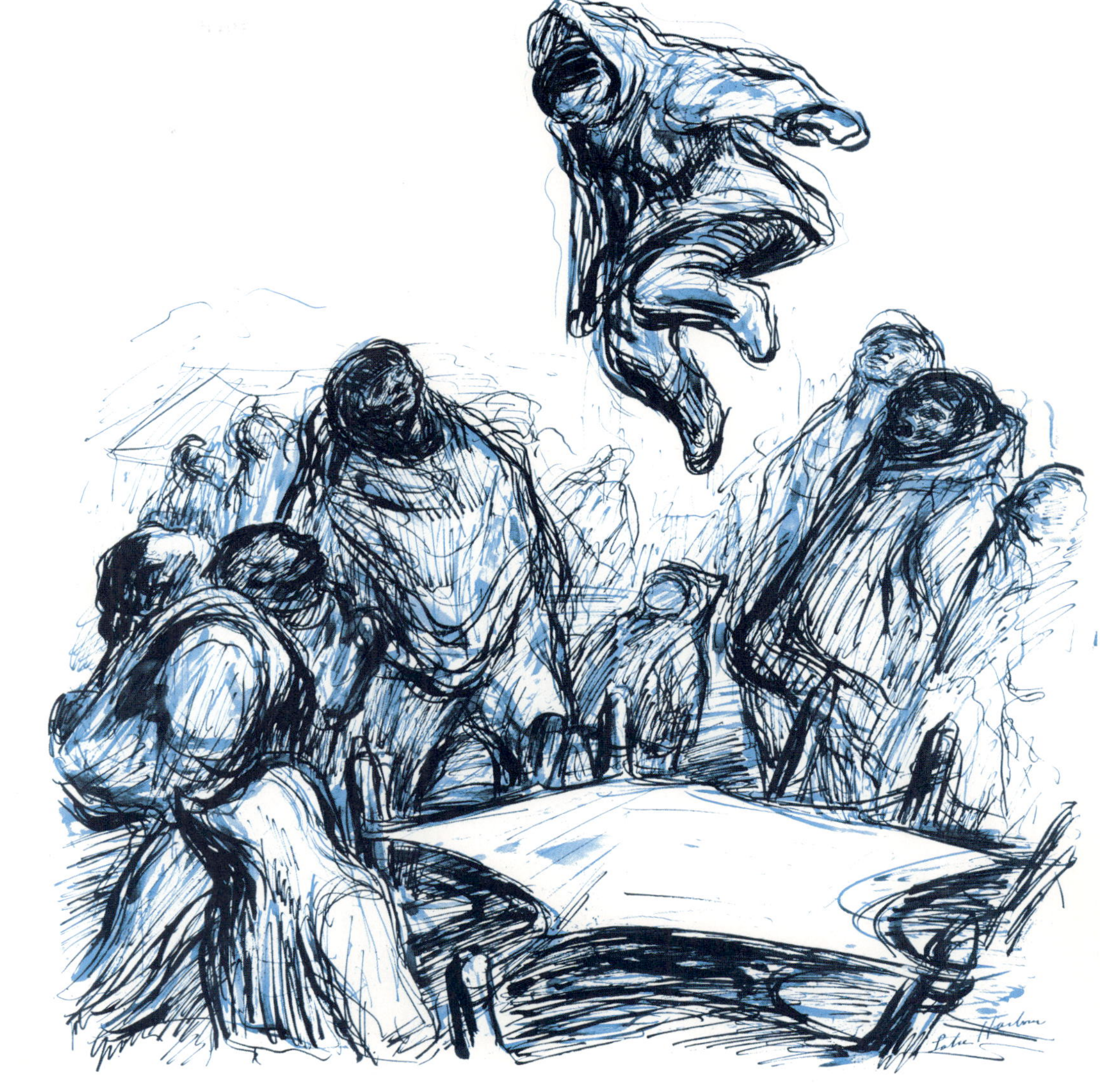

Whipball.

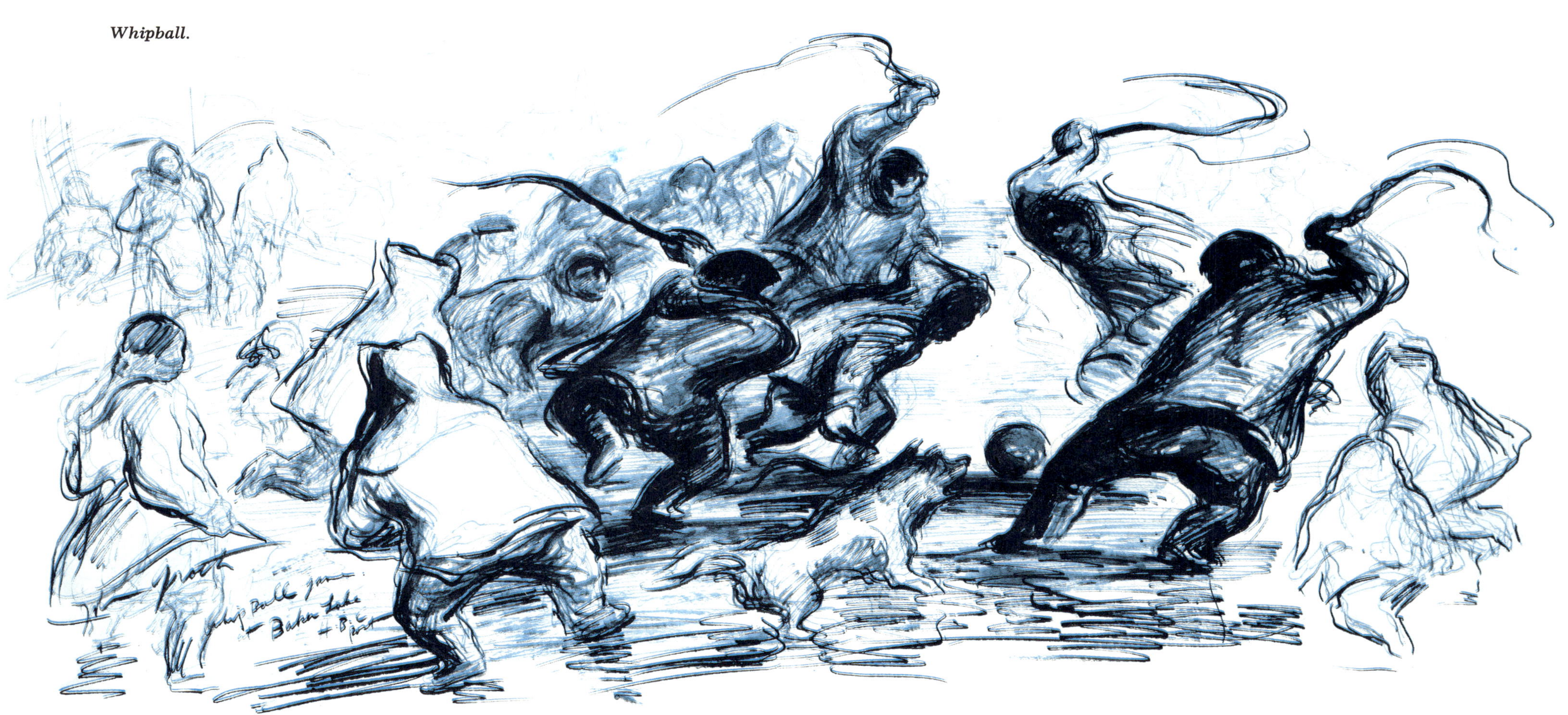

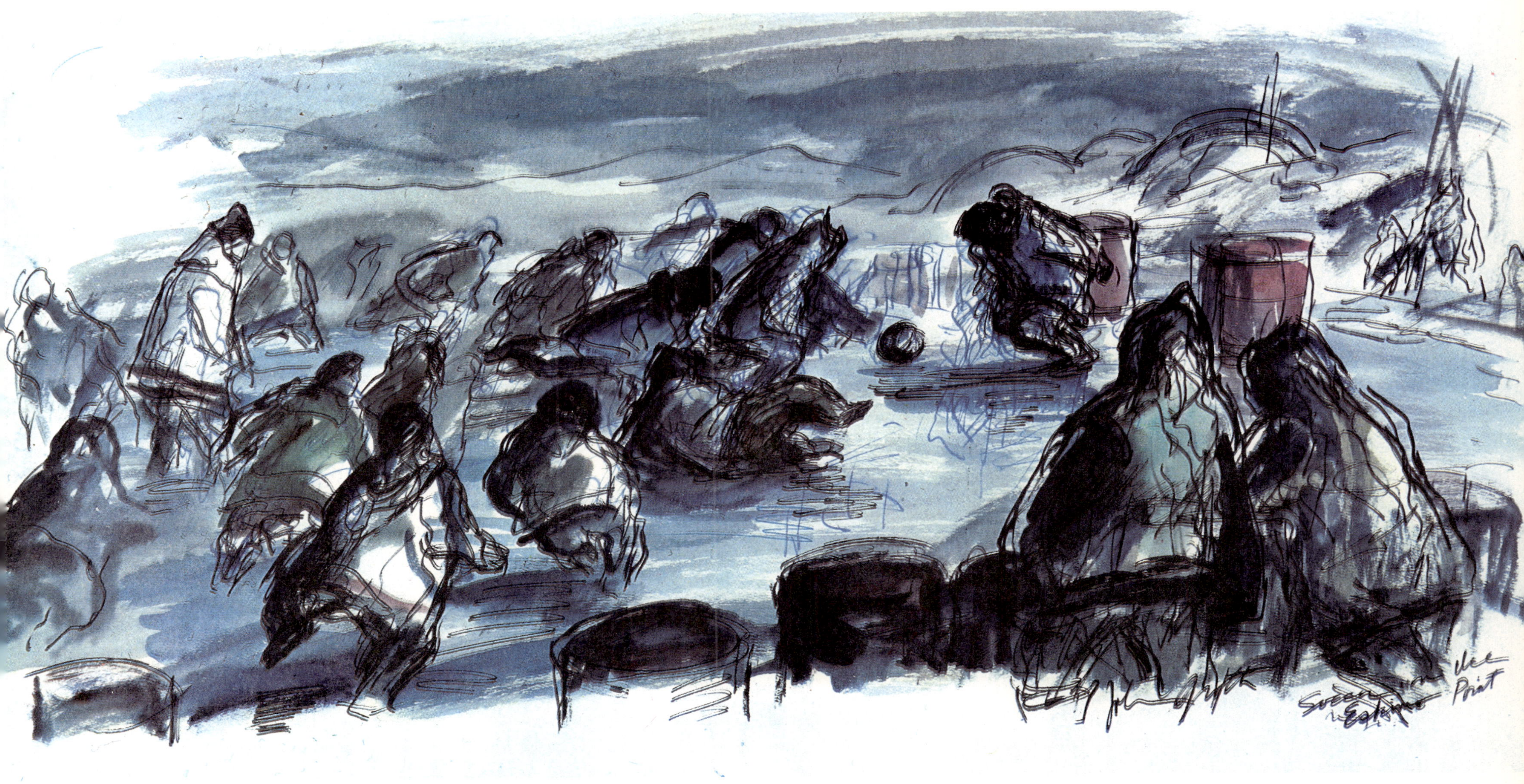

Soccer on the Ice.

Tacraw

Wandering through Bangkok, I saw tacraw *played in every alley and square. It brought back to me my youth on the basketball courts of Chicago's West Side.*

In the slums of Bangkok boys have been playing basketball for some 300 years. Actually it is called *tacraw*, but it so closely resembles the American sport that an ambitious young historian might make a minor discovery if he were to investigate the traveling habits of Dr. James Naismith, the American inventor of the sport. Perhaps more to the point, John Groth—who has been studying athletes all his life —claims that a few of the players are worth a close look by an American scout. "The movements of *tacraw*," says Groth, "are the same as in basketball." Of course, Thailanders rarely reach six feet in height, but, who knows, there could be another Bob Cousy among the boys of Bangkok.

The game is played much as basketball is on the city streets throughout the U.S. Instead of an inflated rubber ball, the *tacraw* ball is fashioned from rattan and is about the same size as a volleyball. The basket—woven from fishnetting—is suspended from a rope strung between two poles. The appropriate number of players per team is six, but the street rules are flexible enough to permit any number of players to participate.

Throughout the day and long into the night under the lamplights, the boys compete on the court at the base of the 42-foot Standing Buddha—passing, feinting, spinning off hookshots, layups and jumpers—while the universal hubbub of city life revolves about them.

The single major difference between *tacraw* and American basketball is that in Thailand there is no dribbling since the rattan ball does not bounce well on the dirt streets. The Bangkok boys have a system of passing and body-blocking and kicking the likes of which no American player has ever seen. Tripping, kneeing and shooting out well-aimed elbows, the little titans of tacraw invariably provide onlookers with as lively a sport as anything ever seen in any urban setting.

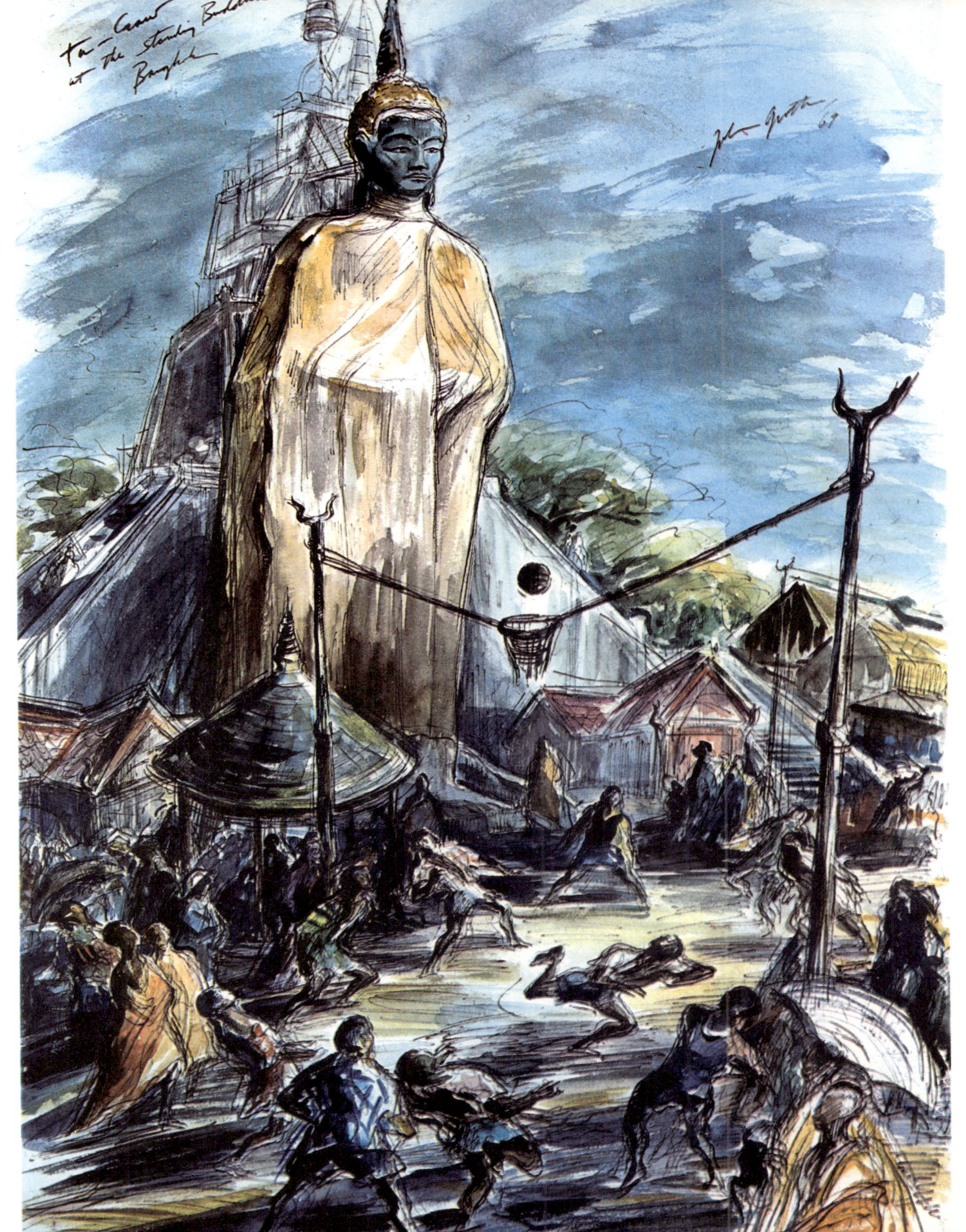

Twilight Match at the Standing Buddha.

71

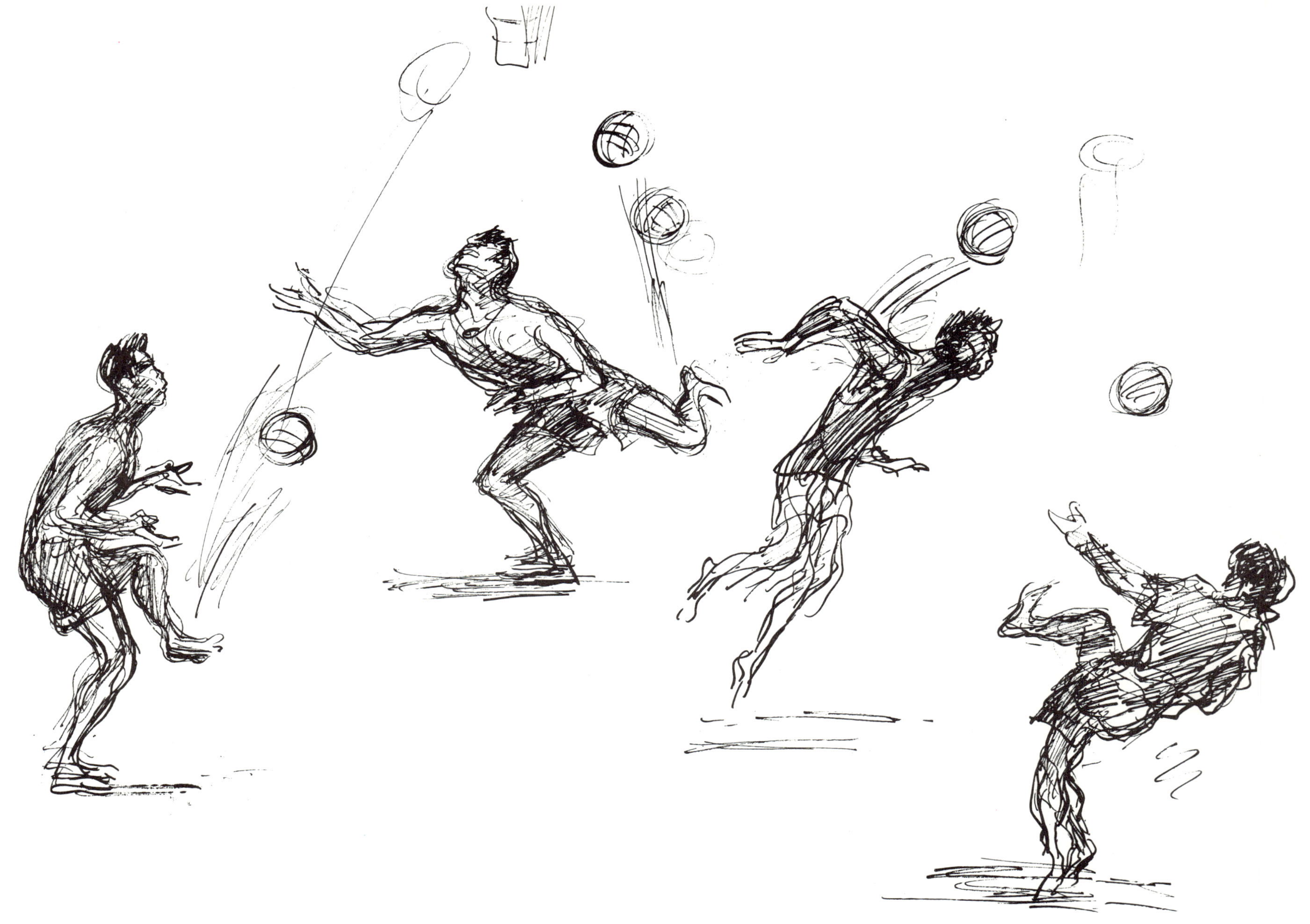

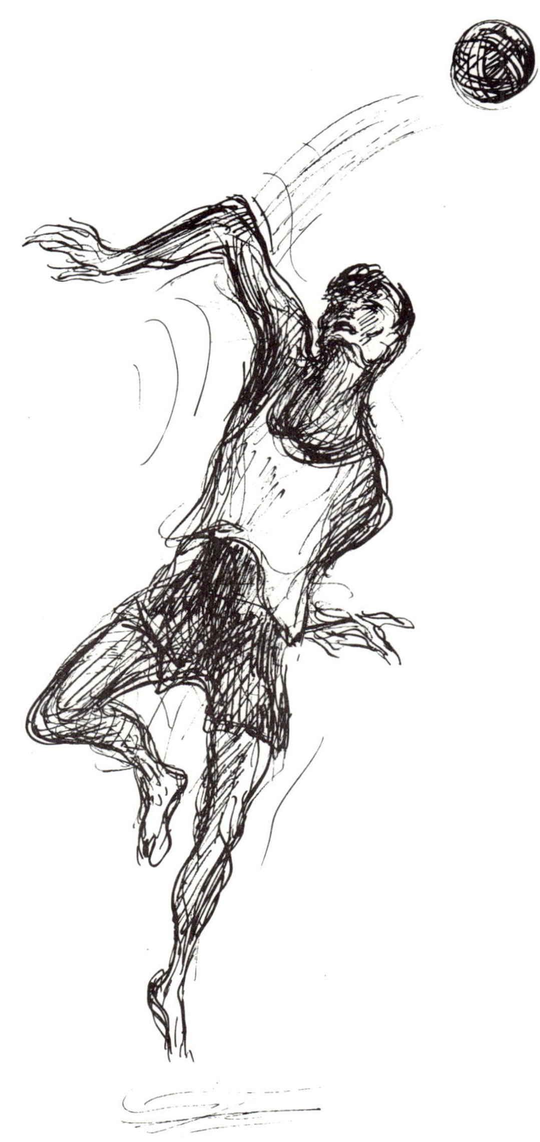

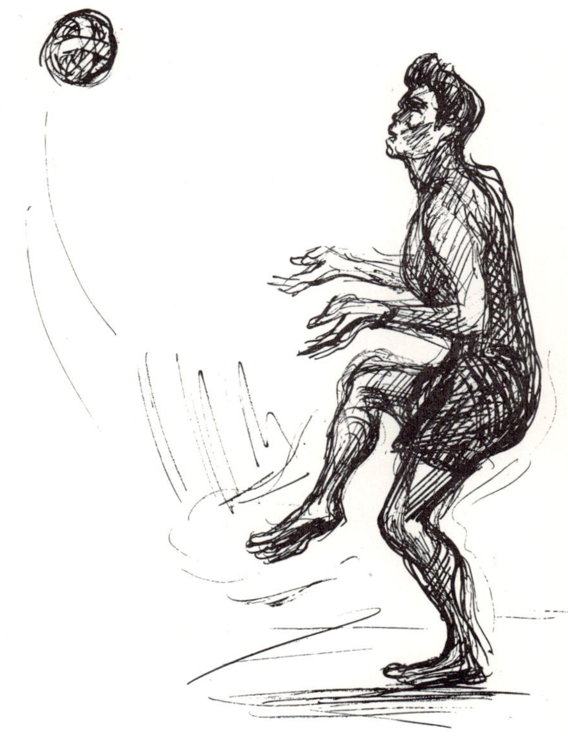

Pig Sticking

My first pig-sticking hunt was sketched from the safety of an elephant's back. A very good place to be, incidentally.

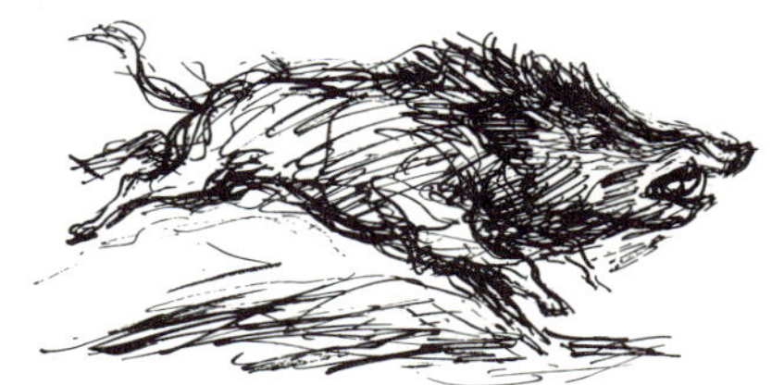

Pig sticking is an ancient hunting sport going back at least as far as the Greek and Roman legions. Numerous bas-reliefs on the walls of tombs stretching from Rome to Sparta depict spear-carrying legionnaires astride galloping mounts in hot pursuit of a scampering pig. Although the sport was a favorite between-battle diversion for his troops, Julius Caesar regarded the pastime as unnecessarily cruel and was conspicuously missing whenever a hunt was held. It is also known, however, that on the night following a successful hunt Caesar could not be deterred from the dinner table for he dearly loved to munch on the victim—after it had been properly roasted and glazed and garnished with an apple or avocado, depending on what part of the world his troops were leveling at the time.

In India, however, pig sticking didn't catch on until the eighteenth century. Before then the fashionable sport had been sticking bears, but as the hunts became more numerous, the bear supply was eventually diminished—and the hunters turned to spearing pigs. Very soon they discovered that the pig was a foe worthy of their steel, providing immeasurably more sport than the comparatively ponderous bear.

Today pig-sticking parties usually number three hunters—called "heats"—who set out into the bush armed with long slender bamboo

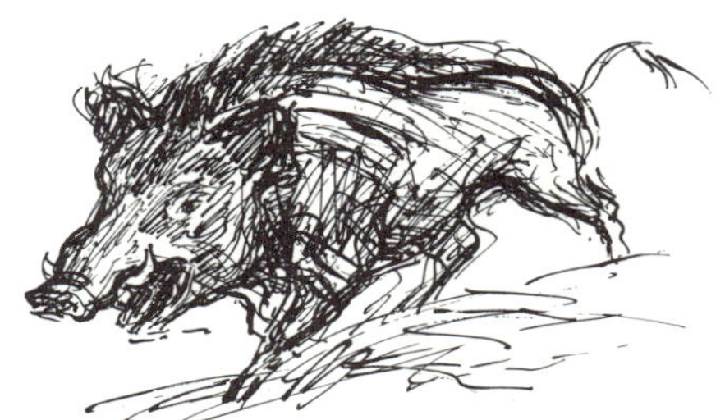

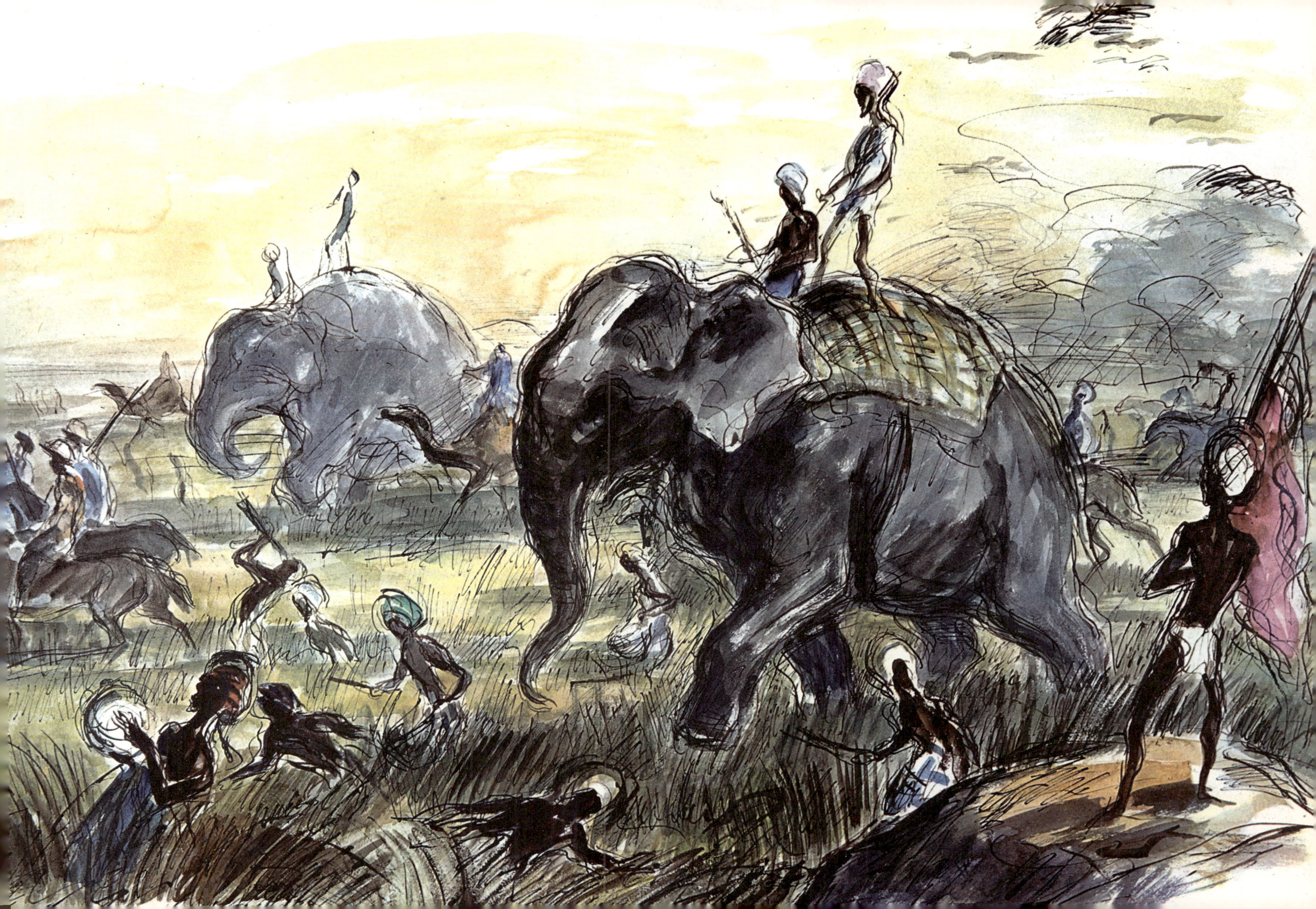

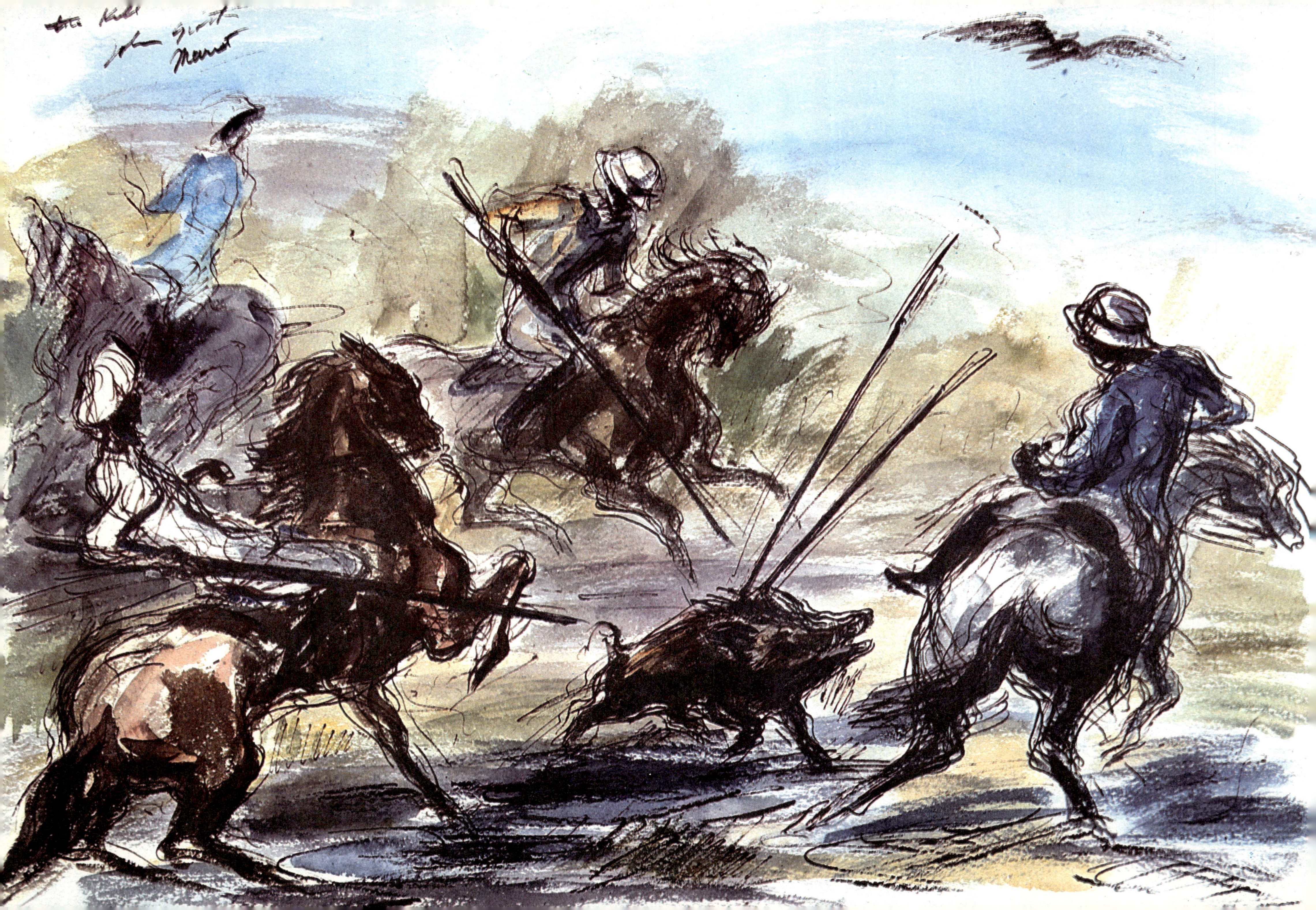
The Kill
John Scott
Mecut

poles tipped with razor-sharp bayonet heads weighted with lead. Village natives are hired to beat the jungle brush and drive the wild boars out into the open, where the hunters await on horseback. If a grass plain is driven, however, the hunters ride adjacent to the beaters, and when a boar is flushed a wild race is touched off.

"I followed my first wild pig hunt from the safety of an elephant's back," recalls Groth. "Within a few minutes after we set out, the first boar broke cover and led the center heat through miles of wither-high tiger grass and jhow [whippy bushes that wrap around the rider's and horse's legs], bounding over hussocks and hummocks, scrambling around anthills and hurling his heavy body into narrow *nuklahs*. For a time the odds seemed to be on the boar."

But eventually the riders began gaining ground on the pig as John followed—sitting like a sultan aboard his quilted elephant. Each of the heats, eager for the honor of "first spear," raced against the other. The middle heat, who had taken up the chase earliest, drew near to the pig and, reminding one of an old-fashioned harpooner cocking and aiming his instrument at the hump of a whale, kept his eye glued on the incredibly swift and artful dodger, flung his spear and sank it deep into the pig's flank.

After receiving his first wound, the pig turned to the attack—spinning on his hind hoof and charging the horse in the hope of unseating the rider. But the rider met charge with charge. An instant before impact the rider urged the horse high in the air and sunk the spear deep into the pig passing directly beneath him. It is a classic move, comparable to a double on grouse, dropping an elephant with a single shot or, more precisely, to a matador finishing the bull with the *muleta*.

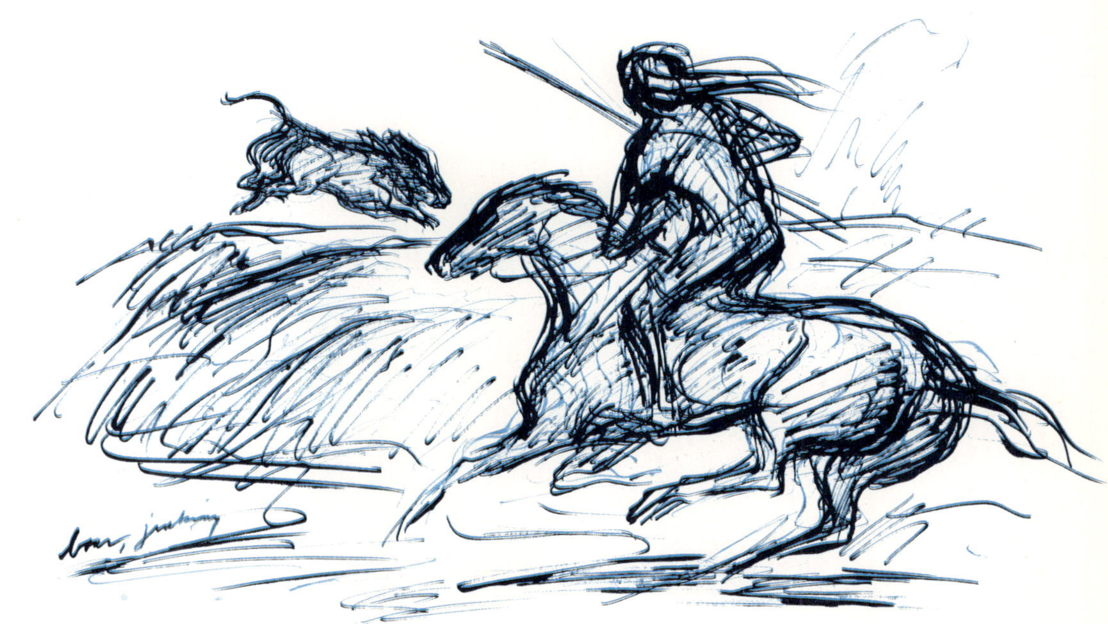

The Kill.

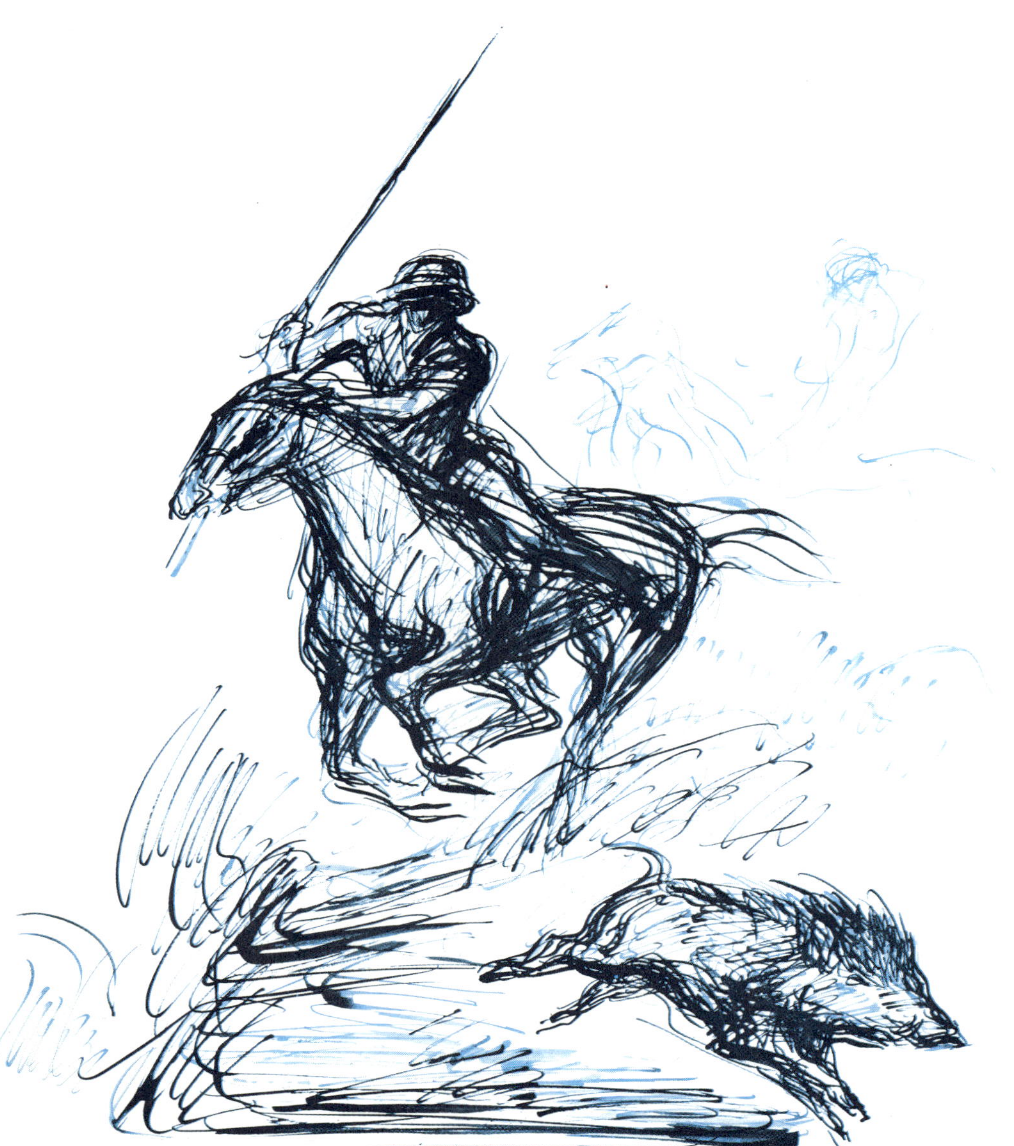

Hunt's End.

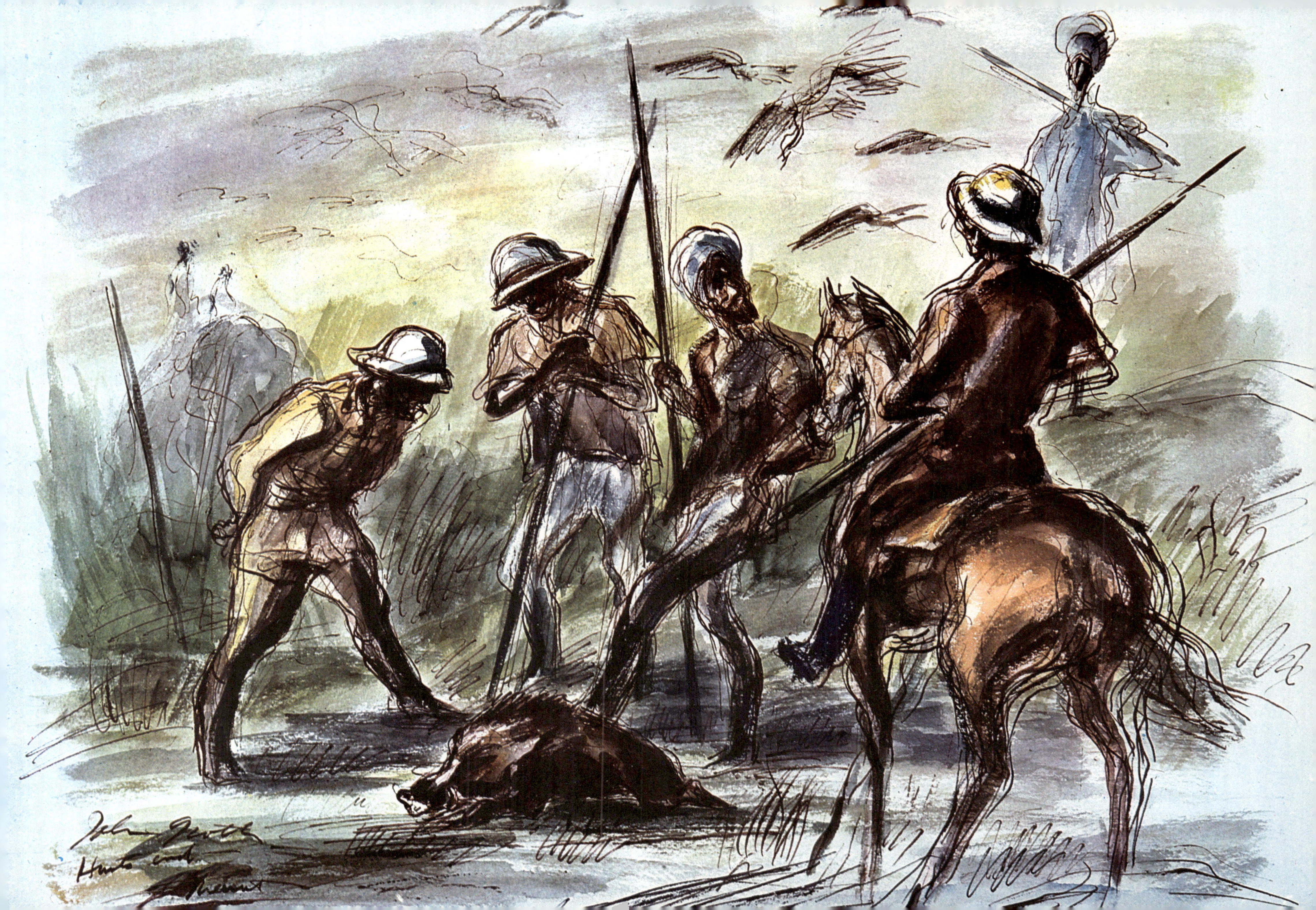

Guks

I heard about the Ethiopian game of guks *while on safari in East Africa. Since it involves horses, which I love to draw, it was worth the detour to Addis Ababa to capture the conflict of this mounted event.*

The sport known as *guks* is less than two centuries old, but its roots run deep into ancient warfare. It is played by the Gulla Tribesmen of Ethiopia twice each year—at the Catholic feasts of Maskal (The Finding of the Cross), in September; and Timkat (St. John the Baptist), in January. Essentially *guks* is a game of mounted fencing played on a field measuring 300 yards by 150 yards, involving two teams each of twenty-five tribesmen on horseback. The men are armed with long, blunt-nosed bamboo lancers and shields made from hippopotamus hide.

The teams line up at opposite end zones, looking like Bengal Lancers about to charge. A member of one of the groups shouts a challenge downfield to the opposition. Instantly the challenged side bursts forward, their bodies hunched behind shields, while the opposition, their lances held high, carefully advance to meet them. The object of the game is for the players of the challenged side to reach the opposite end zone without being touched—or tagged—by an opposing player's lance. For each rider who crosses the goal line in such pristine fashion, a point is scored.

To use a basketball phrase, the game of *guks* is mostly a one-on-one strategy. Each of the challengers picks his foe, then moves in to "tag" him with his blunt-nosed lance. If he ·successfully makes his tag, the challenger may charge off to help out a teammate with his man. But the rider who is tagged is considered a "dead" man and is automatically out of the game. Seldom do more than a few riders reach the goal line unscathed.

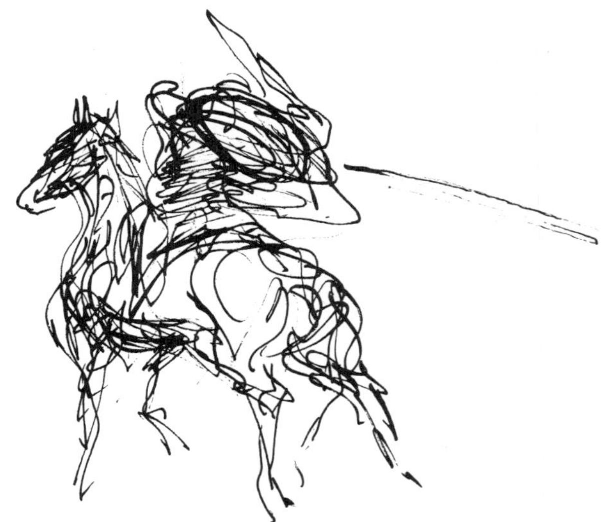

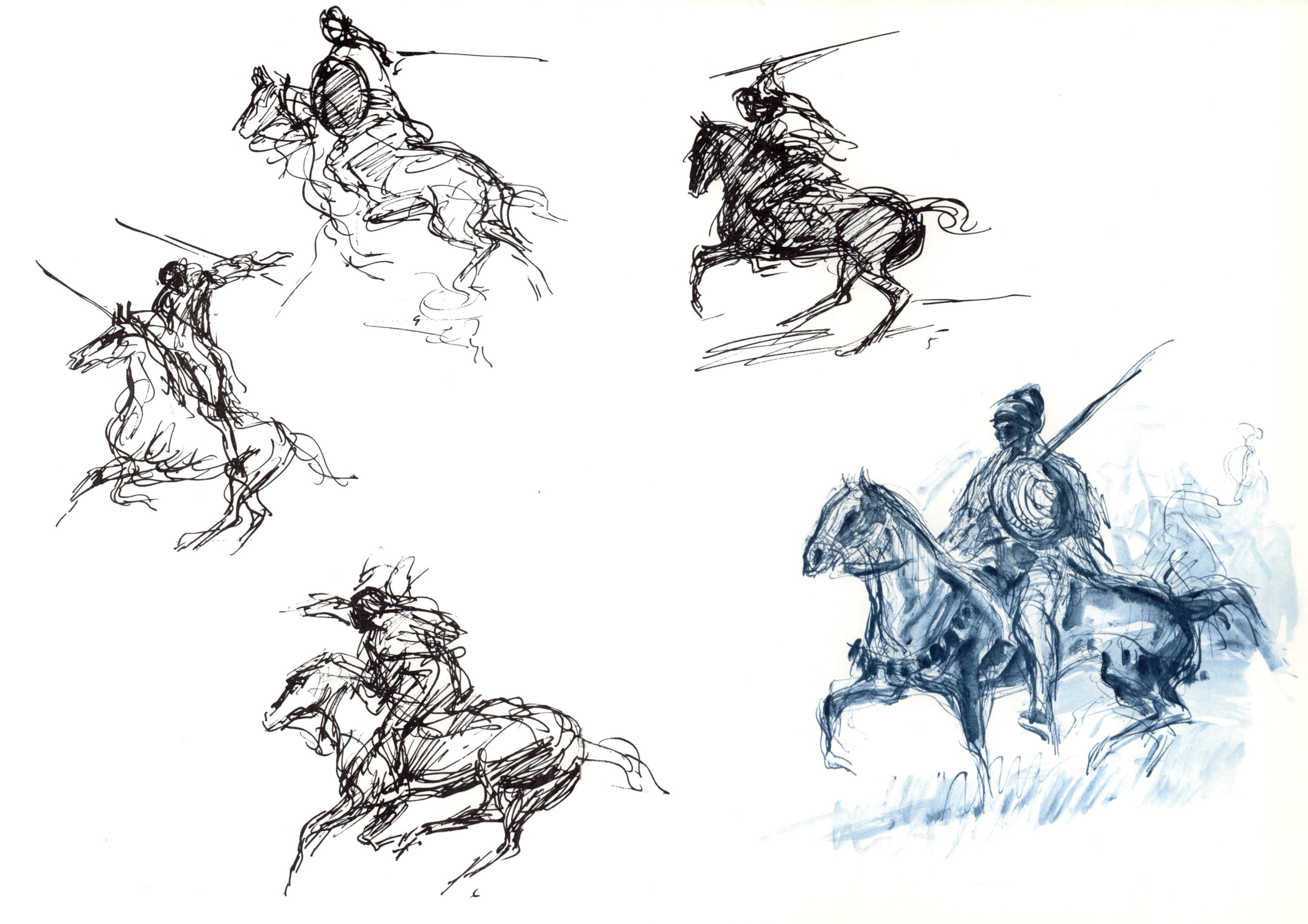

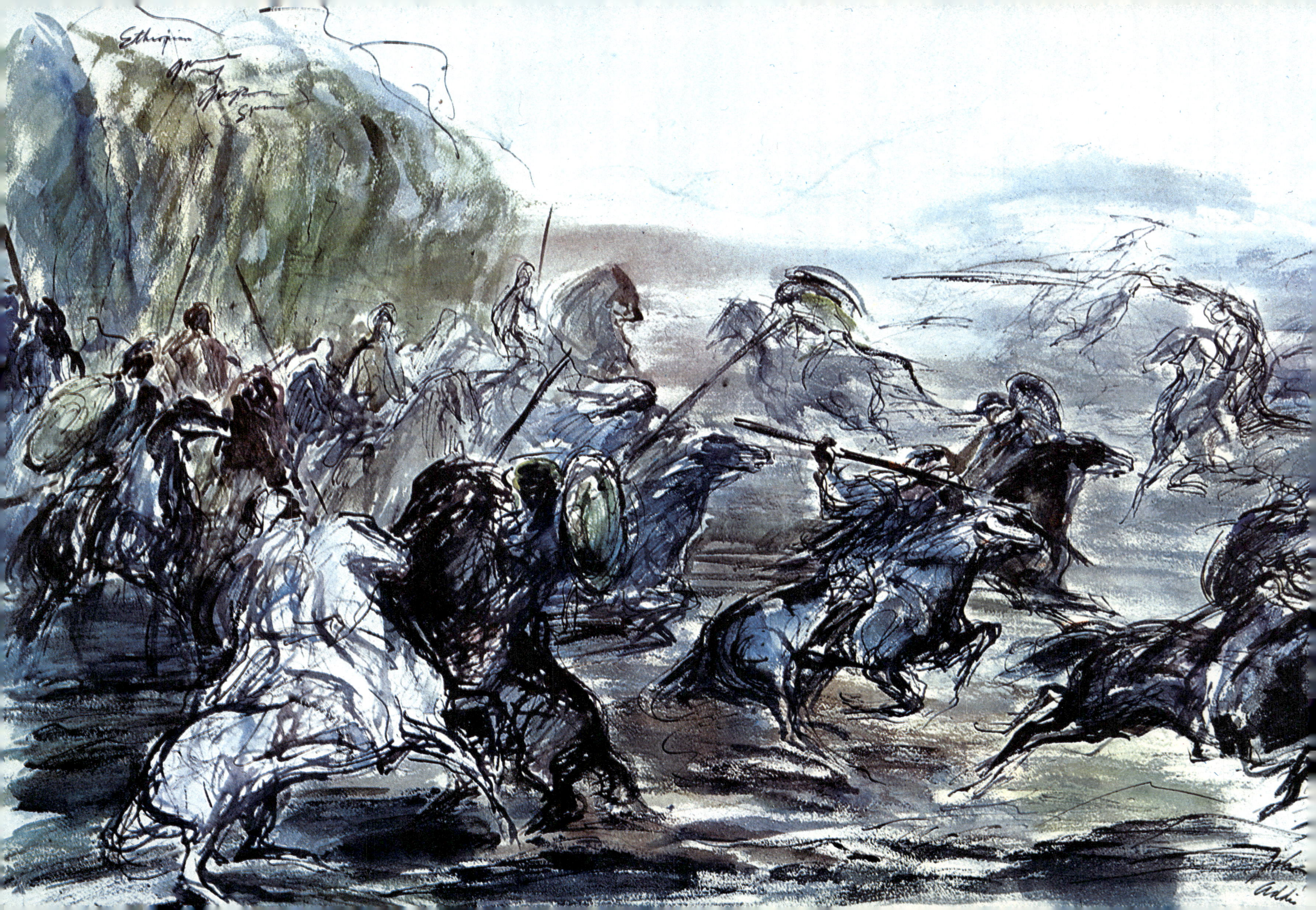

Ethiopian

Imperial Household Cavalry Match.

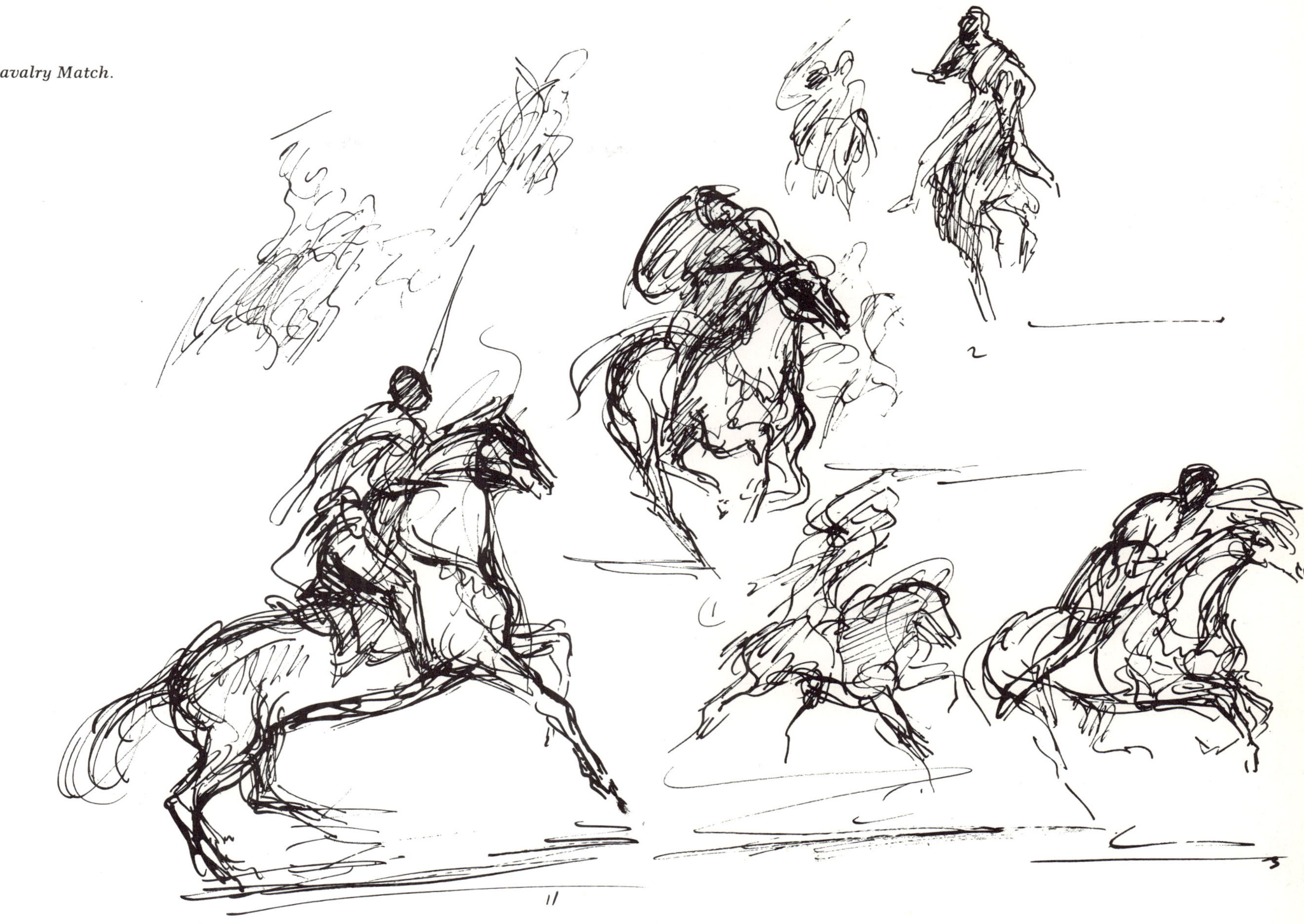

Joust of the Saracens

As a boy I was fascinated by the flash and clash of knights in combat which, of course, I had to draw from imagination. Here, in this time-ripened Italian town, I had my own live models.

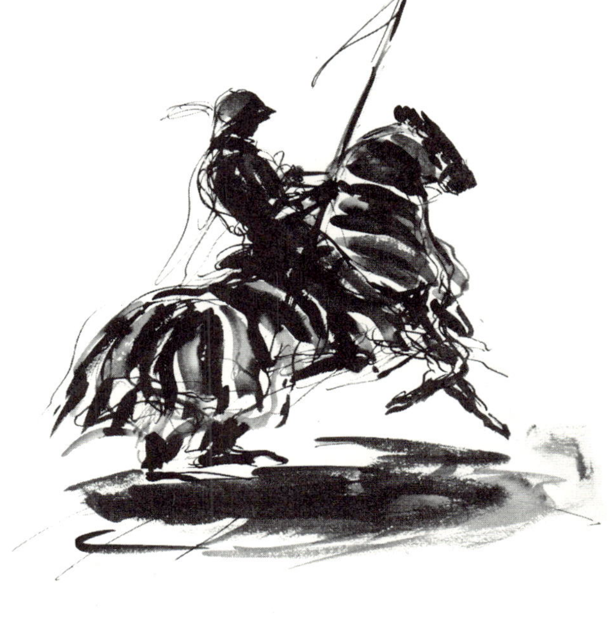

"O Aretines . . . I have seen the starting of raids, the onset of tournaments, and the running of jousts . . . now with trumpets . . . now with drums."
Dante

Twice each year the rich world of Dante erupts in the small, ancient town of Arezzo, Italy, where once again trumpets blare, drums roll, and the thirteenth century awakens and lays siege to the present. The dates of this twin renaissance are June 4th and September 3rd—before and after summer invades this mountain country—and on each morning the townsfolk, costumed as heralds, foot soldiers, bowmen and maidens, fill the cobblestone streets, flinging high their medieval flags, parading on horseback and hawking their wares.

In the afternoon the main event is held: the Joust of the Saracens.

The joust dates back some seven centuries to when the Crusades were imposing their own bloody brand of religious fervor on all heretics within reach. Highest ranked among their many enemies were the Saracens.

The hatred continues even today. To the cheers—and jeers—of the crowd modern men clad in eighty-pound suits of armor are hoisted aboard their steeds. Armed with long heavy lances the jousters take turns charging their common enemy, "the King of the Saracens," a wooden man set on a well-oiled swivel. To score, a knight must spear a paper bull's-eye set in the center of the wooden enemy's shield while simultaneously avoiding a smashing blow from a knout tipped with heavy wooden balls, the wooden victim's instantaneous response to his wound. If he places his lance exactly right, he won't get hit. If he misses—and many of the amateur jousters seem to have more enthusiasm than skill—the blow comes quick and sure.

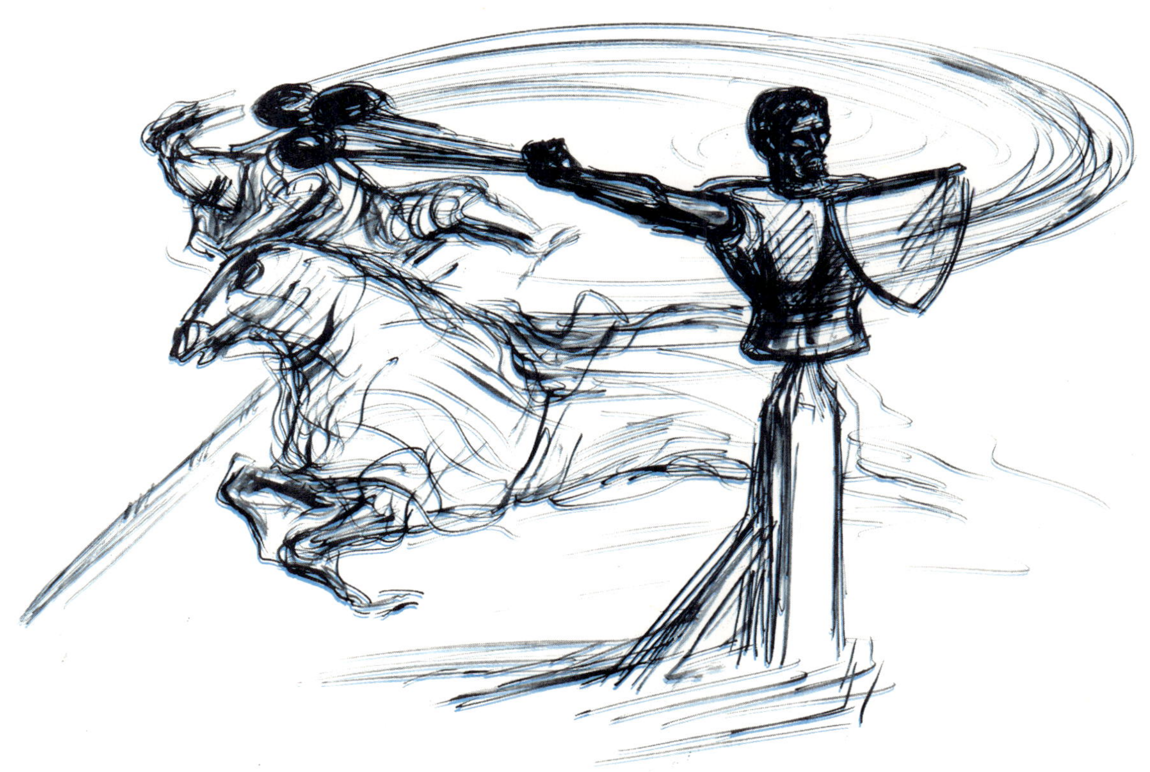

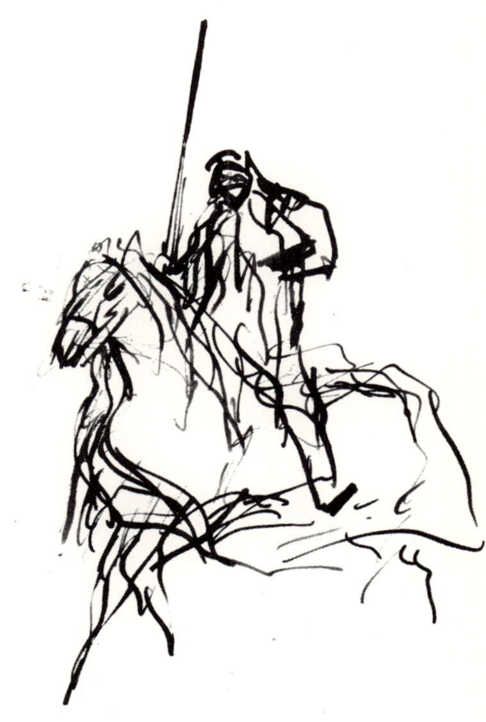

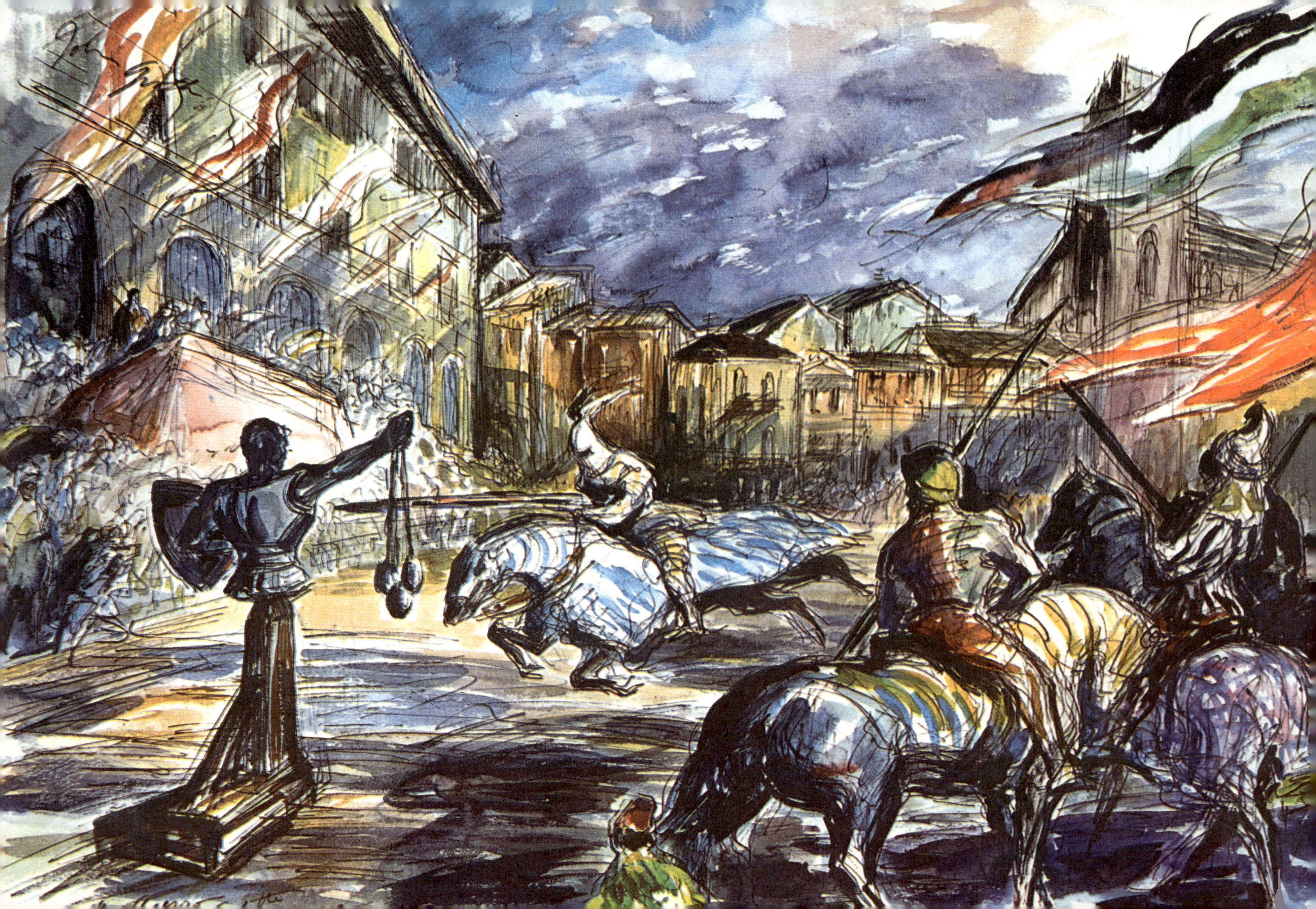

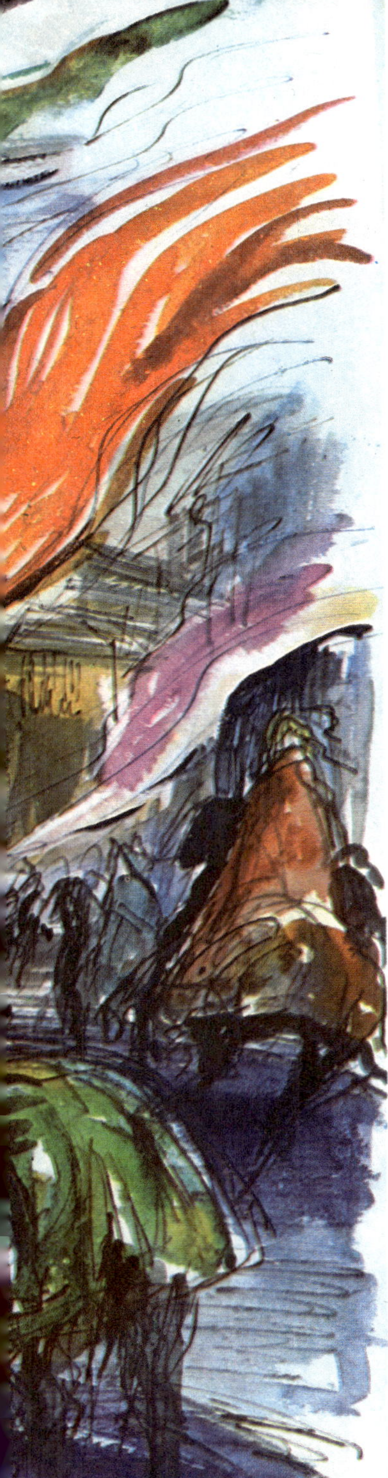

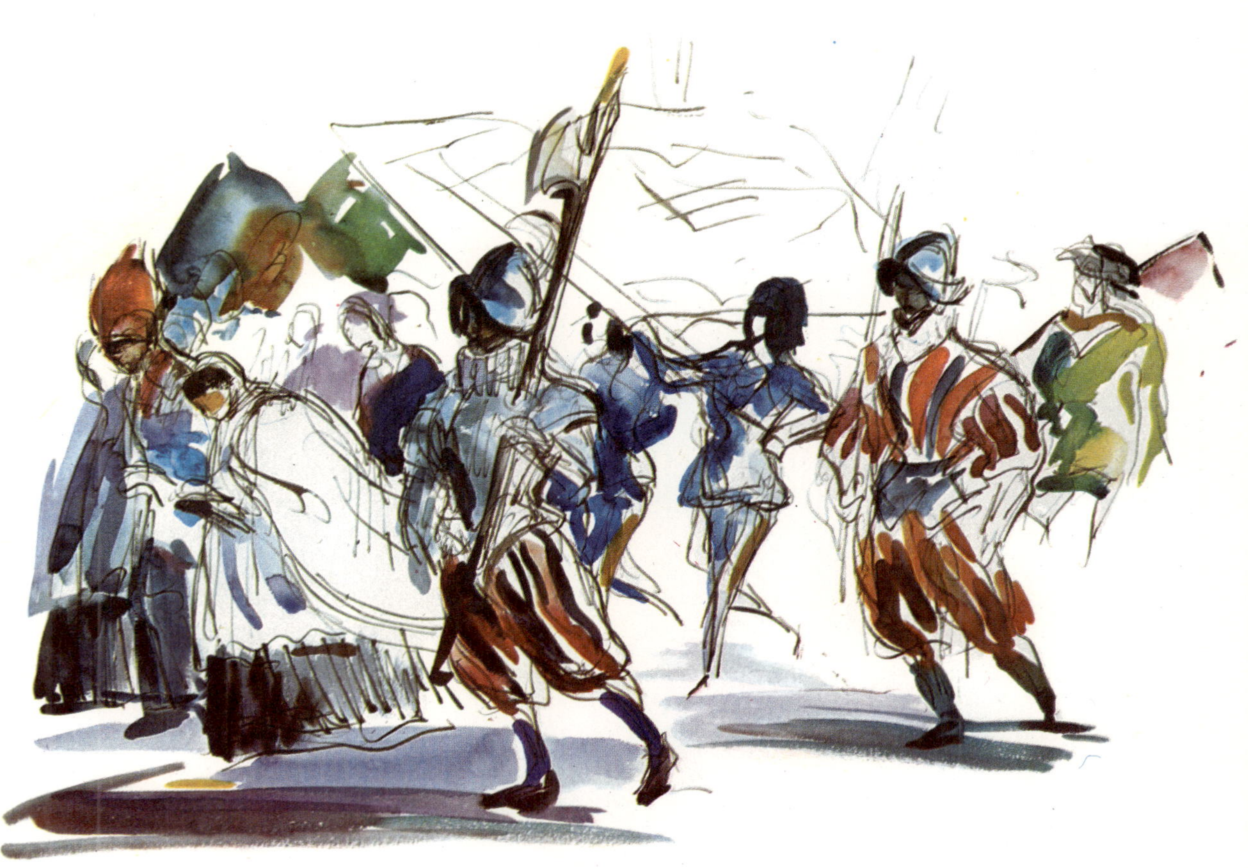

Opening Procession.

Crossbow

*While doing the sketches I felt like an artist in the sixteenth century.
The entire city was a perfect medieval stage.*

Each year during May a colorful company of men from Sansepolce in the northern Italian province of Arezzo travel south to Gubbio, in Umbria, to take up an ancient rivalry waged with the crossbow. Richly costumed in sixteenth-century style—shorts flaring over brilliant tights, mail shirts and plumed mountaineer hats—these men whose lineage goes back to the Middle Ages gather in the central square and compete against the best bowmen of Switzerland, Austria, West Germany and Belgium. Thronging the medieval square is the entire population of Gubbio—and very nearly everyone is decked out in appropriate historical garb. Although the main event may not be among the most famous in Europe, it is certainly one of the most ancient—and genuine.

To be sure, the crossbow is genuine enough. When it was developed more than 600 years ago, the crossbow was generally feared as the "total weapon"—just as the atom bomb was in its time. Using crossbows that could send an armor-piercing dart accurately to 400 yards, infantry invariably decimated cavalry. Even though it took as much as 20 seconds to load each time, the weapon was so terrifying that in 1139 the Pope banned its use "except for shooting infidels."

At Gubbio the crossbows are leveled at wooden targets placed some forty yards away from the marksmen. To load the crossbow the bowstring must be cocked with a special instrument called a "martinette" —a small type of jack operated by a screw thread. Because of its heft —it often weighs as much as 60 pounds—the crossbow generally is fired from a benchrest, much as in rifle competition. Compared with modern rifles and shotguns, shooting a crossbow is an extremely demanding task. Besides dexterity and a good eye, experience is essential to fire crossbowmanship; the slightest change in humidity or temperature can produce notable variations in the delivery of the arrow for which the bowman must learn to compensate.

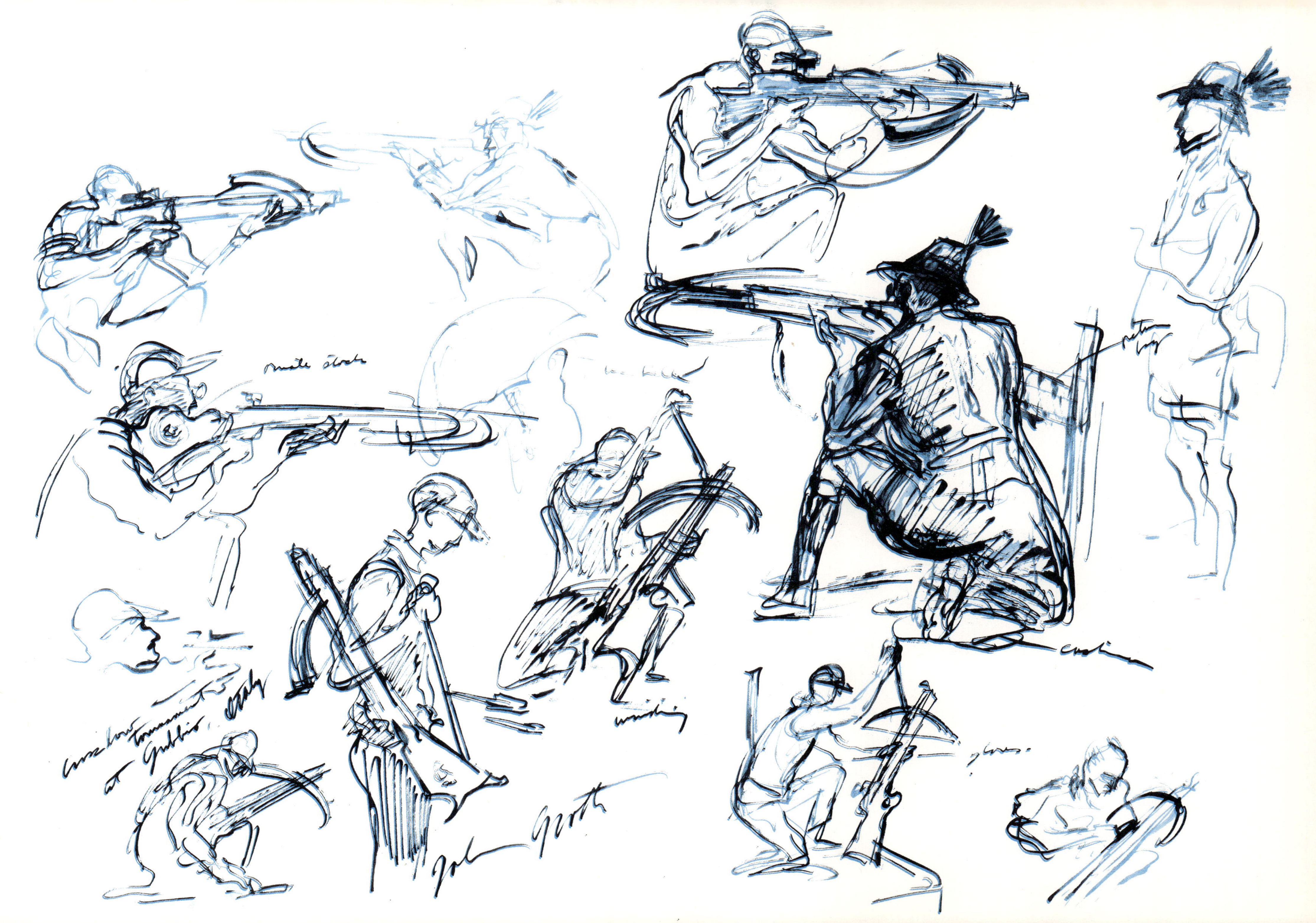

crossbow tournament
at Gubbio, Italy
John Groth

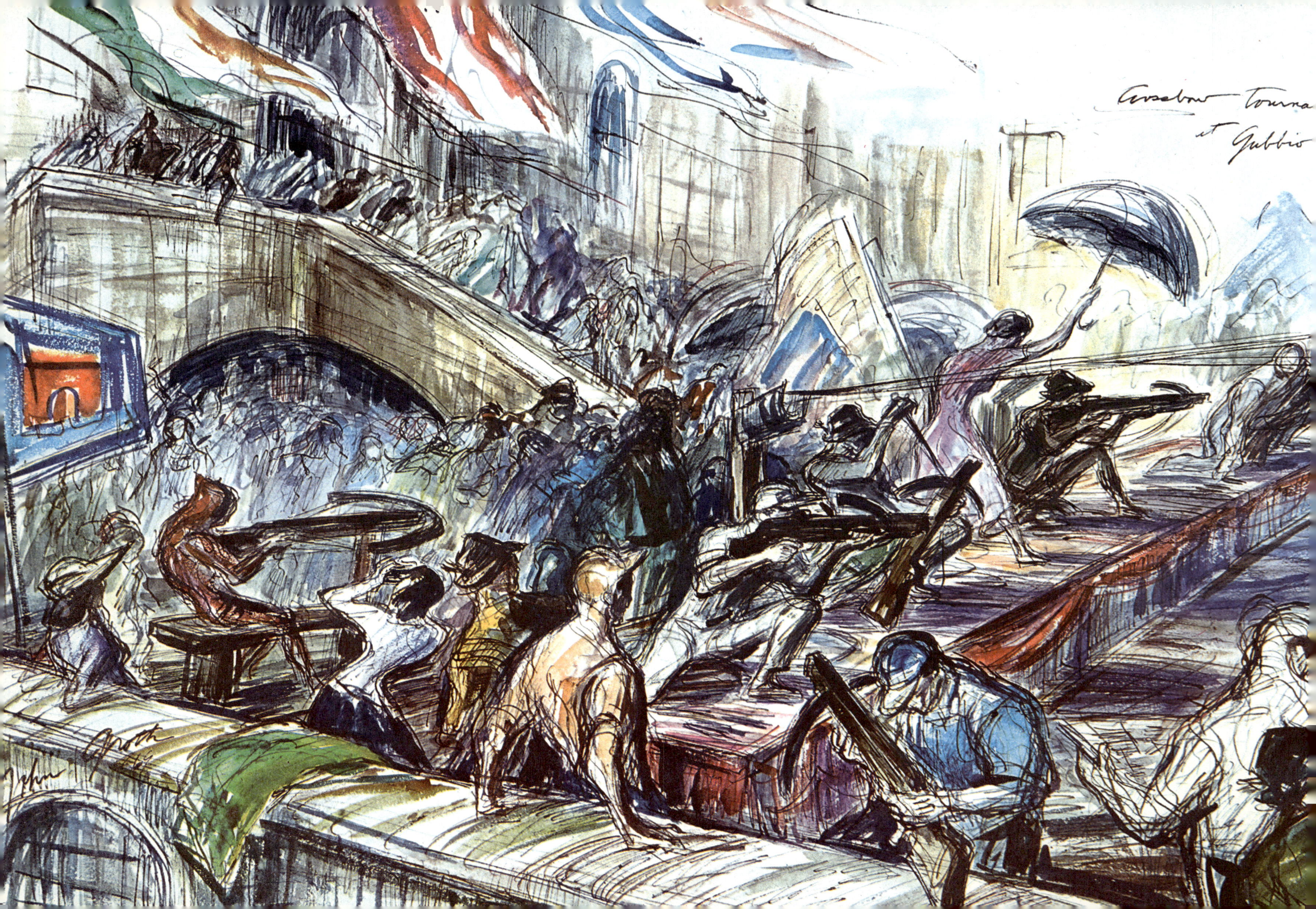

Crossbow Tourna
et Gubbio

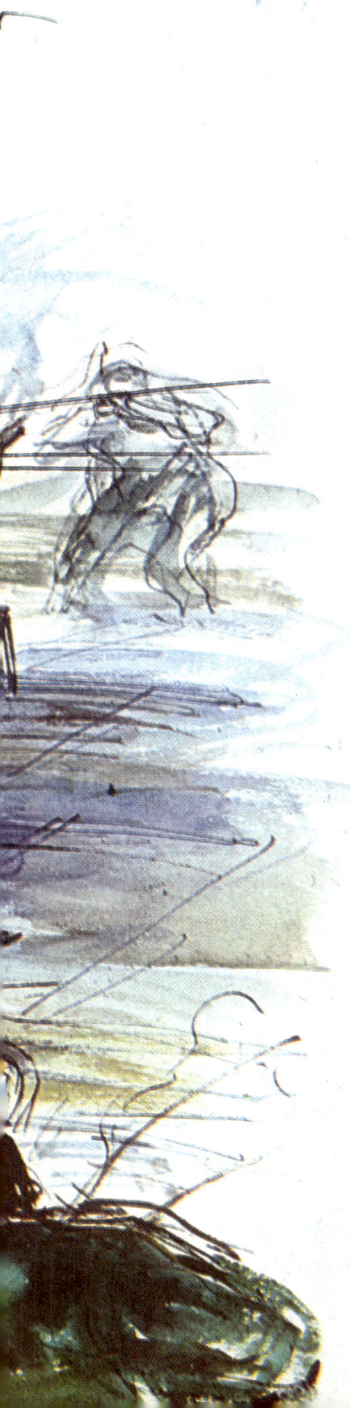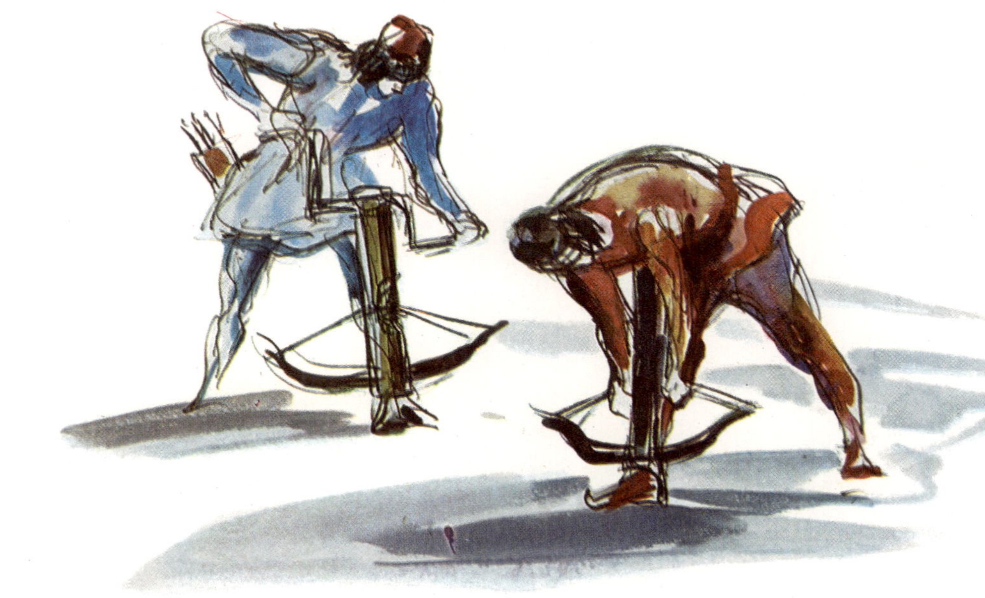

Tournament at Gubbio.

Mideast Sports

Most of the Mideast sports were sketched on the run. I caught pyramid climbing between planes; whip fighting from the window of a bus; Nubian water bugs on a tour of the Aswan Dam.

Except for the occasional liberated lady playing tennis in a Cairo country club or schussing across the waves off the beach at Beirut, the sporting life in the Mideast remains the private preserve of men. Which is a very good thing, because a great many of the sports indigenous to this primitive part of the world involve such a high degree of ferocity as to send shivers down the spine of the fairer half of the species.

While a few of the sports are organized team efforts, most of them are impromptu affairs played casually on streets. One of the on-the-spot games is stick fighting, a traditional pastime enjoyed particularly by Yemeni bedouins that goes back to the days when their Saracen ancestors did bloody battle with great, curved scimitars. In the modern version the contestants employ long sticks in place of the scimitars, felt gloves instead of mail gauntlets and small wooden shields rather than heavy palladins fashioned from hammered metal. A touch on the body scores a "wound"—and although the wounds are usually bloodless, a young stick fighter often pays painfully for his acquired skill with a mountain sunset of high bumps and purple bruises ranging over his body.

Even more savage is a snappy little diversion known as whip fighting. Played primarily in Syria, Lebanon and Iraq, the game's object is quite simple: to flail the skin off one's opponent with a frighteningly long bull whip. "I kept trying to figure out the point-scoring system of the game," says Groth, "until I realized there wasn't one. Apparently, the game is over when one of the boys has had enough—and admits it.

In Iran a curious form of partridge hunting requires a kind of horsemanship possessed by few of the well-seated swells of the foxey set. Roughly, the hunt resembles a cavalry charge. The shooters—usually mounted on Arabian horses—gallop across the valley floors in this mountainous land, hoping to flush a covey of Asian partridge. When the birds explode from the knee-high grass, the marksmen drop their reins and, still going at full tilt, blaze away with their shotguns, often creating, as they say, a "rain of dropping game."

The organized sports, however, usually tend to be relatively civilized. Visitors to the Aswan Dam, for example, are often treated to a pastel parade of tiny boats (usually eight feet long) known as Nubian Waterbugs. Piloted expertly by small boys, the waterbugs—looking like so many bright-colored beetles on the blue expanse of Aswan—are a welcome relief from the lustier sports. "I had a chance to think and draw in more delicate terms," recalls Groth.

Still another nonviolent sport is pyramid climbing. In the 1900's a traveler, writer and critic of his time—and ours—observed the sport and wrote:

The traditional Arab proposed, in the traditional way, to run down Cheops, cross the eighth of a mile of sand intervening between it and the tall pyramid Cephron, ascend to Cephron's summit and to us at the top of Cheops, all in nine minutes by the watch, and the whole service to be rendered for a single dollar.

. . . He started. We watched. He went bounding down the vast broadside, spring after spring like an ibex. He grew smaller and smaller till he became a bobbing pygmy, away down toward the bottom—then disappeared. . . . There he goes; Too true—it was too true. He was very small now. Gradually, but surely, he overcame the level ground. He began to spring and climb. Up, up, up —at last he reached the smooth coating—now for it. But he clung to it with his toes and fingers like a fly. He crawled this way and that—away to the right, slanting upward—away to the left, still slanting upward—and stood at last, a black peg on the summit, and waved his pygmy scarf! Then he crept downward to the raw steps again, then picked up his agile heels and flew. We lost him presently. But presently again we saw him under us, mounting with undiminished energy. Shortly he bounded into our midst with a gallant warwhoop. Time, eight minutes, forty-seconds.

Mark Twain, *Innocents Abroad*, 1869

When Groth arrived at the timeless site where Twain had paid a dollar to watch a very small man perform a herculean feat, he gazed at Cheops, rising 450 feet and stretching some 700 feet at the base, then at Cephron, its equally huge companion. John shook his head and reconsidered the old saw about men being better in the old days. To find out (and also test the journalistic integrity of one Mr. Clemens), Groth hired a six-man team from nearby Cairo for five dollars, positioned himself atop Cheop's pointed pate, yelled "go" and set to work with speedball and pad.

Under the heavy desert sun the six nut-brown racers began scrambling over the same course as Twain's man had negotiated almost a century before. Down they flew, as if their feet never touched the steps. Up, up, up they went—until only their bright green sleeveless track shirts were but specks on the great stone slants of Cephron. Then down, down, down. Then up again—all of them completing the course under seven minutes, twenty-one seconds. His sketches completed, John happily paid the price and returned to his hotel in Cairo with his faith in human progress restored—along with his trust in the veracity of America's greatest writer.

Stick Fighting.

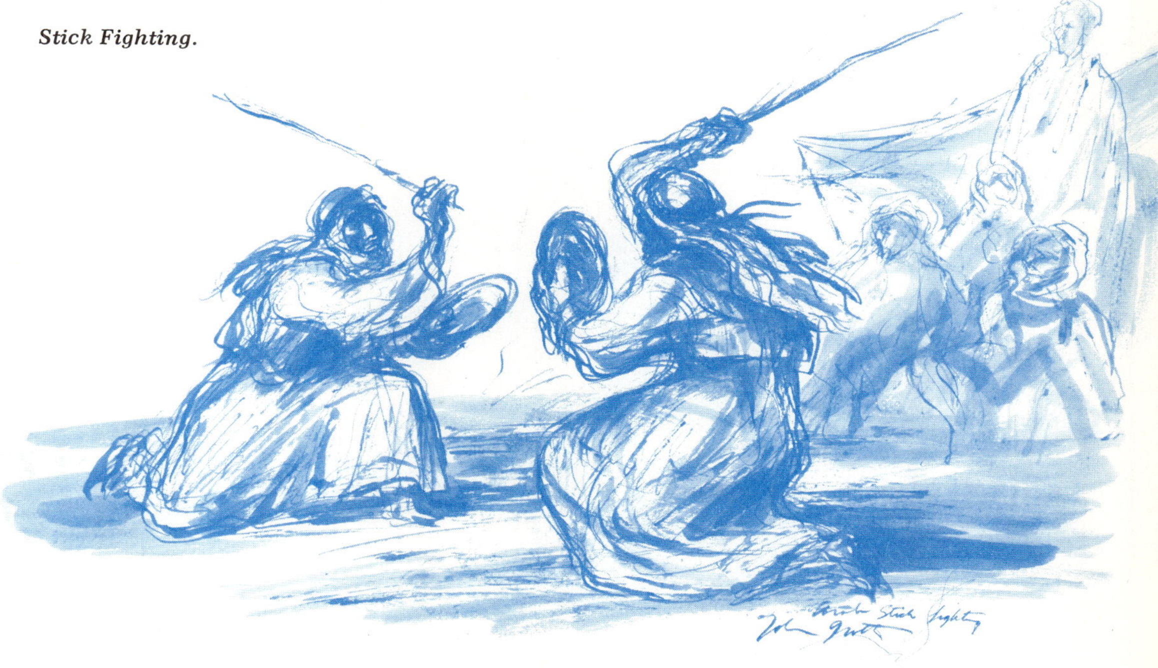

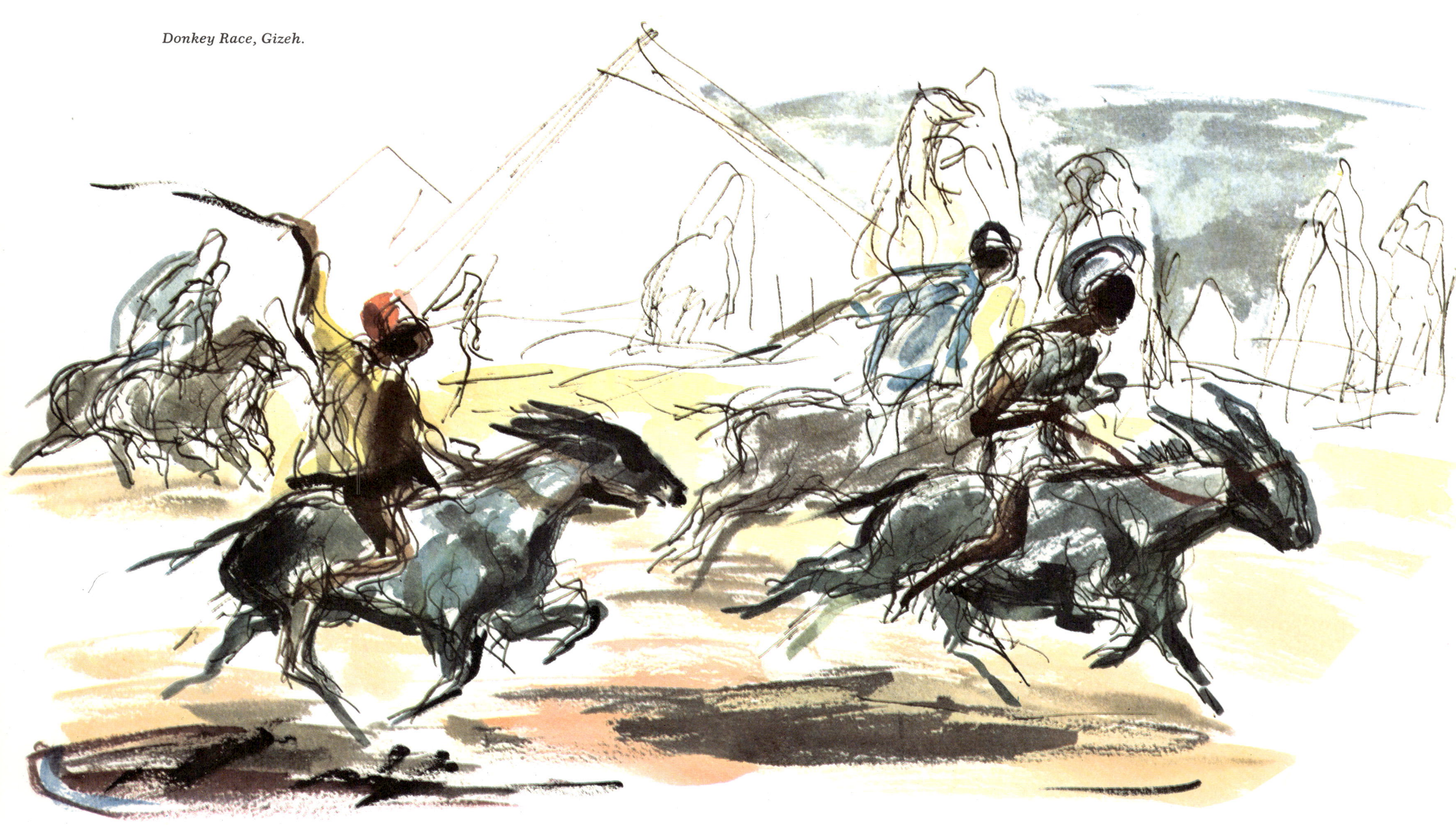

Donkey Race, Gizeh.

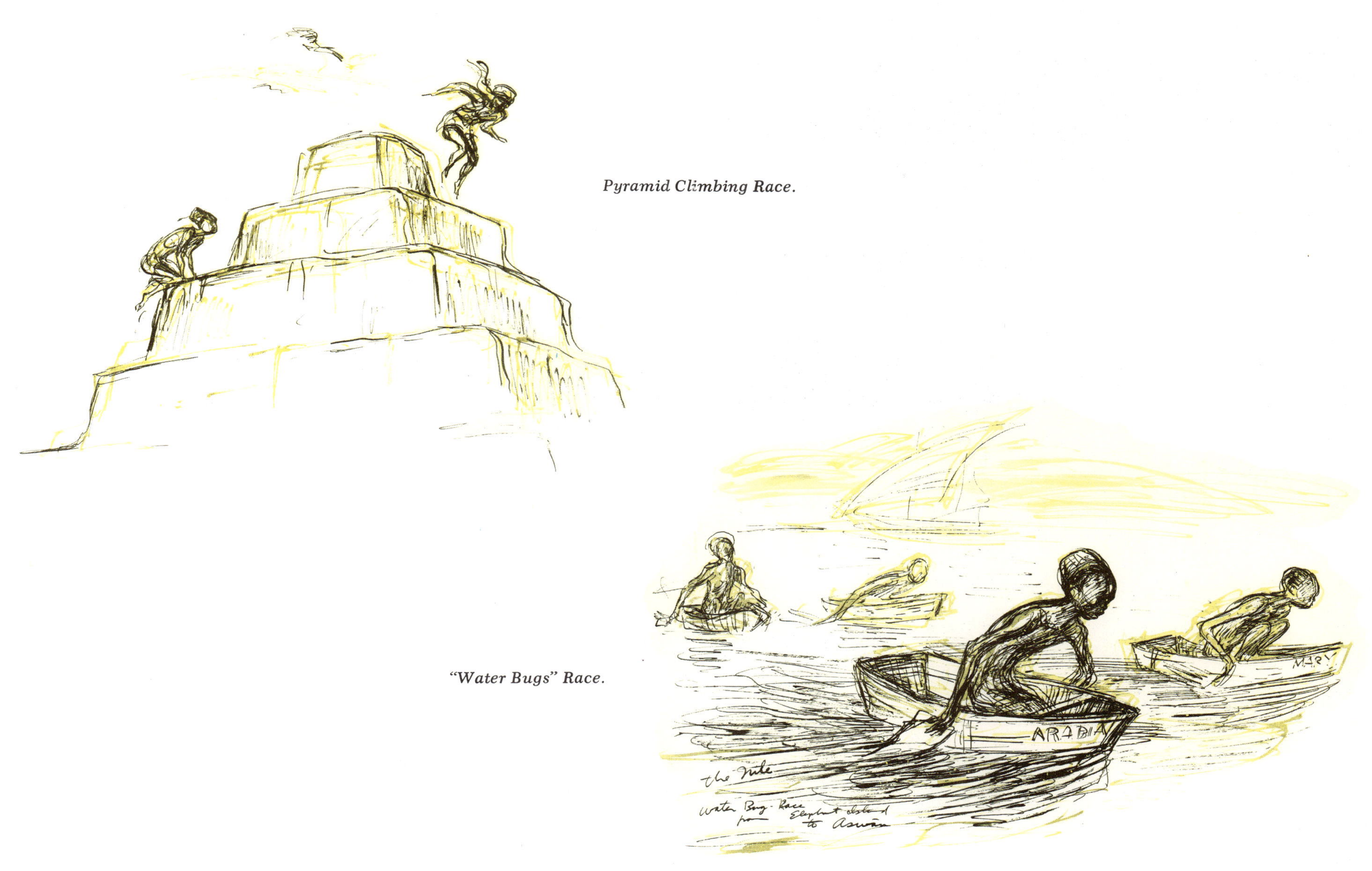

Pyramid Climbing Race.

"Water Bugs" Race.

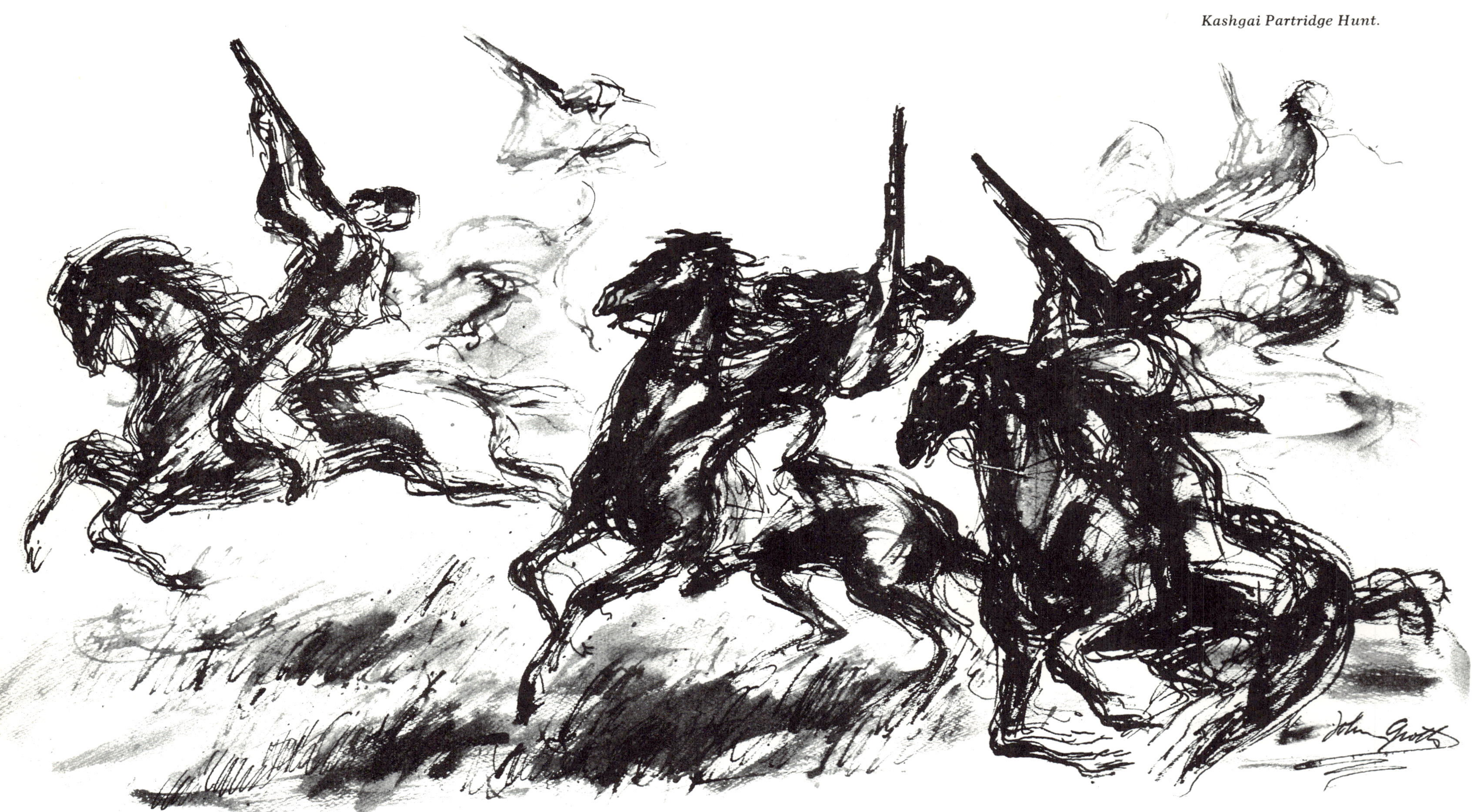

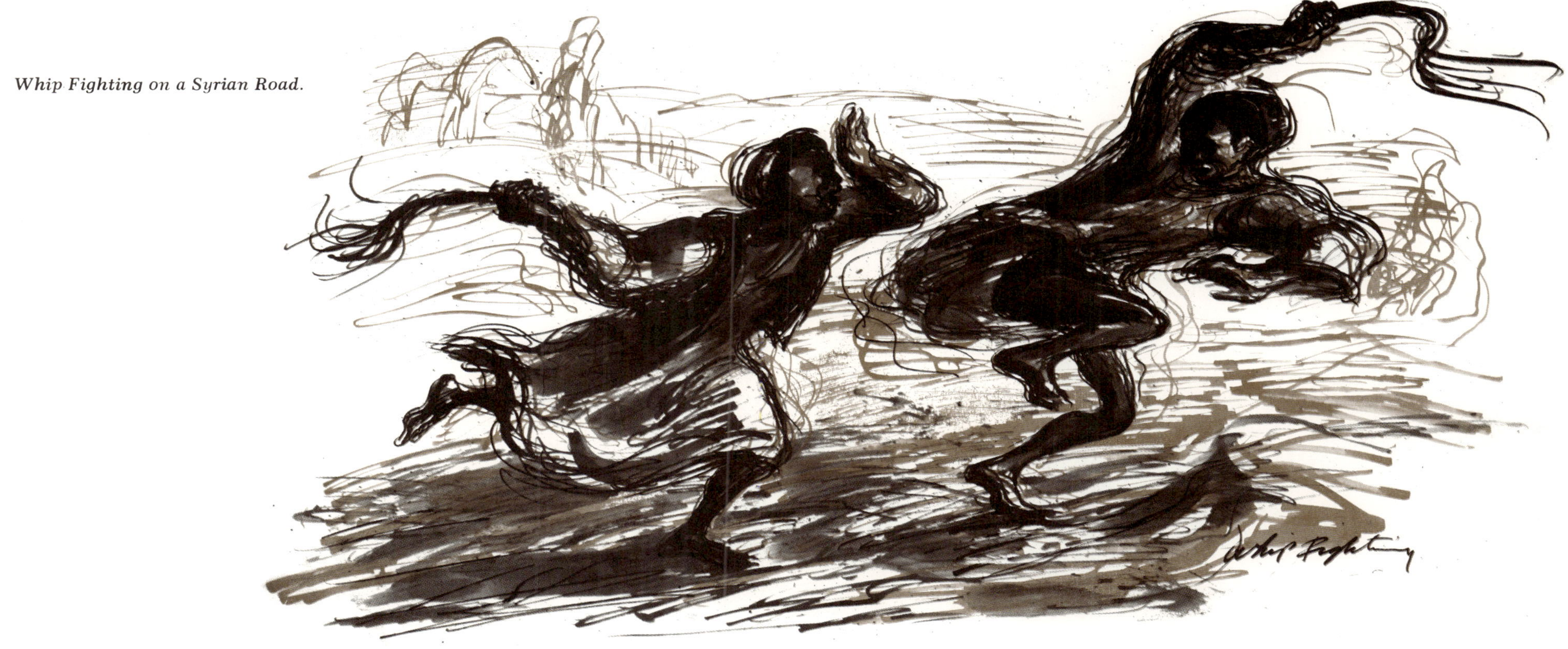

Whip Fighting on a Syrian Road.

Palio

I've seen a lot of horseraces. But this was easily the most rousing of them all, from the colorful pre-race ceremonies to the raucous post-race squabbles.

No racing fans anywhere can claim a race so old and so rousing as Sienna's Palio, run sometime during July or August—except, of course, during a time of plague or a siege—for four centuries. Held in the main square, its cobblestones carpeted for the event with tons of soil, the opening ceremonies are worth a visit by themselves. While a team of freshly scrubbed white oxen haul the treasured victory banner—the Palio—around the makeshift track, a procession of representatives of the city's seventeen boroughs is led about by a mounted brigade of armored knights and men-at-arms clad in costumes straight out of the Middle Ages.

The race draws nearly every one of the city's 60,000 residents, and each cheers madly for the horse representing his borough. The horses are picked as much for endurance as speed. Certain partisans for the rival boroughs—which bear such symbolic names as Goose, Worm, Giraffe, Unicorn and Snail—occasionally attempt to hypo the energies of their charge with a sneak-shot of dope. But the rumor of a possible doping only seems to heighten the interest. Others seek Divine help. Some borough bigwigs bring their horse to church the morning before the race—leading him up to the altar for the Padre's blessing. (It is considered a healthy omen if the horse happens to relieve himself during the ceremony.)

At post time the jammed square erupts. Last-minute bets are placed. Tourists and Siennese jam the rails shoulder-to-shoulder, cheering on their choices.

Just as their ancestors have done since the time of de Medicis, the seventeen horses and their riders circle the track three times (in all, about five furlongs). As always, the steel-helmeted riders battle for the lead not only with speed but by slashing one another with short whips made of beef sinew. The horses—slipping on the exposed cobblestones—bump and slam together, very often unseating a rider, who is deemed extremely lucky to escape unscathed.

The race usually takes less than a minute and a half. The winning horse is ceremoniously covered with the heavy Palio while the jockey receives his purse, 360 lire (about 55 cents). The losing jockeys, however, must survive still another battle—convincing their backers that they rode an honest race.

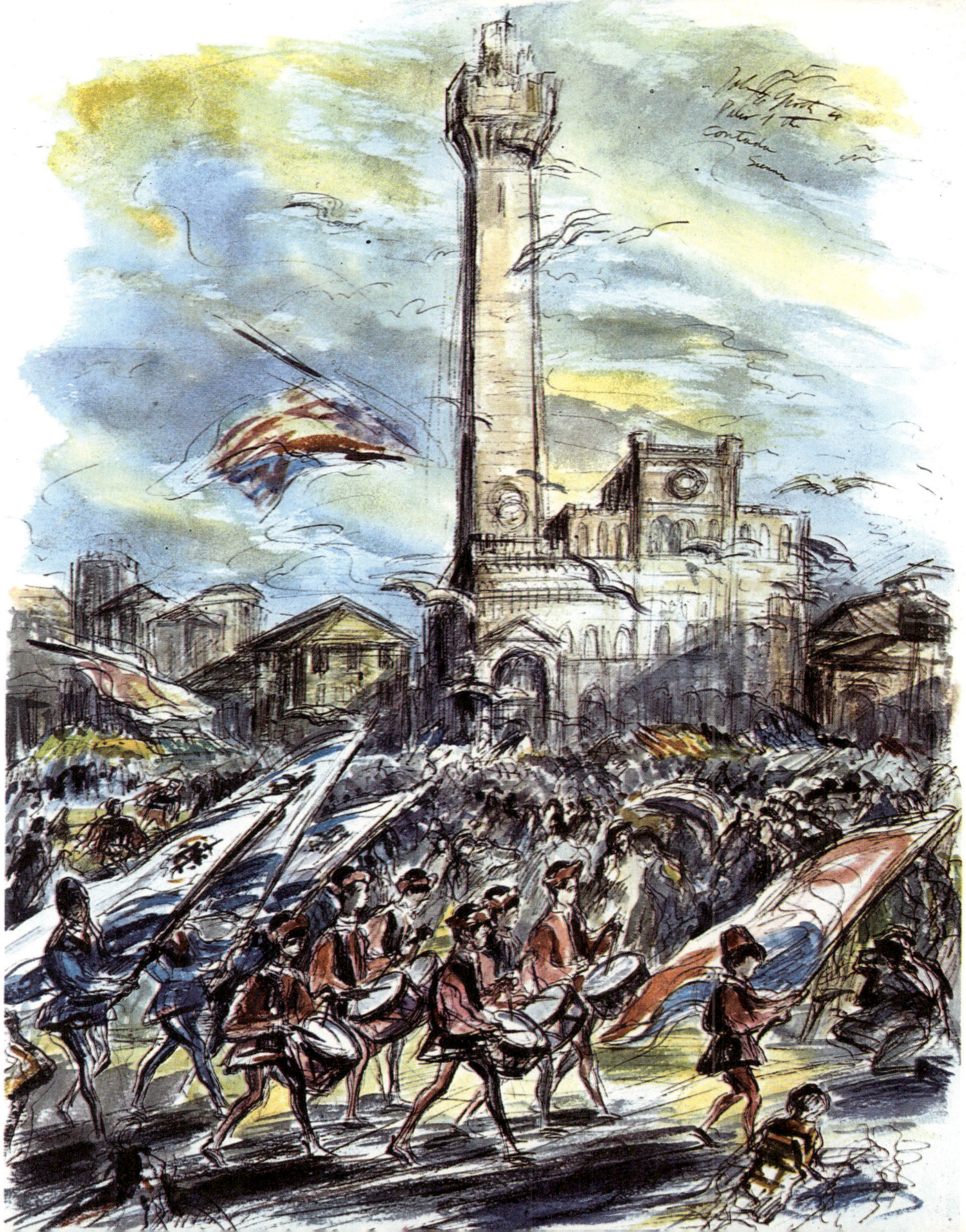

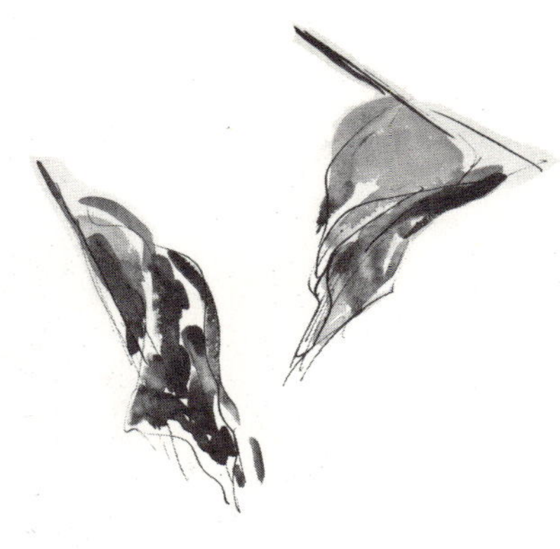

Parade of the Contradas, Sienna.

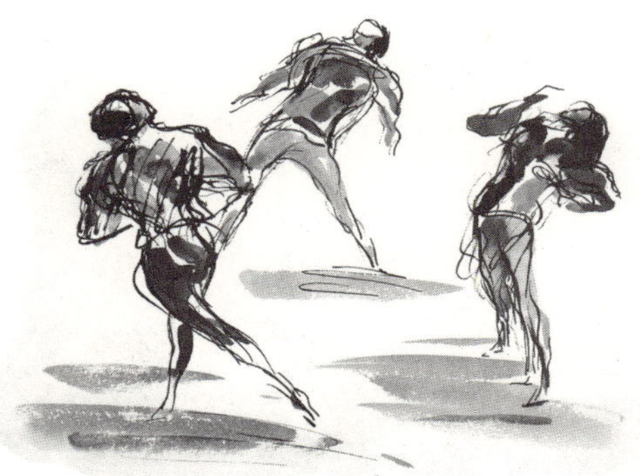

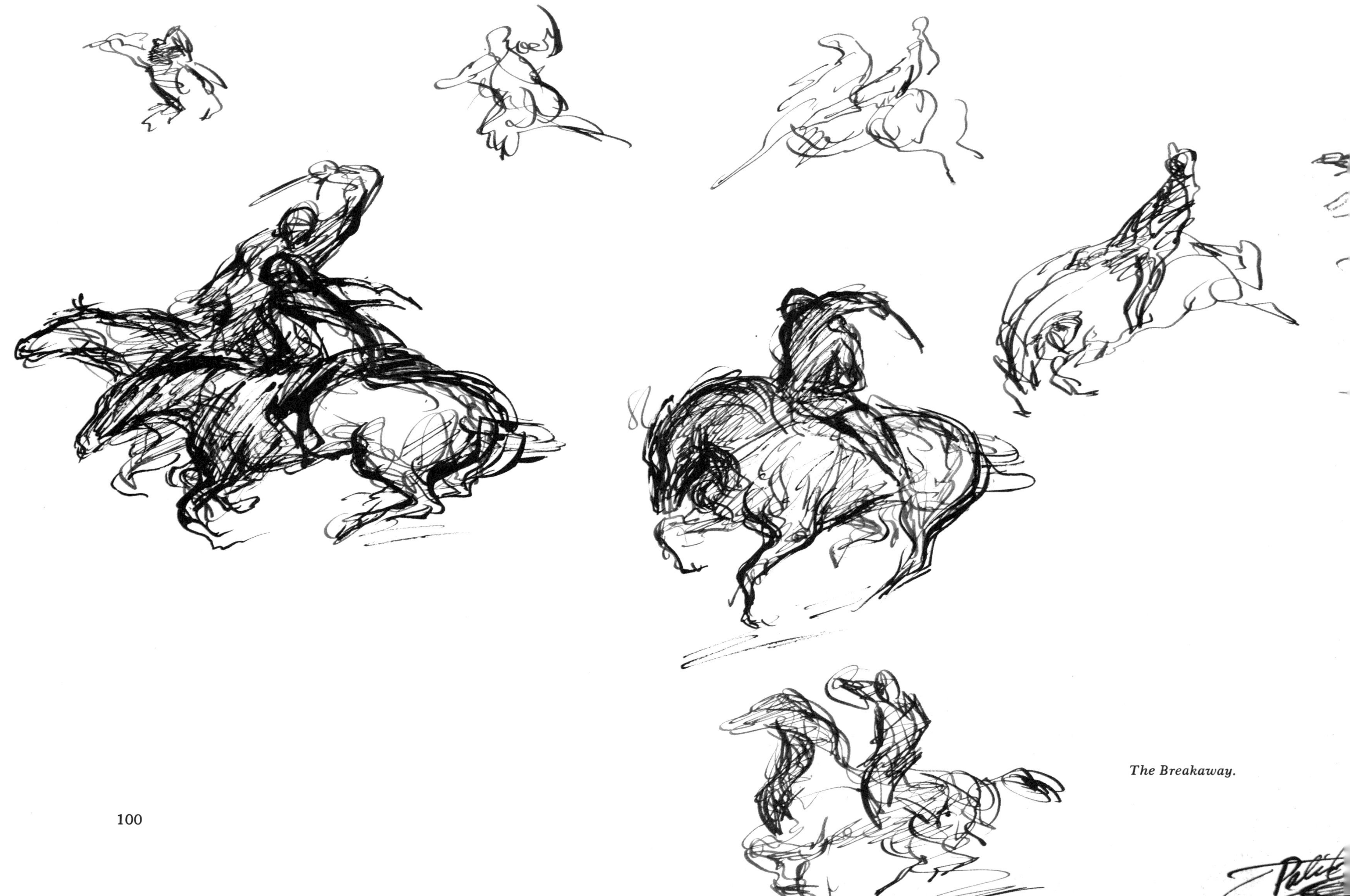

The Breakaway.

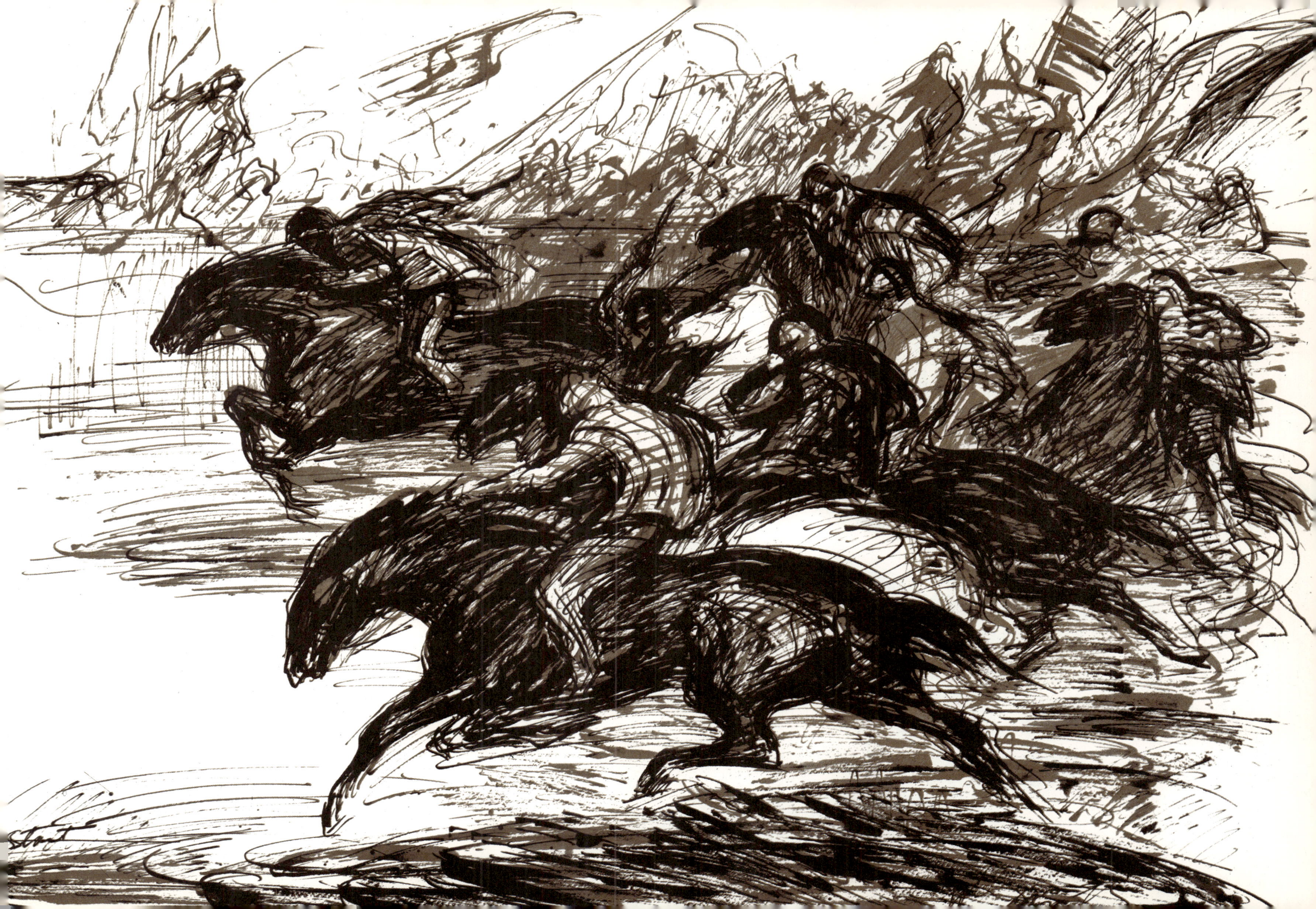

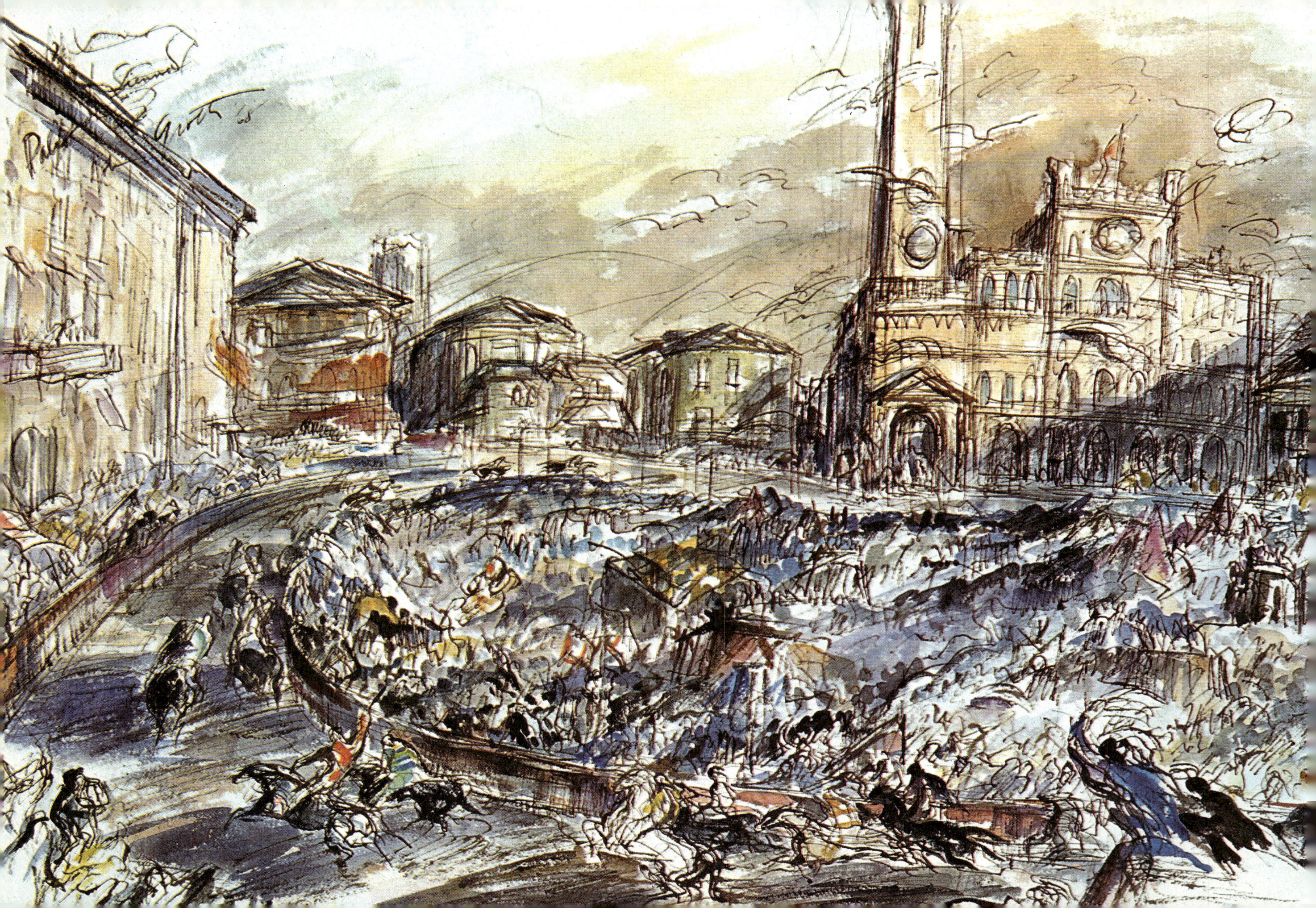

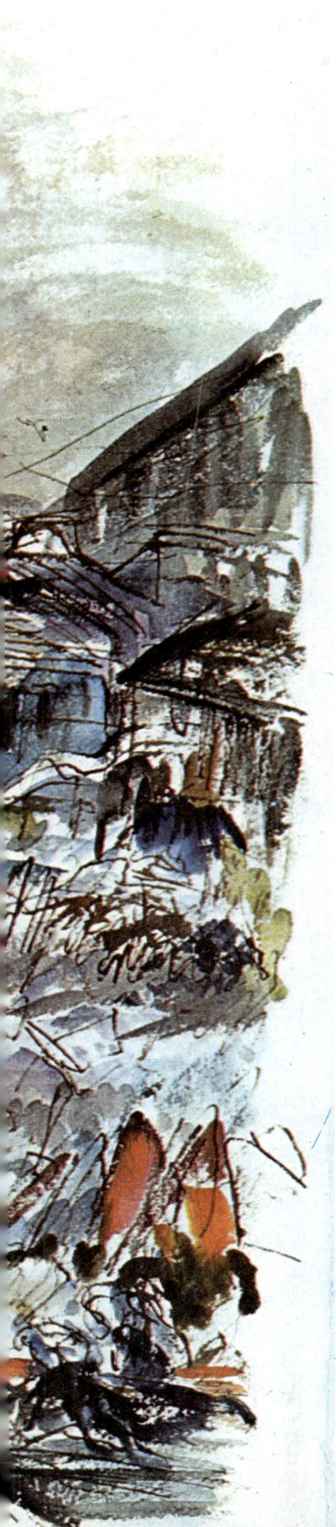

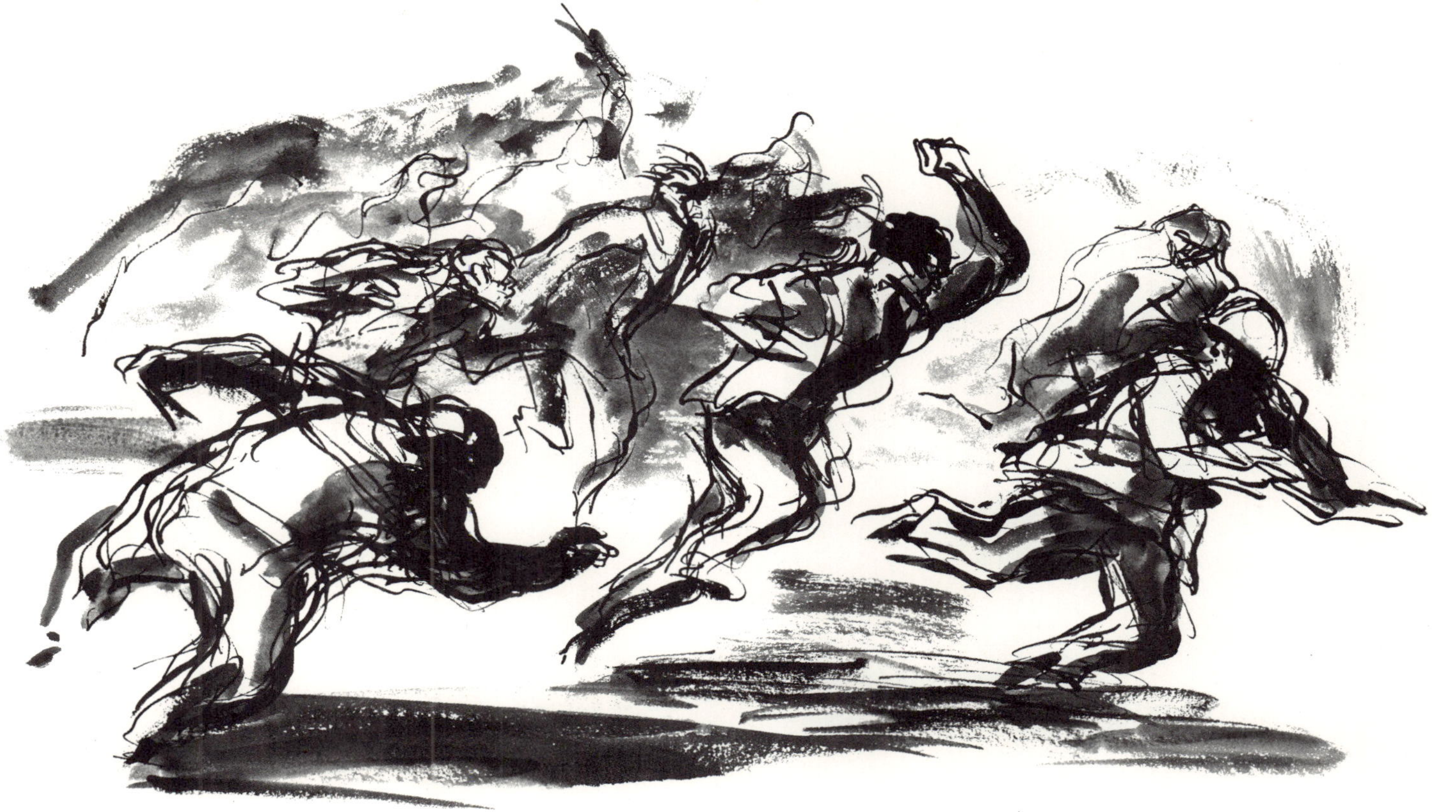

The Palio.

Running of the Bulls

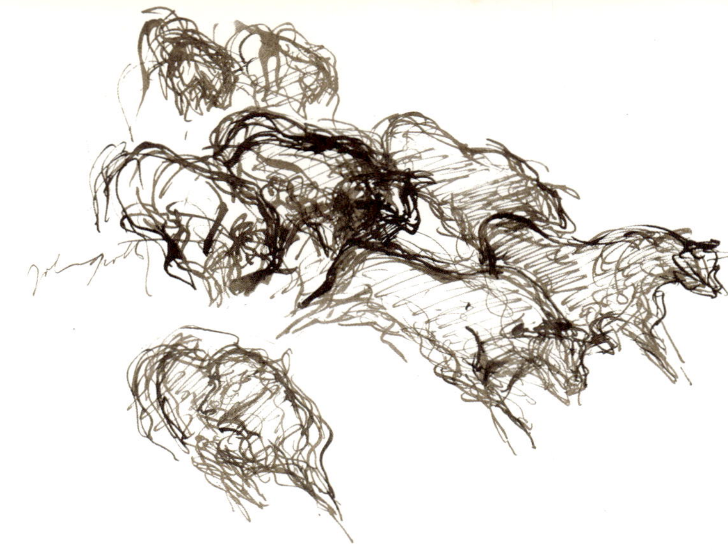

At 7 A.M. the rocket is launched from the Plaza de Toros, signalling the start of the *encierros*. With wide-eyed women jamming the balconies and wined-up men, called *valientes* and armed with rolled-up newspapers, lining the chutelike *avenidas* leading to the plaza, the six bulls—and their steers—that will die that day in the arena are released for the crazy, thronging charge of just under a mile into the holding pens. Those not so fortunate as to have been to Pamplona during the ten-day Fiesta of San Fermín certainly know of it from accounts in newspapers, magazines, books and on films. Others have had people attempt to describe it to them, attempt to explain why the running of the bulls is one of the most explosively memorable experiences in the world. But try as they may, Pamplona veterans know deep down that all their words and the most artful photos cannot begin to tell it like it is.

However, there is one combination of picture and word that comes as close to the truth as a bull's horn does to a matador during a perfectly performed veronica—Groth and Hemingway. In *The Sun Also Rises* Hemingway wrote:

". . . Everything looked sharp and clear, and the town smelt of the early morning.

"The stretch of ground from the edge of the town to the bull-ring was muddy. There was a crowd all along the fence that led to the ring, and the outside balconies and the top of the bull-ring were solid with people. I heard the rocket and I knew I could not get into the ring in time to see the bulls come in, so I shoved through the crowd to the fence. I was pushed close against the planks of the fence. Between the two fences of the runway the police were clearing the crowd along. They walked or trotted on into the bull-ring. Then people commenced to come running. A drunk slipped and fell. Two policemen grabbed him and rushed him over to the fence. The crowd were running fast now. There was a great shout from the crowd, and putting my head through between the boards I saw the bulls just coming out of the street into the long running pen. They were going fast and gaining on the crowd. Just then another drunk started out from the fence with a blouse in his hands. He wanted to do capework with the bulls. The two policemen tore out, collared him, one hit him with a club, and they dragged him against the fence and stood flattened out against the fence as the last of the crowd and the bulls went by. There were so many people running ahead of the bulls that the mass thickened and slowed up going through the gate into the ring, and as the bulls passed, galloping together, heavy, muddy-sided, horns swinging, one shot ahead caught a man in the running crowd in the back and lifted him in the air. Both the man's arms were by his sides, his head went back as the horn went in, and the bull lifted him and then dropped him. The bull picked another man running in front, but the man disappeared into the crowd, and the crowd was through the gate and into the ring with the bulls behind them. The red door of the ring went shut, the crowd on the outside balconies of the bull-ring were pressing through to the inside . . ."

The running of the bulls occurs every morning of the Fiesta of San Fermin, which runs its jubilant course from July 6th to July 17th, celebrating the life of San Fermin, a third-century saint who is credited with converting the region to Catholicism—and who was martyred for his deed.

A typical festival day begins with band music and the caping of the calves in the arena at 5:45 A.M. Coming fast on its heels is the running of the bulls at 7; then a concert of Basque music followed by a comic bullfight in the Plaza de Toros; each afternoon, beginning at 5:30, the *corridas* are held, usually involving three matadors who each fight two bulls. Throughout the history of the festival, the world's best bullfighters have worked in the ring at Pamplona—from Juan Belmonte to Antonio Ordonez, whose style Hemingway described as "slow magic" in his final treatment of bullfighting, *The Dangerous Summer* (1959). After the bullfights there is more band music in the plaza, and at 10:30 a giant bull constructed of fireworks is paraded through the streets. At 11 the night explodes with a fireworks display to rival anything ever performed at the Chinese New Year. Throughout it all the official liquid is wine—red or white—drunk deeply from communal skins.

But the running of the bulls has remained the major event for over 400 years—and each morning the *valientes*, many of whom have imbibed and serenaded all night, arrive to test themselves in order that they may continue to drink through the day with a feeling of having earned the privilege. Well aware of this—and also of the fact that bulls invariably run faster than men—the local government has devised a set of rules for the early-morning madness.

Listed among the twenty-two paragraphs of instructions; no one under 18 is permitted to run; all must have suitable shoes; no one may run either behind the bulls or directly at them; no runner should be drunk! It is forbidden to carry any objects—capes, shirts, etc.—for the purpose of inciting the bulls to riot. (The last rule tacitly recognizes that the matadors would be in considerably more danger in the afternoon if the bulls learned to follow any large piece of cloth.)

There has not been a death during the running of the bulls in twenty-four years. But each year the crowds at festival get bigger and bigger and the local officials are worried that eventually there will be a tragedy during the early morning at Pamplona. "It has got to happen," says one Pamplona policeman. "Someday someone is going to fall and the entire crowd will pile up and then the bulls will come and some people will die."

Despite the drinking, the danger, the crowds, the lack of sleep, the very often poor accommodations, the occasional brawls—or perhaps because of it all—Pamplona is quite a place to be beginning July 6th. You may love it and you may hate it. But whichever, you can probably credit your trip to the incredible public relations job that Hemingway did for the festival. In recognition of his efforts the government placed a granite bust of Hemingway in Plaza de Toros, near a street recently christened Paseo de Hemingway. On the bust, the inscription reads:

"Ernest Hemingway, Nobel Prize Winner. Friend of the people and admirer of their fiestas, who knew how to describe and so to make them known; The City of Pamplona, San Fermin, 1968."

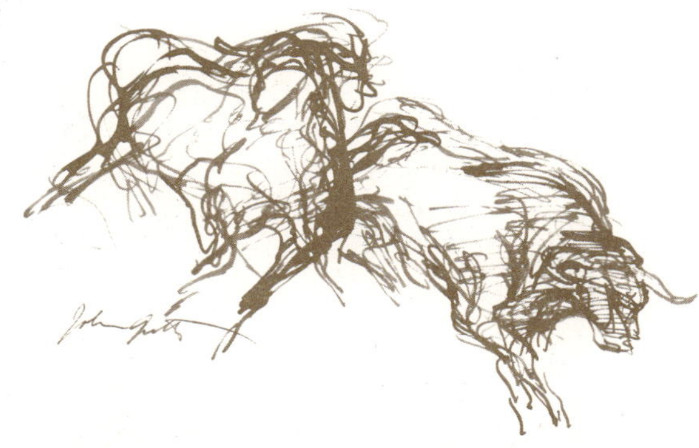

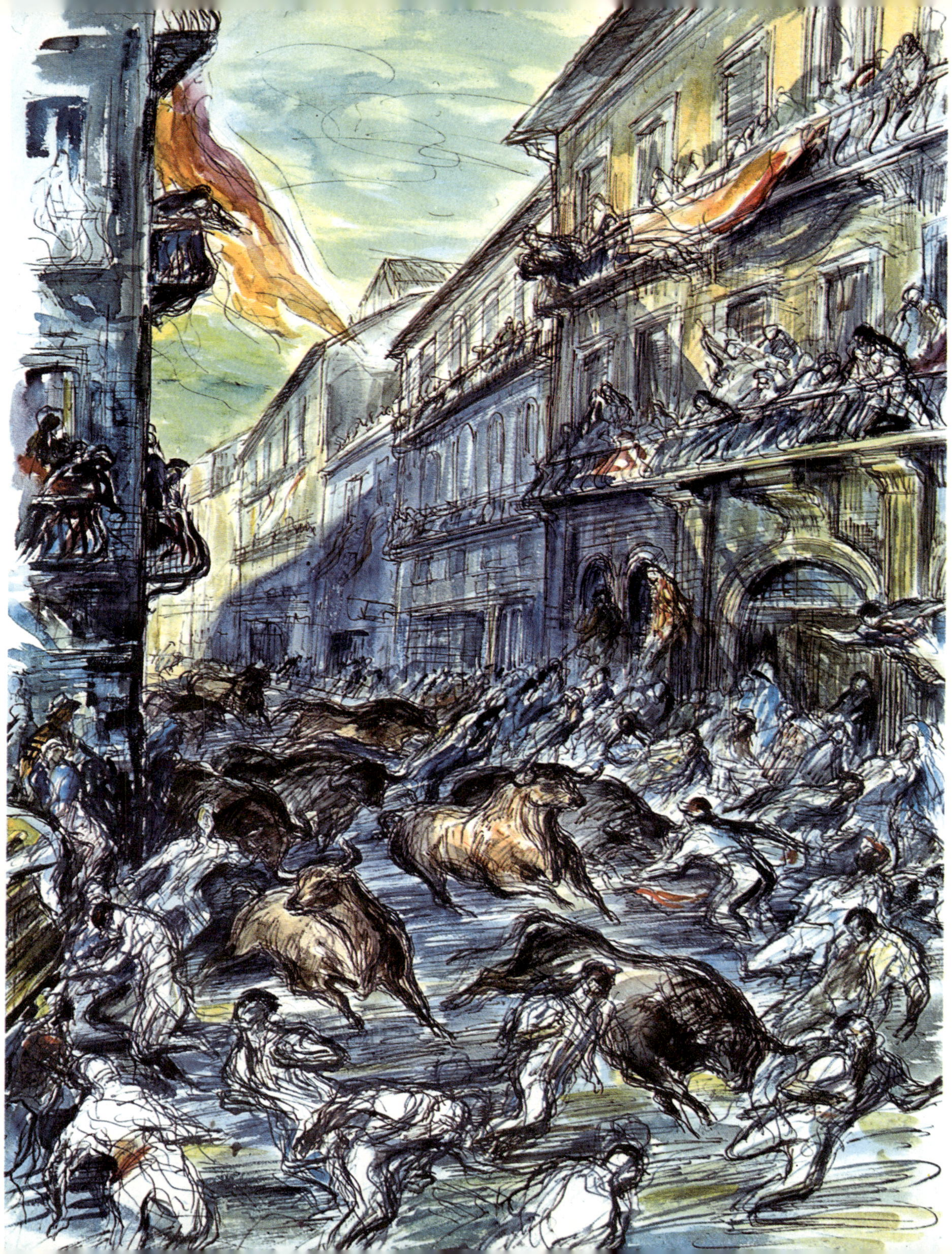

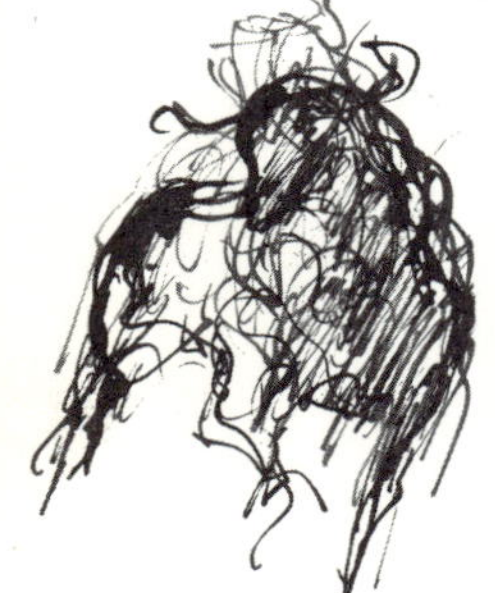

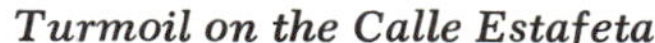
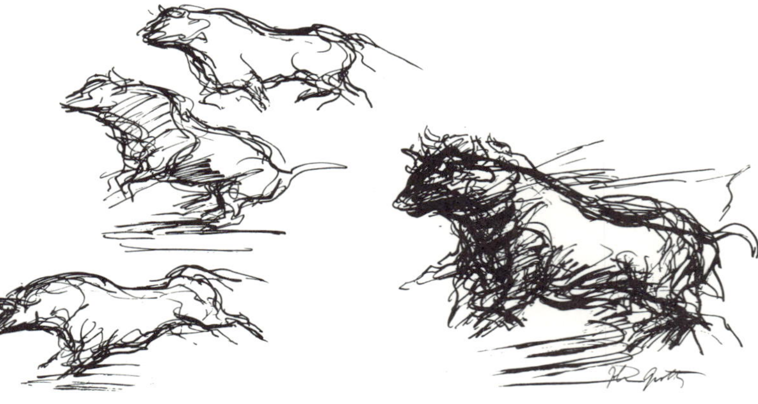

Turmoil on the Calle Estafeta.

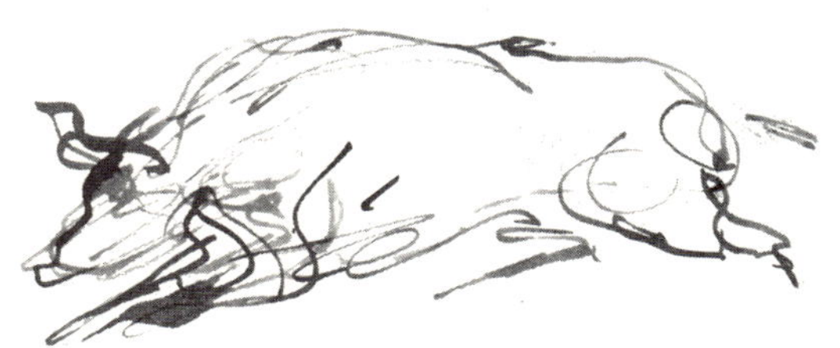

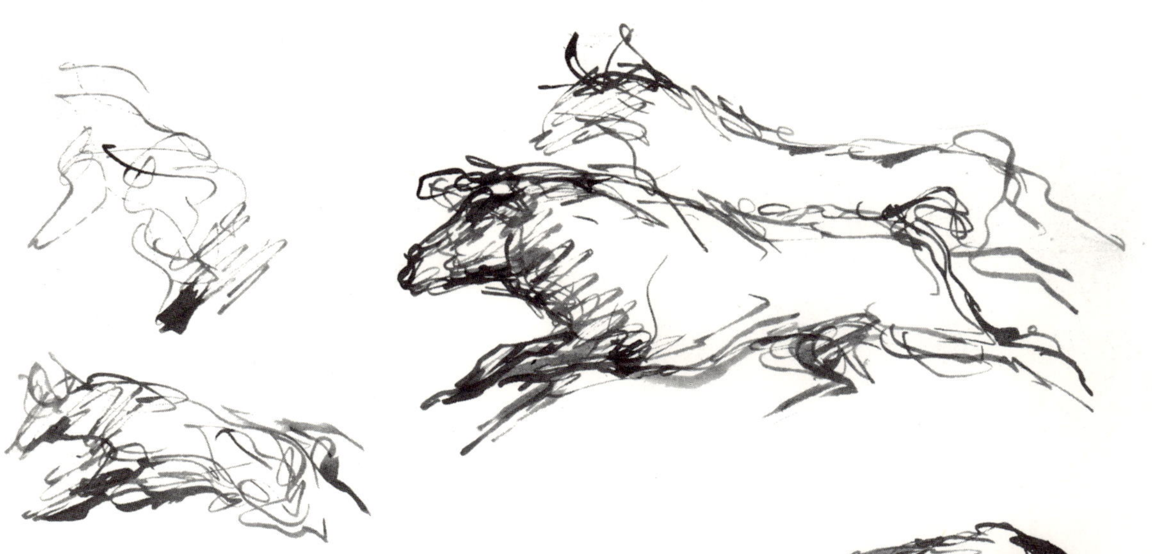

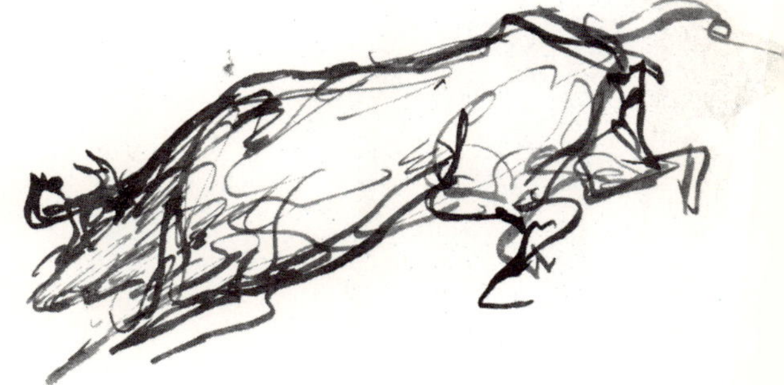

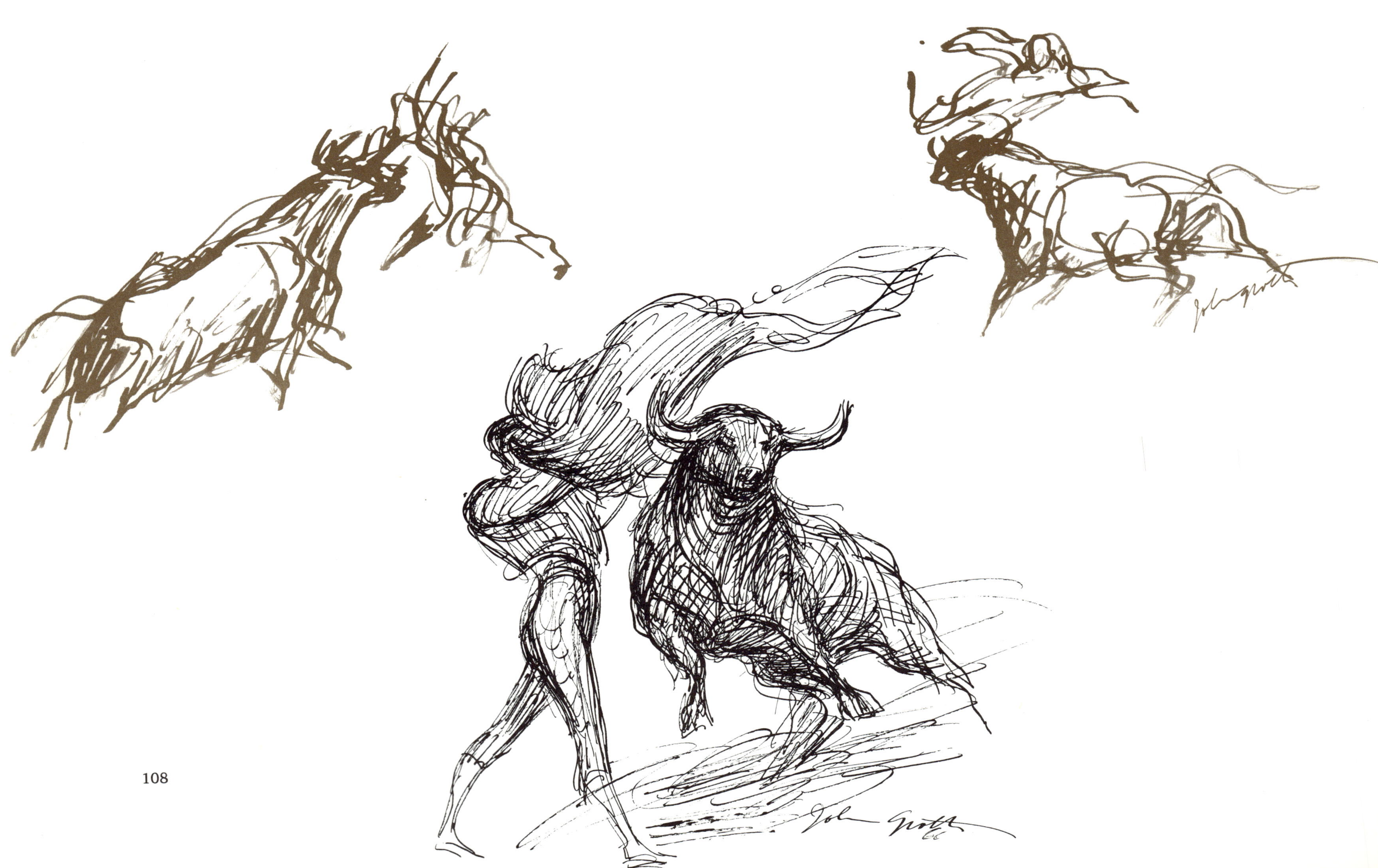

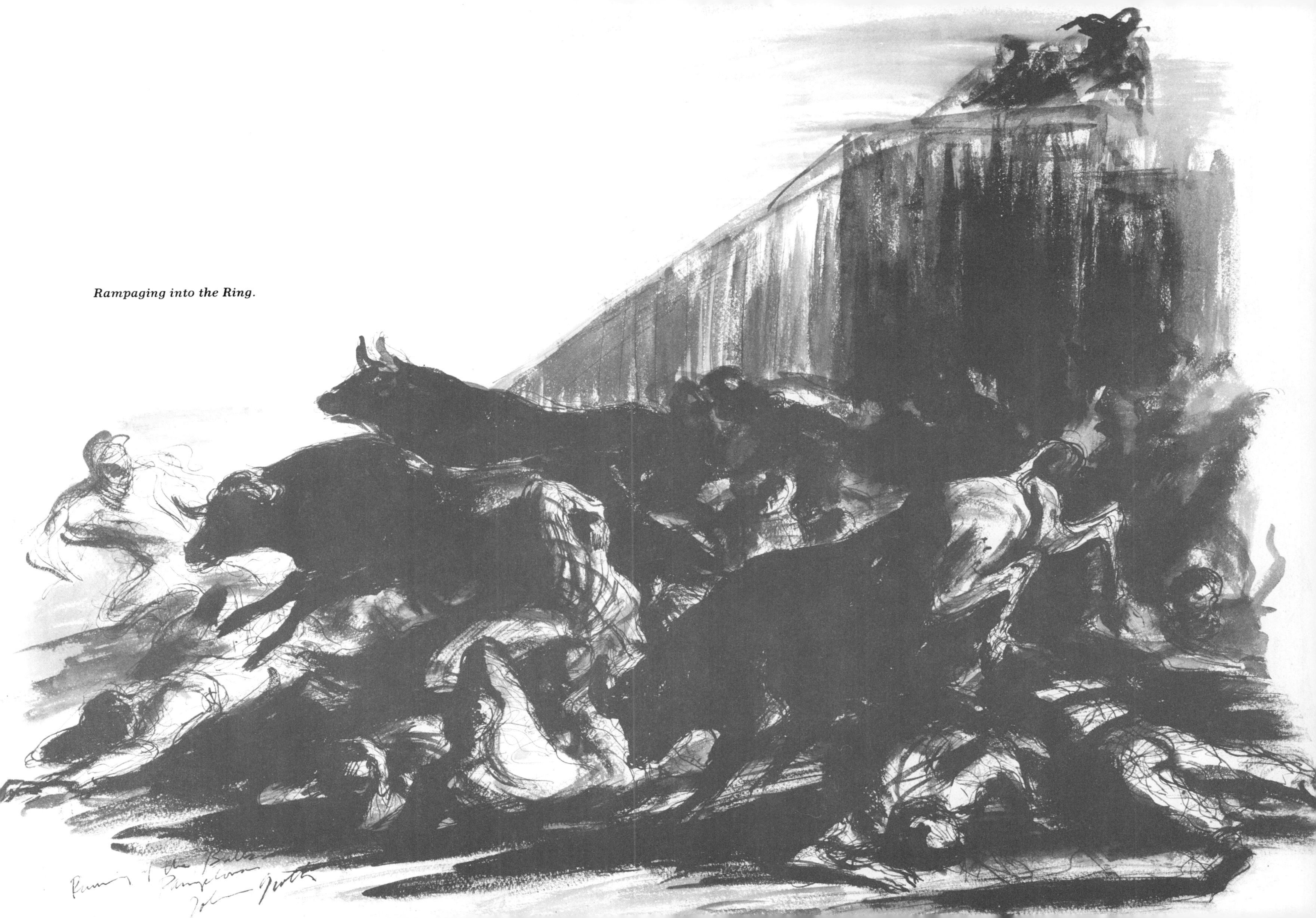

Rampaging into the Ring.

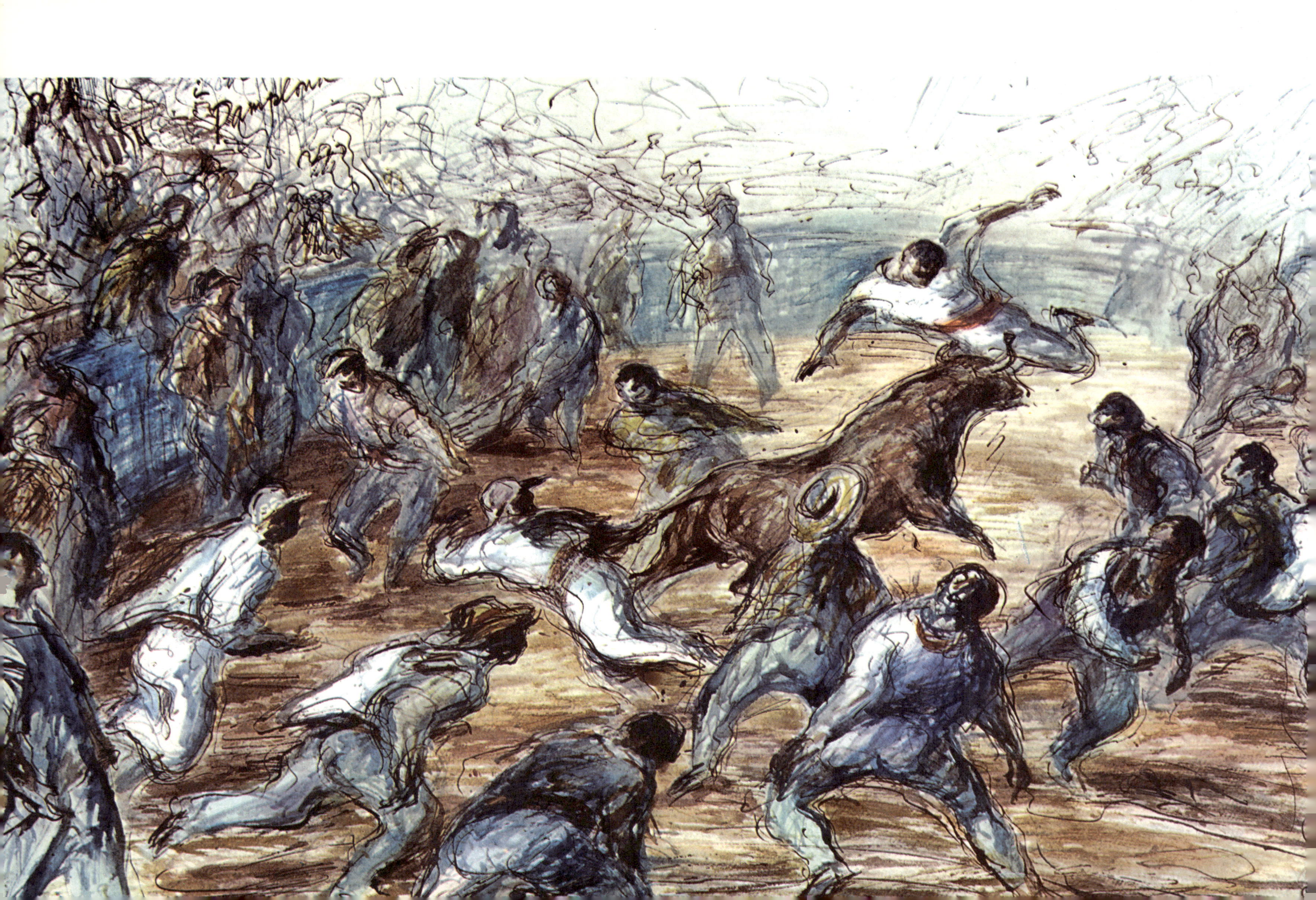
Pamplona

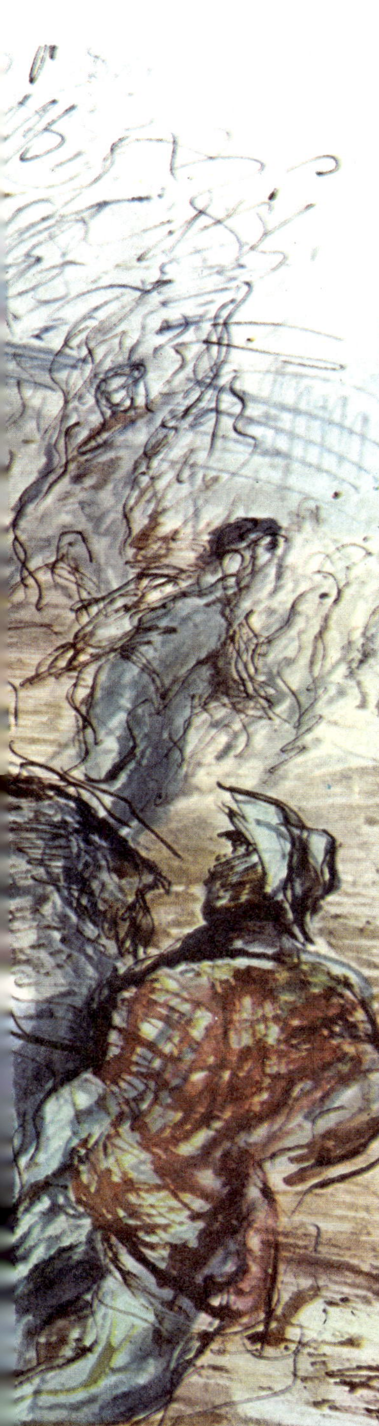

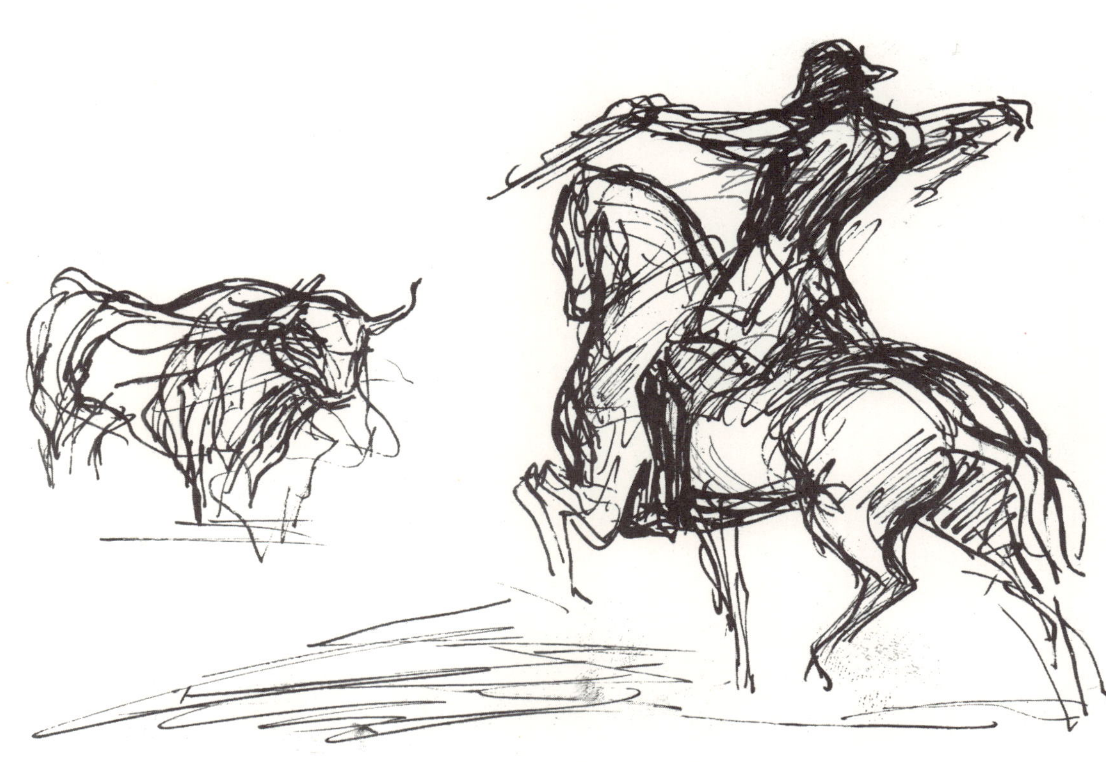

Encierros.

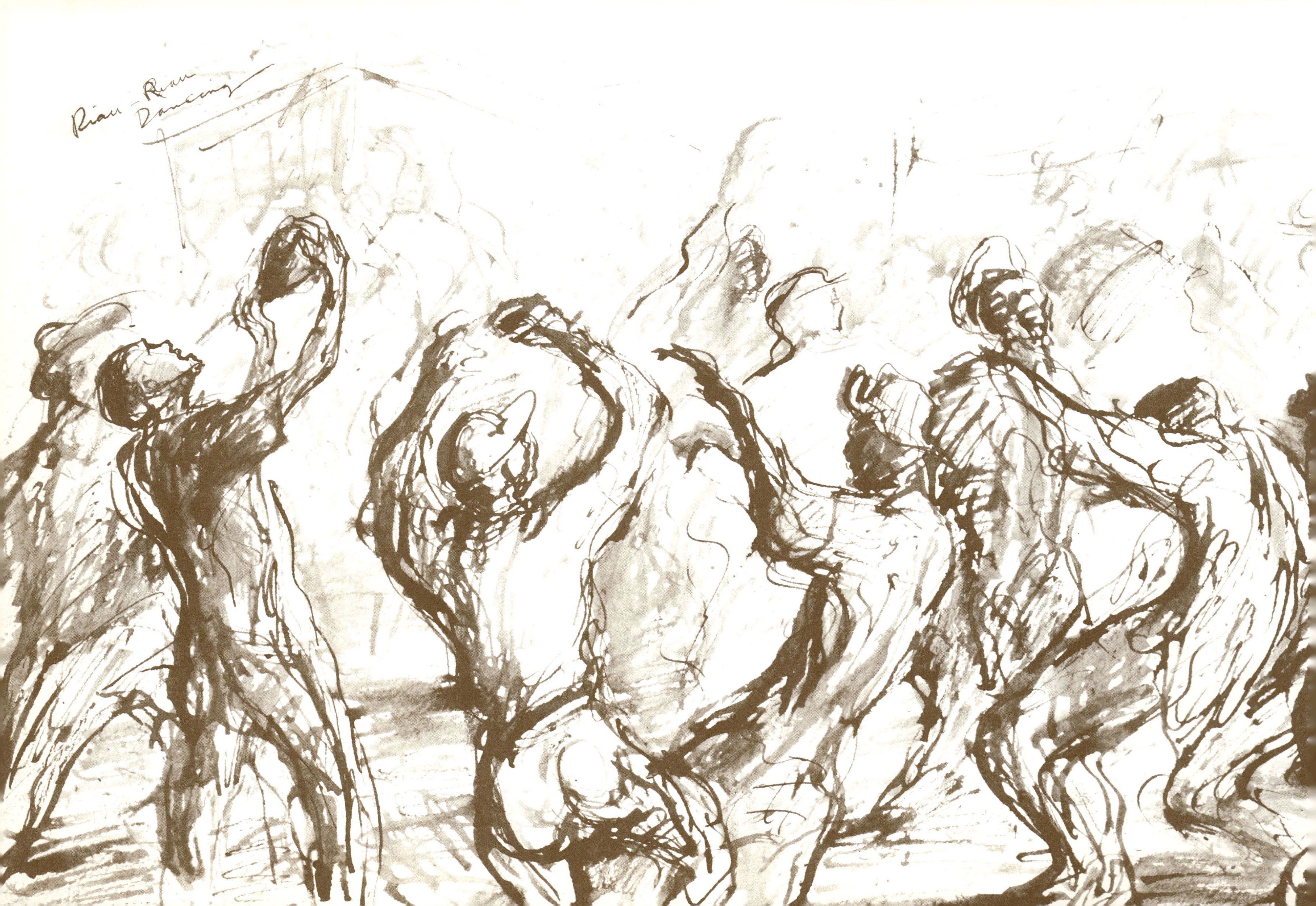

Riau-Riau
Dancing

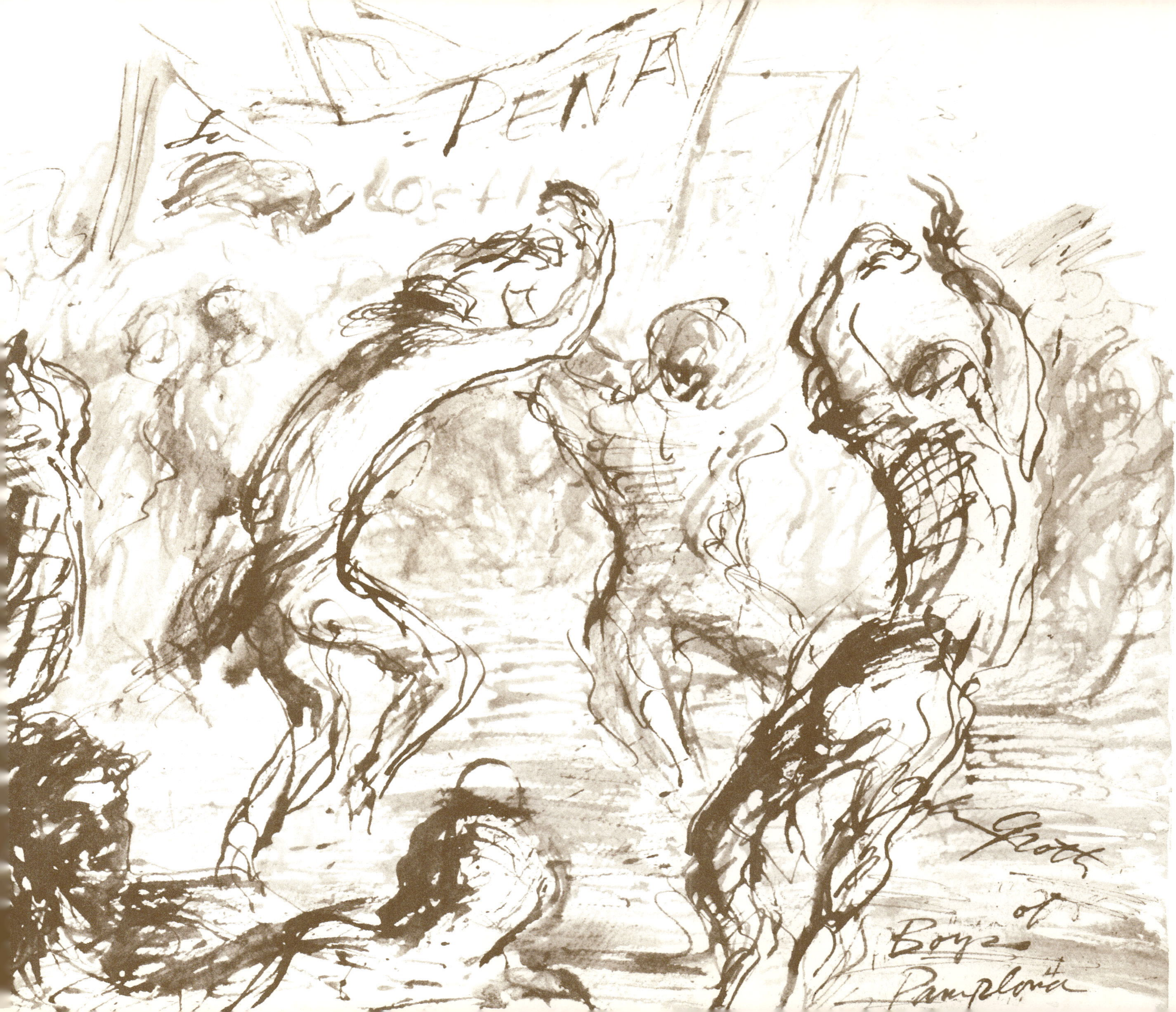

The Riau Riau.

113

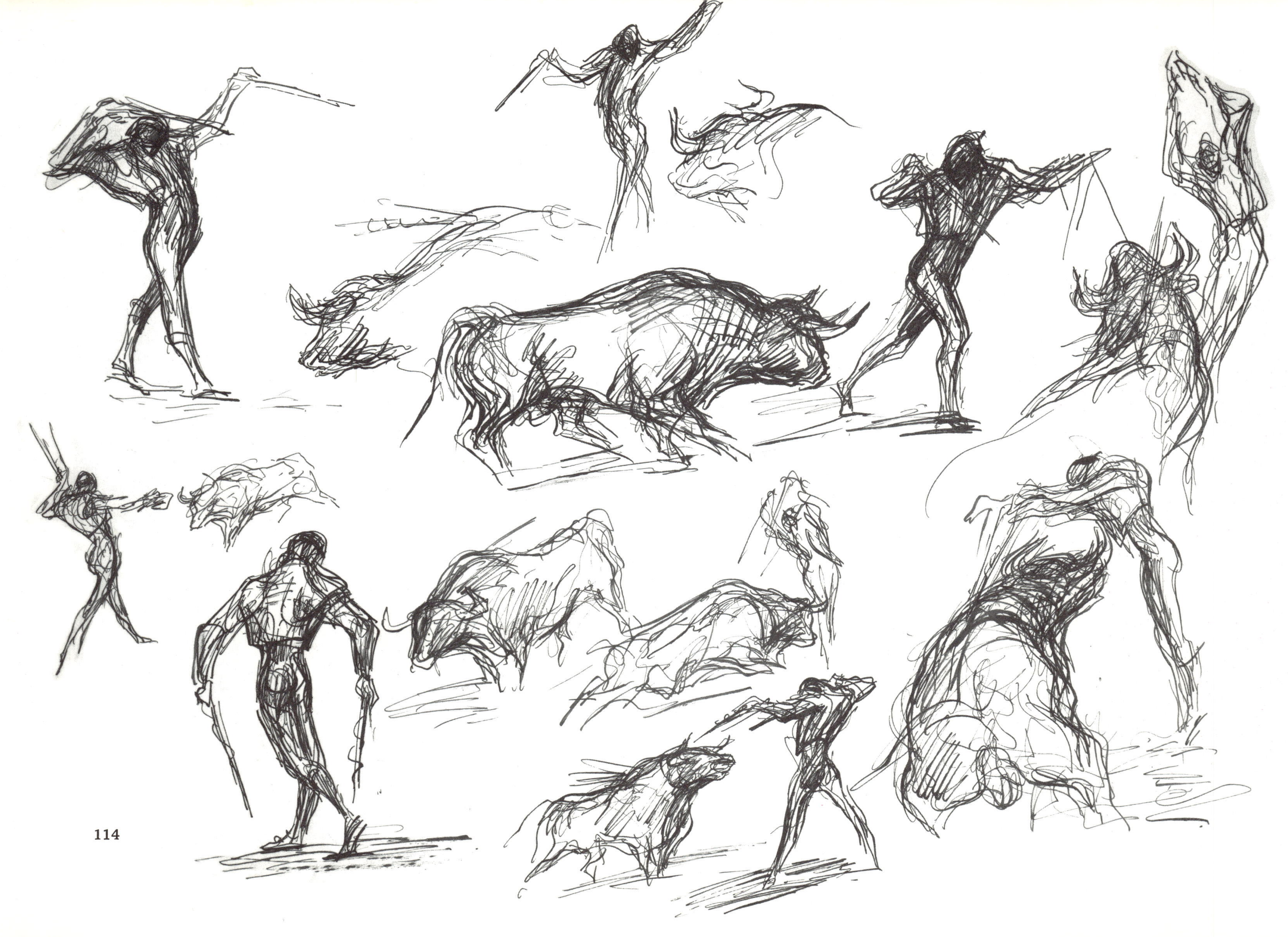

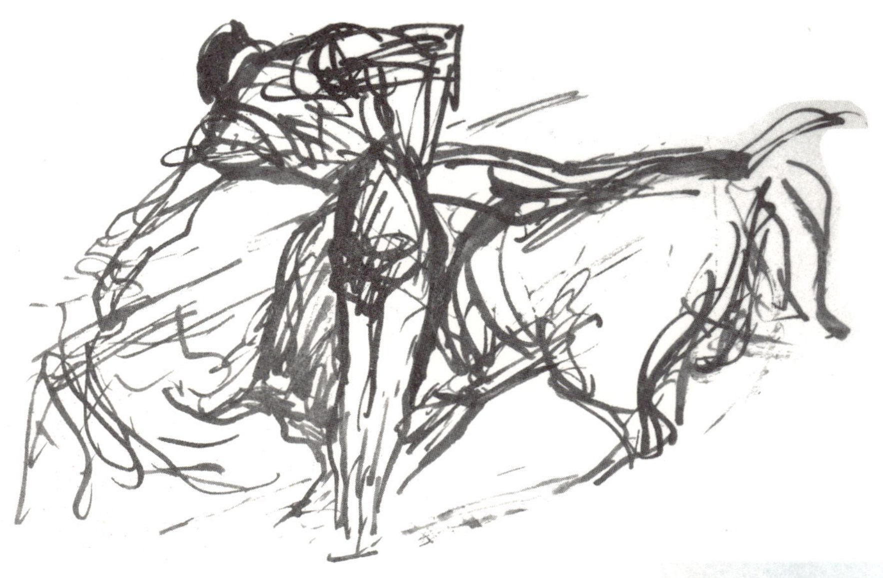

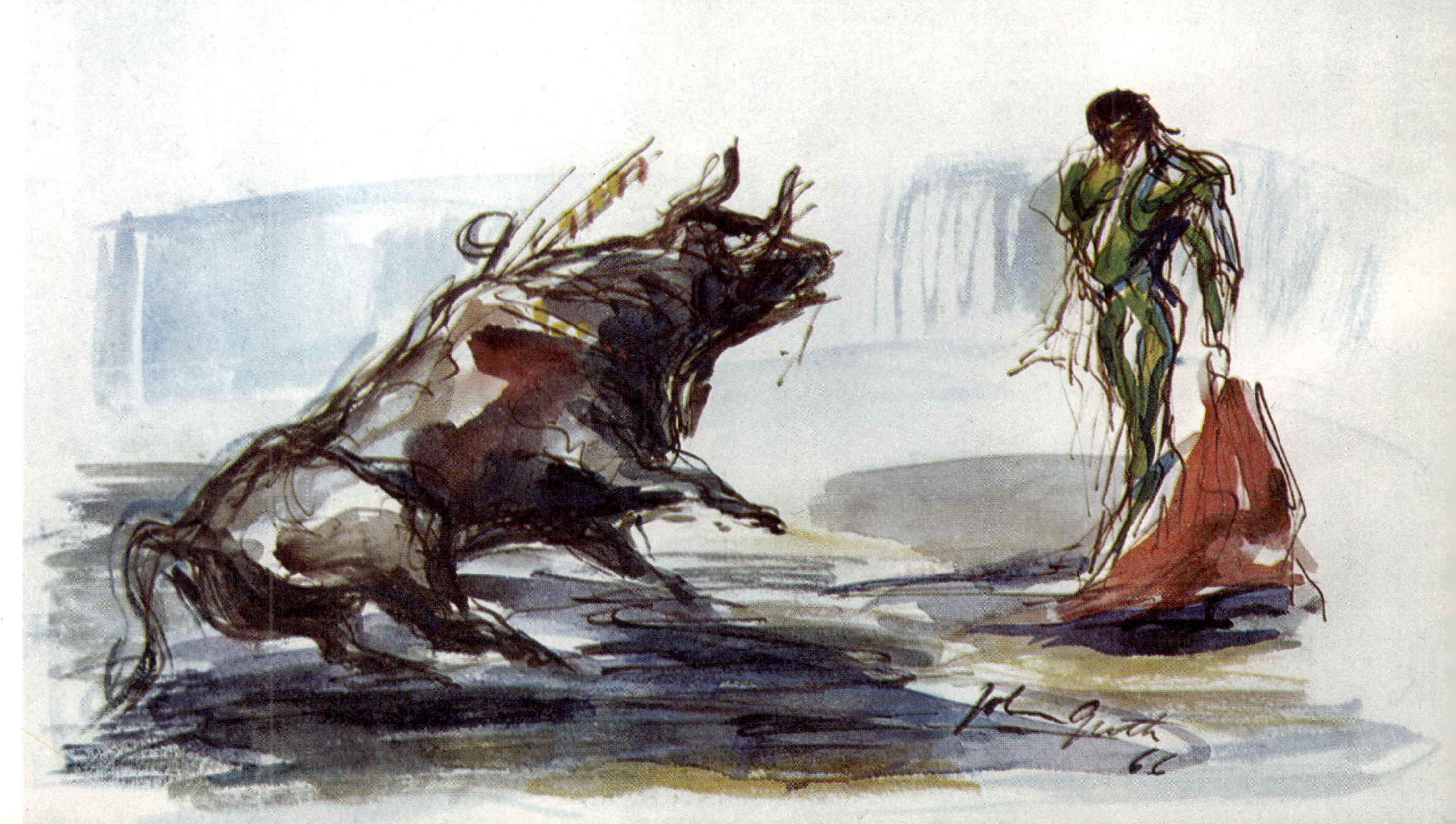

Tour de France

As an old cyclist, I could almost feel a throbbing ache in my thighs
as the racers sludged by in the rain on a hairpin turn in the Pyrenees.

There are bike riders and there are cyclists. In the Tour de France there are nothing but cyclists—hundreds of them pedaling their way over a grueling 2,641-mile course covering every conceivable type of terrain, including two of Europe's highest mountains and running through four countries—France, Switzerland, Italy and Germany. Usually held during July, the marathon is Europe's most celebrated sports spectacle—dominating television, doubling newspaper circulation and involving some seventy-five major companies who contribute to the event's million-dollar budget. "At those prices," says one manufacturer, "those damned cyclists better break the sound barrier."

Indeed, despite the expense to the companies, the Tour de France is the proletariat's Le Mans. All a competitor needs is a well-oiled bike, a pair of strong legs, a sponsor and a benevolent boss who will let him off for twenty-two days running. The route varies each year and villages vie to have the cyclists run through their streets. For the privilege, a township must fork over $5,600. According to one veteran observer, "Some towns depend entirely on the tourist trade brought by the race. They couldn't survive without it."

Besides thousands of peripatetic bike buffs and tourists who follow the event from town to town, thousands of salesmen, whose companies sponsor the riders, scramble along, pushing their products in some of the more remote areas. The Tour de France is a mobile village—an anarchy with its own law and customs—a territory some 30 kilometers long and as wide as the road.

Each Tour produces memorable stories. In 1966 Belgian bikeman Herman van Springel was well ahead of the strungout competitors near the end of a particularly grueling 100-mile stretch—but when he rolled up to the entrance of the stadium at Turin, Italy, where some 30,000 fans awaited to applaud his entrance, a traffic cop outside the walls blithely directed him into a parking lot. By the time the hapless van Springel found his way through the main gate, he was well out of contention. Some of the instances, however, do not suggest humor. For example, on the treacherous roadways in the Italian Alps, where the cyclists achieve speeds of 50 miles per hour, the history of the Tour de France is marred by fatal accidents—caused mostly by pileups after a lead rider has broken a tire or lost control of his throbbing vehicle.

Beyond the racers themselves—whizzing through every kind of countryside, collecting in knots, piling up and, always, hunching over the turned-down handlebars, legs pumping, twisted faces reflecting minds forcing tired bodies to work some more—there is the spectacle of the crowd. At every village the entire population lines the roadway hours before the first cyclists come barreling into view. As they pass the riders are treated to showers of cool water shot from a fire hose, bottles of chilled wine offered on the run from comely young girls and perhaps an extra push from a few of the men. Usually, the riders wave away the villagers—if an official spots them getting a push he will level a fine on the rider—not the pusher.

The final sprint into Paris begins at the crest of St. Bernard Mountain and drops some 32 miles to the finish line. Often enough, the leading cyclist will make a fatal error on this treacherous home-stretch. The record speed for the Tour de France was set in 1966 by Lucien Aimar, who finished the course in 117 hours 34 minutes and 21 seconds, averaging about 23 miles per hour.

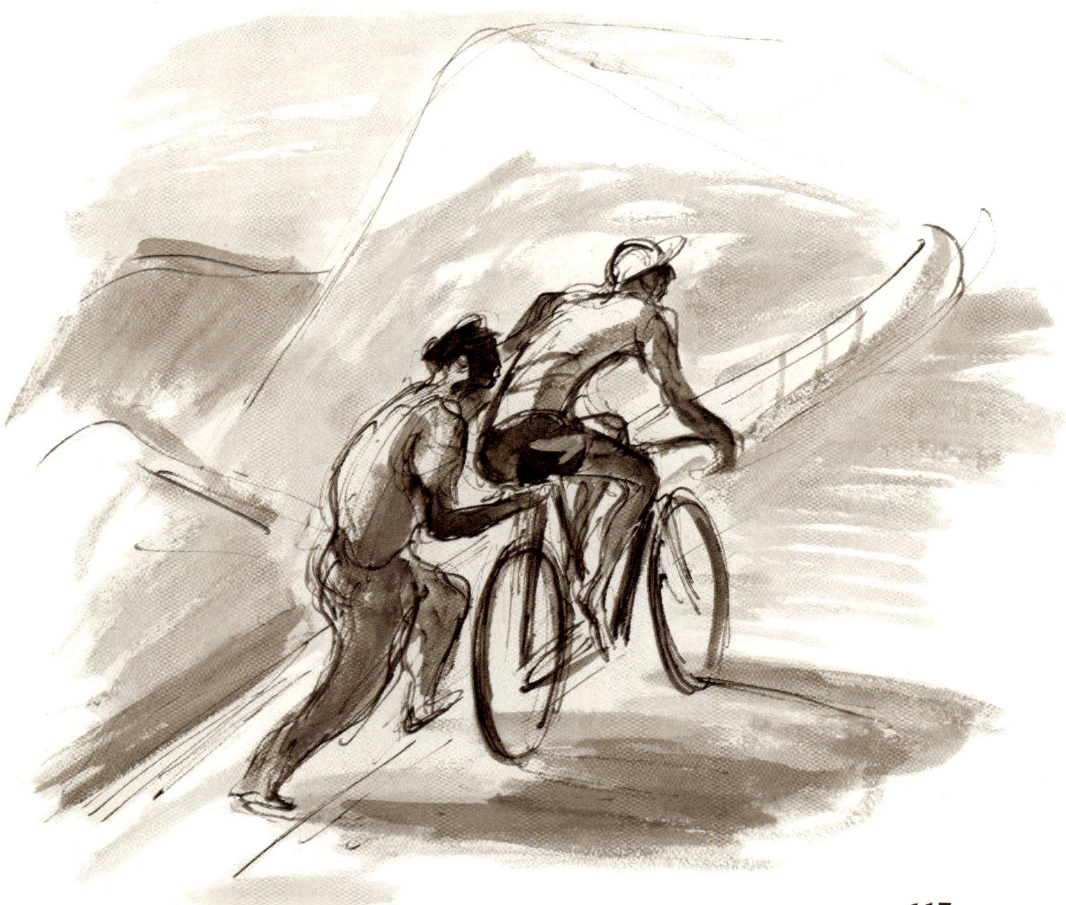

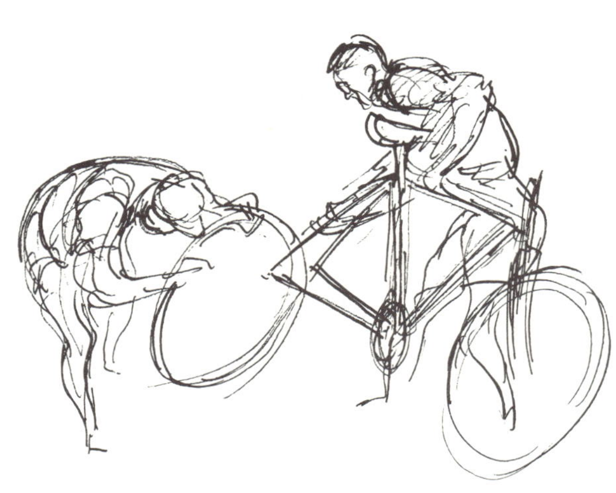

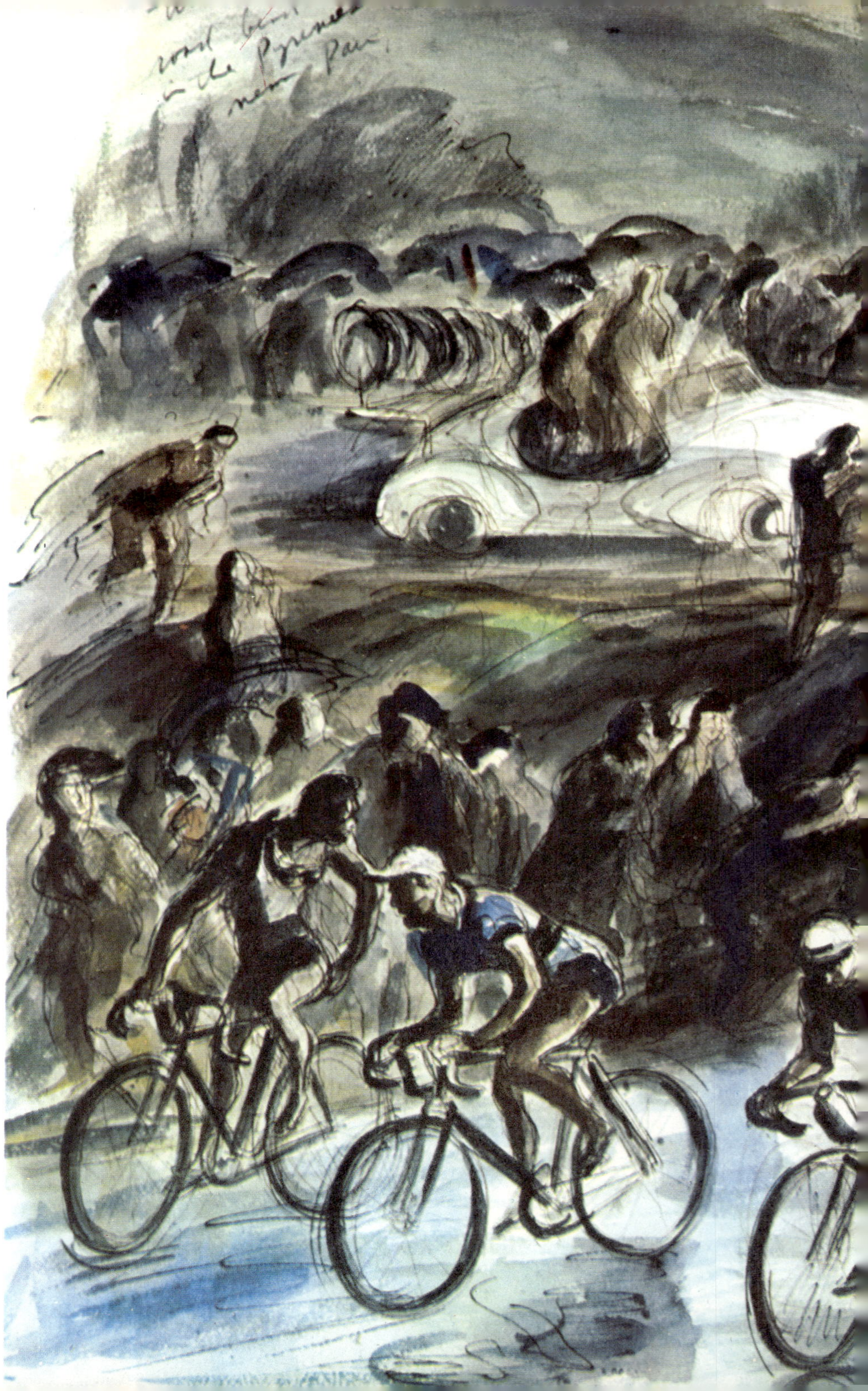

Hairpin Turn in the Pyrenees.

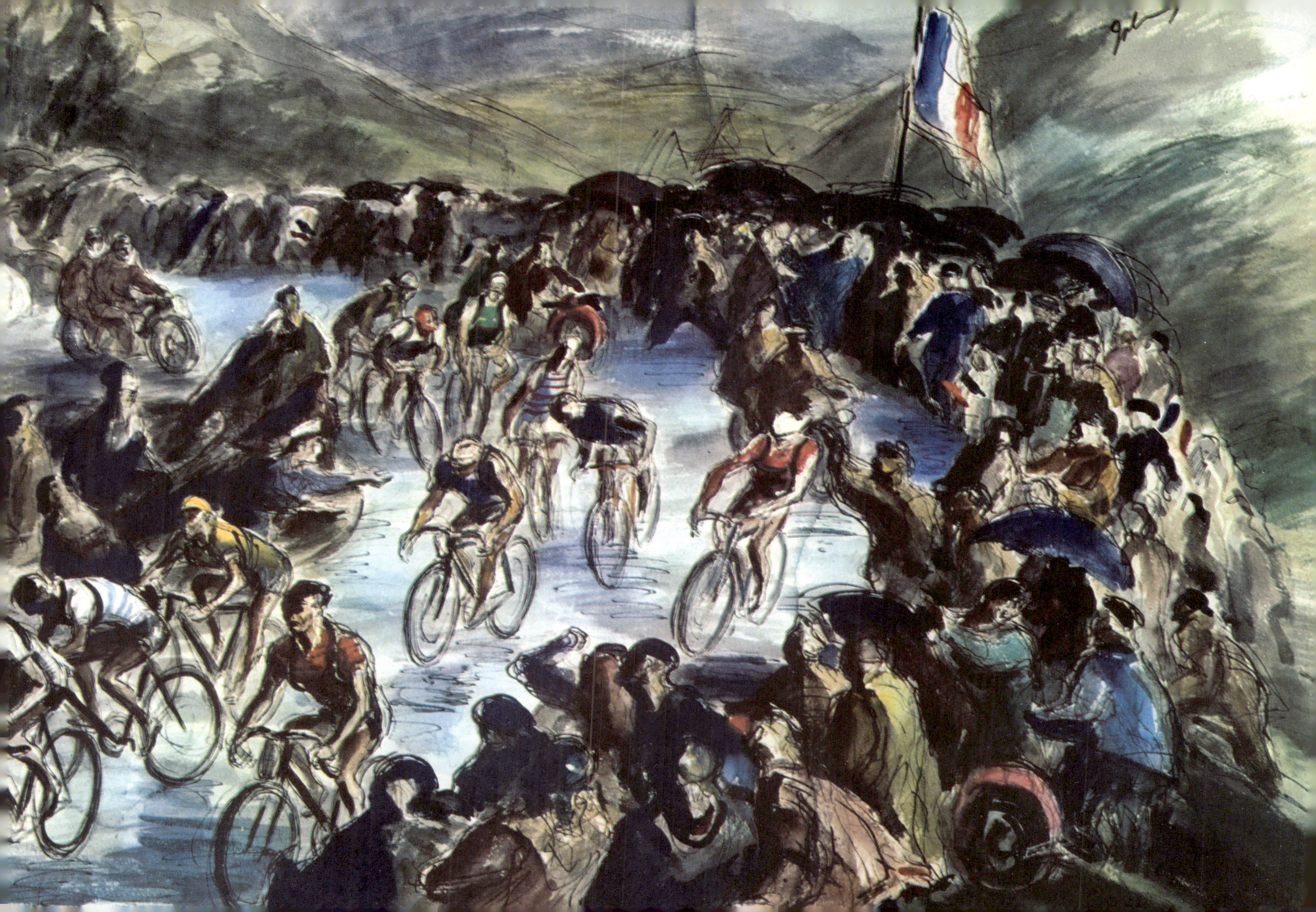

Pile Up.
Cafe Stop at St. Gaudens.

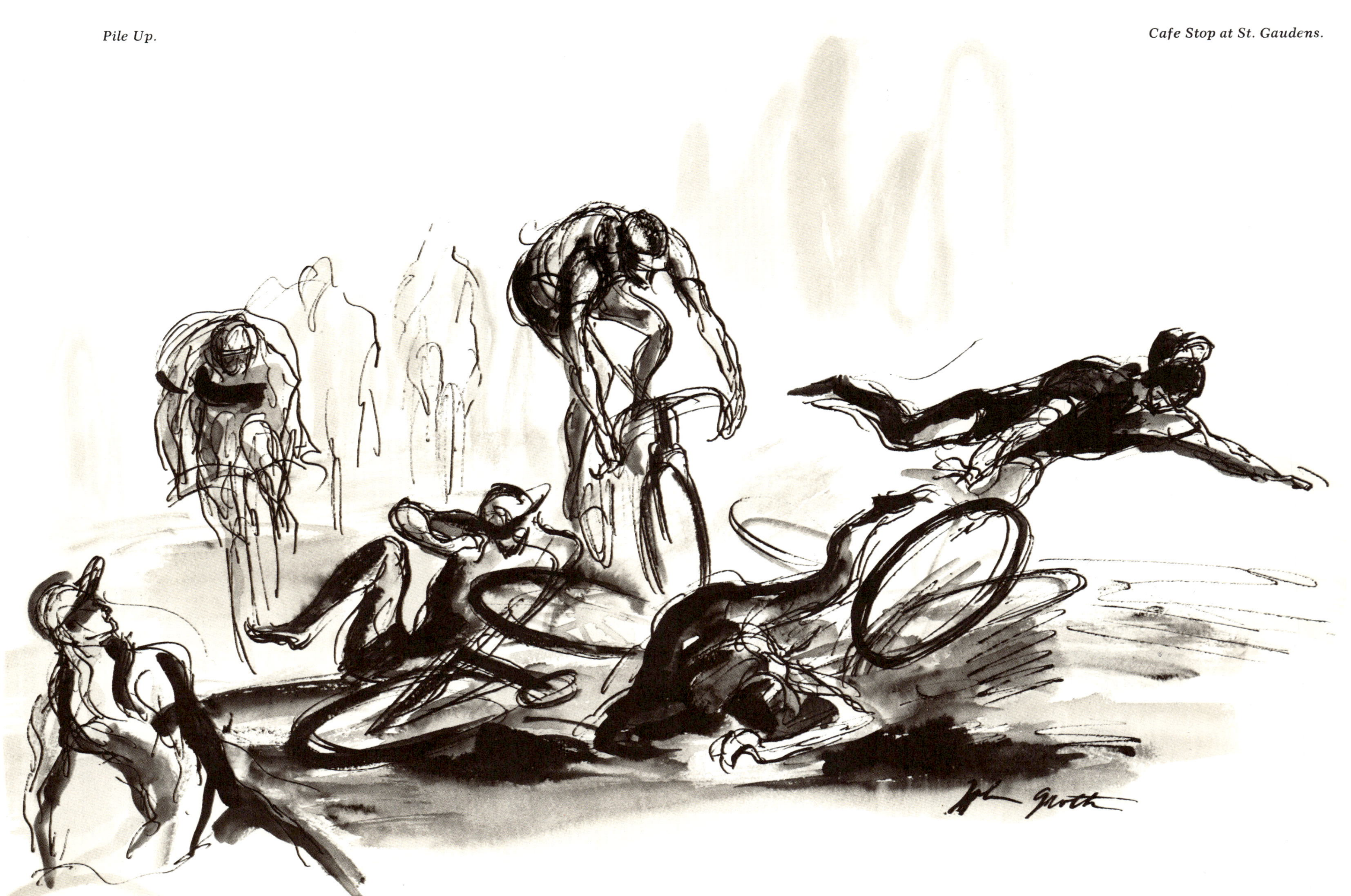

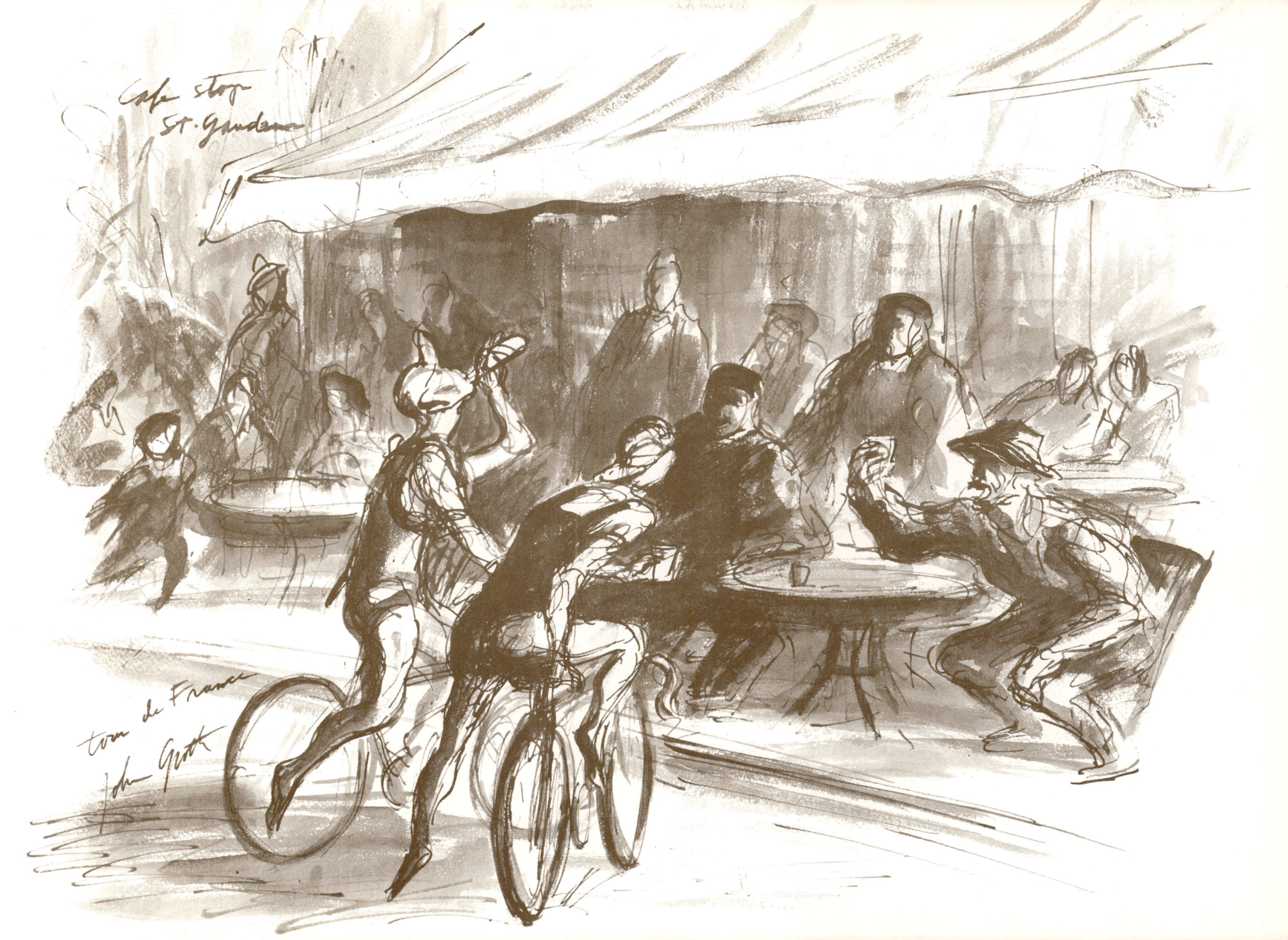

Cafe stop
St. Gaudens
tour de France
John Groth

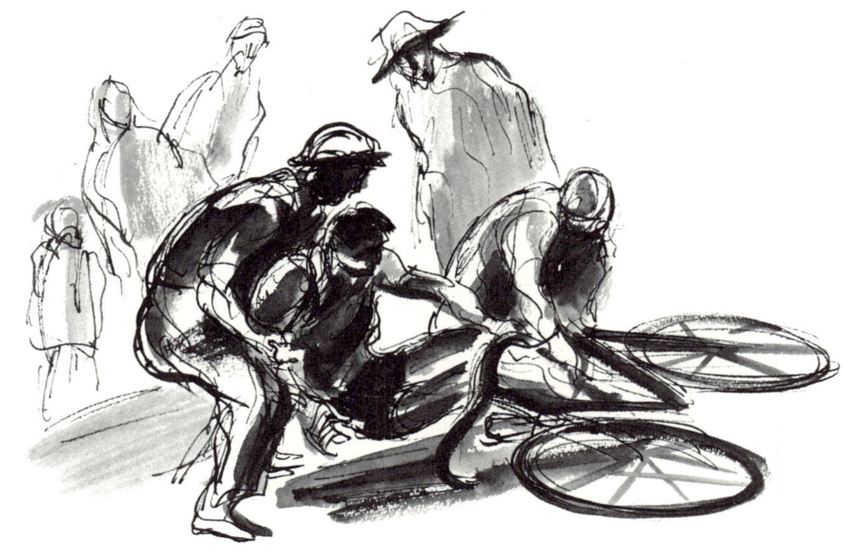

"Hosing Down," Orthez.

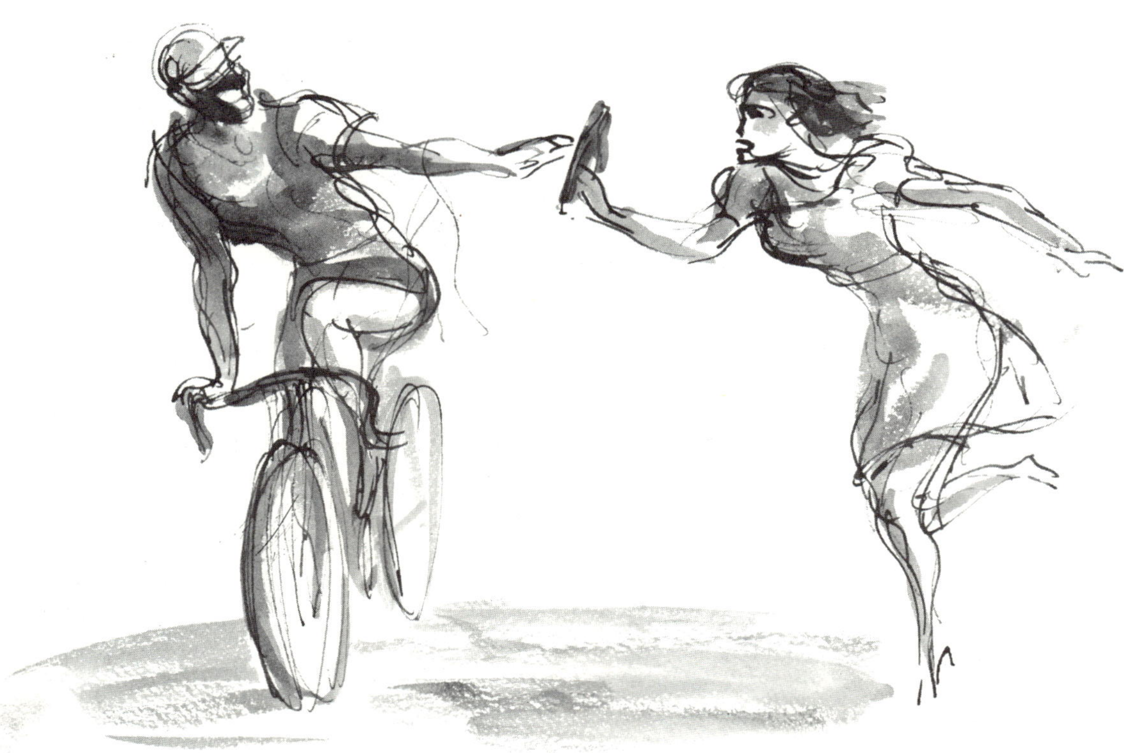

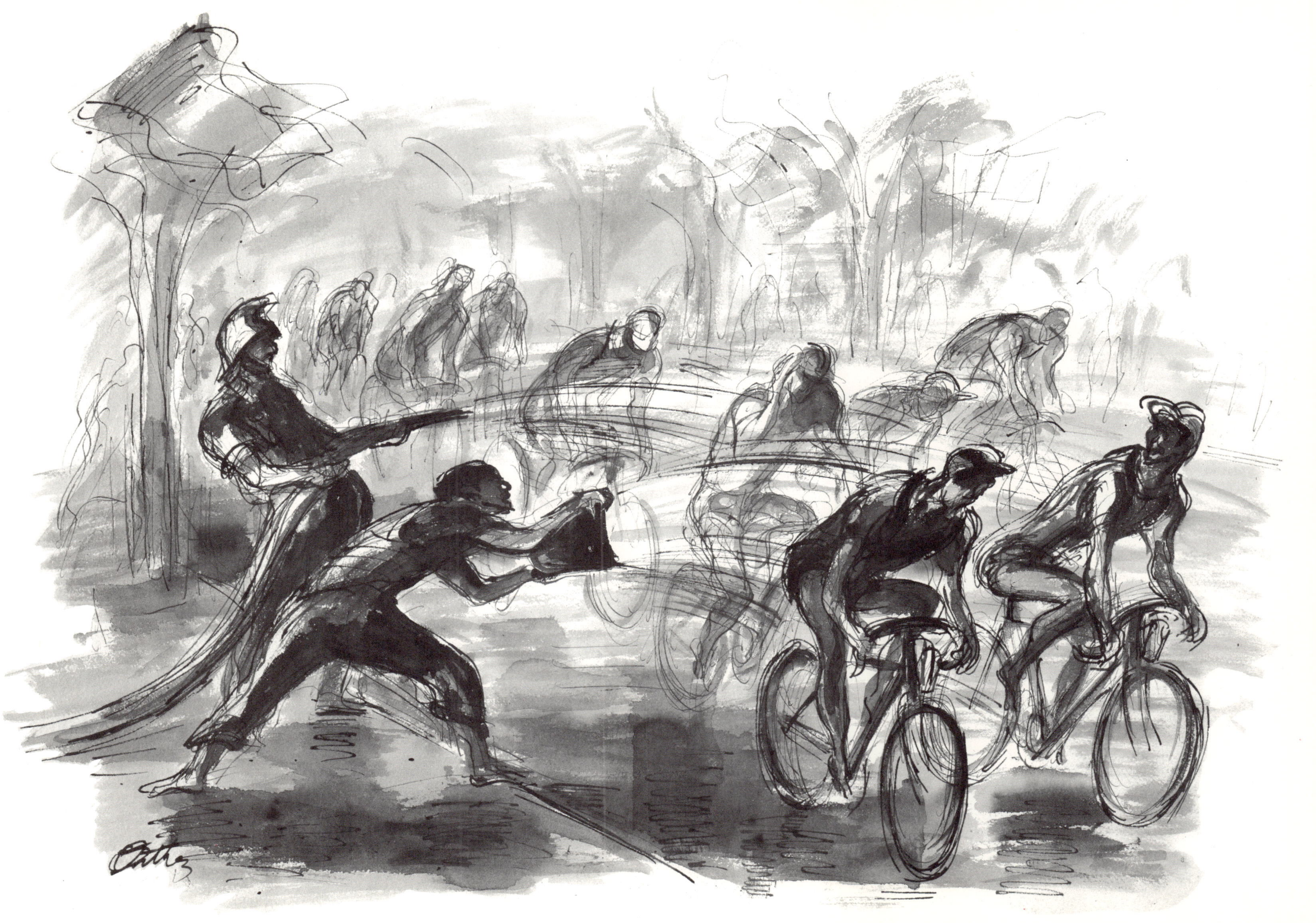

Falconry

One of the most arresting scenes for me as an artist was two mounted tribesmen silhouetted against a dying day, releasing a Falcon on its search-and-destroy mission.

If one sport more aptly than any other demonstrates man's compulsion to dominate and control, it is falconry, or hawking—the training of birds of prey to seek and destroy at their masters' bidding. Certainly such a sport would be considered cruelty at its zenith by a majority of nonparticipants, yet it is one of the most ancient hunting techniques, dating back to the time before man learned to write, and though it has had its periods of decline almost everywhere in the world, it has always made a soaring resurgence.

Today it is widely practiced in Arab and Asian countries, but most European and American regions also have their enthusiasts. It is a sport that involves virtually all sixty species of hawks belonging to the family *Falconidae;* their captors, who are men of great training skill and infinite patience; and, of course, their unfortunate prey, which include rabbits and hares, ducks, quail, partridge, doves and, in fact, most flying or ground animals smaller or less agile than they.

The falcon normally takes off from his trainer's fist, climbs with strong wingbeats for altitude greater than that of his intended prey, then, much as a pelican does over a school of fish, closes its wings and plummets earthward, its fierce talons clenched. When it strikes its victim, whether a streaking duck or a dodging quail, it kills on contact, punching the prey with its fisted talons. The speed of its dive, or "stoop" in the language of the falconer, often reaches an incredible 180 miles an hour. Having made its kill the birds (with the exception of some eagles) will not retrieve, and it is often necessary for the huntsmen to follow on horseback for the pick-up.

Of all the species of hawks, the most popular is the peregrine, a true falcon that can adapt to almost any climate. It is most easily trained and has been called the Bird of Nobility because of its lofty bearing and the fierce alertness of its eyes. The peregrine is a handsome creature, about the size of a large crow with a black head, a bluish-gray back, a buff breast and white patches on its cheeks. It is barred with black overall except at the throat.

The sport of falconry has a checkered past. It was practiced in Egypt during the period of Sargon II around 700 B.C., and by 800 A.D. it had spread to Western Europe and the British Isles. For almost 1,000 years, the sport flourished there, but in the nineteenth century falconry was again grounded because of a shortage of herons, the favorite prey of the broad-winged killers.

Today the British Falconers' Club has 150 members, and less than a third of these keep and fly falcons. In the United States the sport fell victim to the nemesis of every activity that demands open space— the fence. Huntsmen can no longer ride across country at breakneck speed in pursuit of their soaring birds, and many enthusiasts have retired from the sport.

Throughout the unfenced plains of Asia and North Africa falconry lives. In Arabia desertmen still train hawks to course the swift game of the sands. In coursing gazelles as many as five hawks are used, along with as many dogs for the actual kill—the hawks bewildering the game until the dogs can catch up. These desert hawks are fed from the eyesockets of a calf, fantastically enough, they naturally lunge for this vital spot in their quarry. Still another desert diversion is coursing the bustard, a chase that often covers many miles over the blindingly bright, rough terrain where only the staunchest horse can follow. The size and stamina of the quarry—combined with its tendency to run rather than fly—make the kill a difficult and danger-ous maneuver for the small "lanner" hawk used in this hunt; there is so little room for the bird to swing back up into the sky after he strikes. Groth's painting of coursing on the next spread was done in Bamian, Afghanistan.

The golden eagle is used to hunt foxes in the mountain reaches of Kazakstan, near the boundary between the Soviet Union and Chinese Turkestan. The Kazak sportsman usually wounds the prey first, then lifts the hood from his killer eagle, allowing the handsome bird to mount into the sky—and plunge, with incredible speed, to strike the limping game with its fisted talon and beak.

In the Near East, particularly in Georgia, the most popular bird is the goshawk, the fiercest and most competent killer of all. Unlike the true falcon, the short-winged goshawk hunts ground haunting quarry, gripping its victim in its claws and shielding it with its spread wings, squeezing until the animal is dead, rather than killing on impact. "Red Queen," a famous goshawk of the "Old Hawking Club," had an authentic record of sixteen hares out of seventeen struck in a single morning.

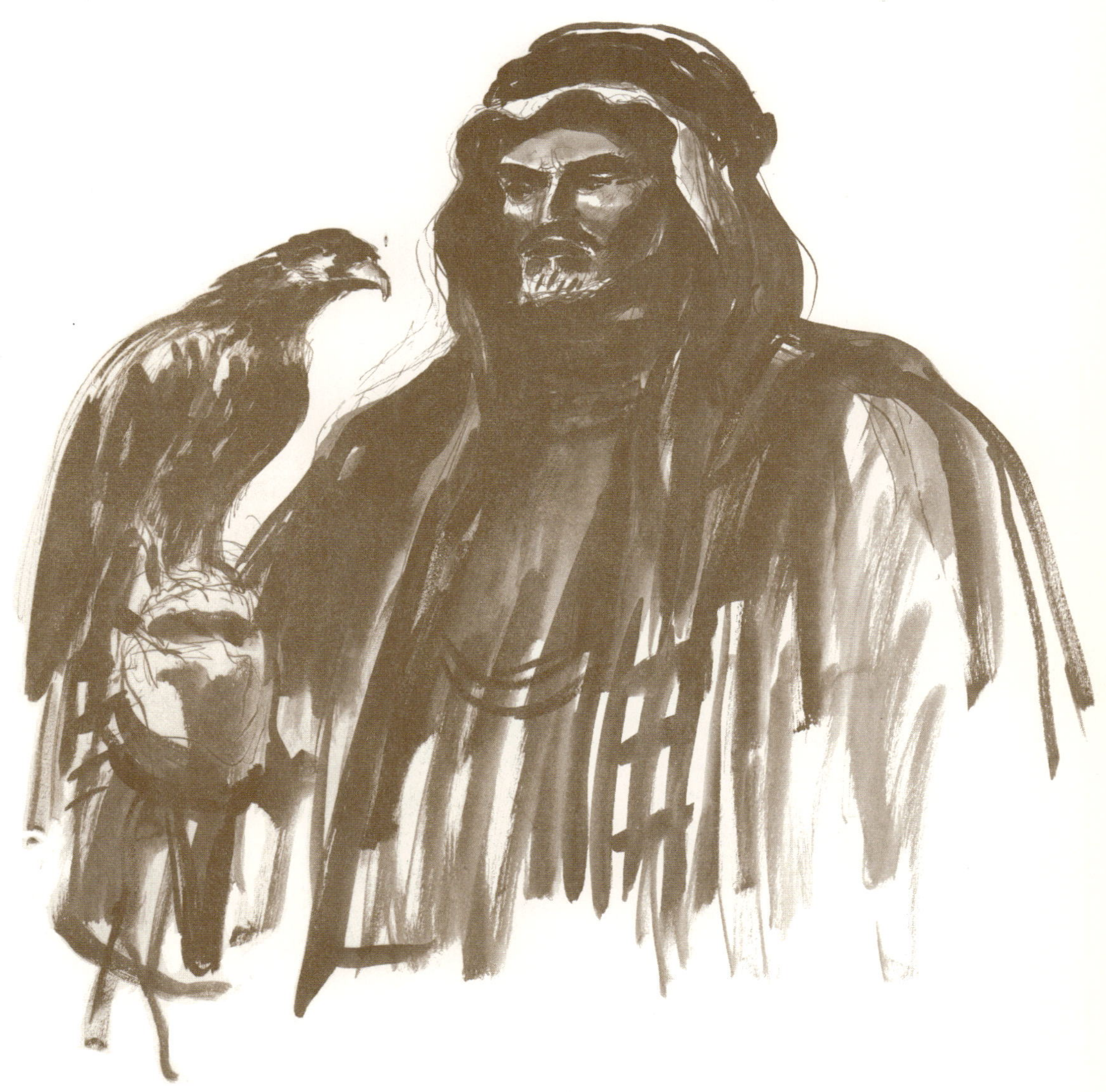

A Sheik of Kuwait.

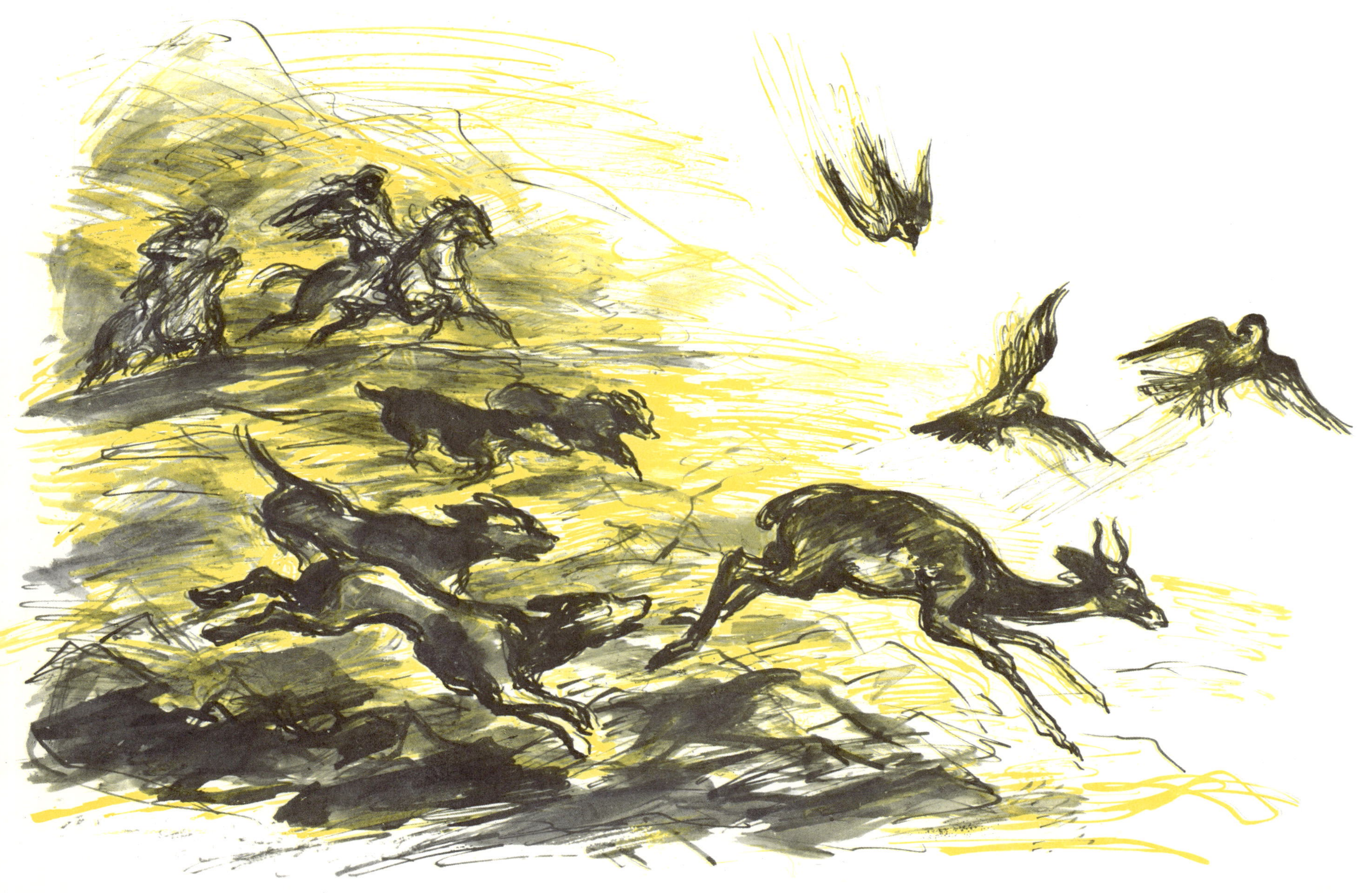

Coursing the Gazelle.

Afghan Falconers.

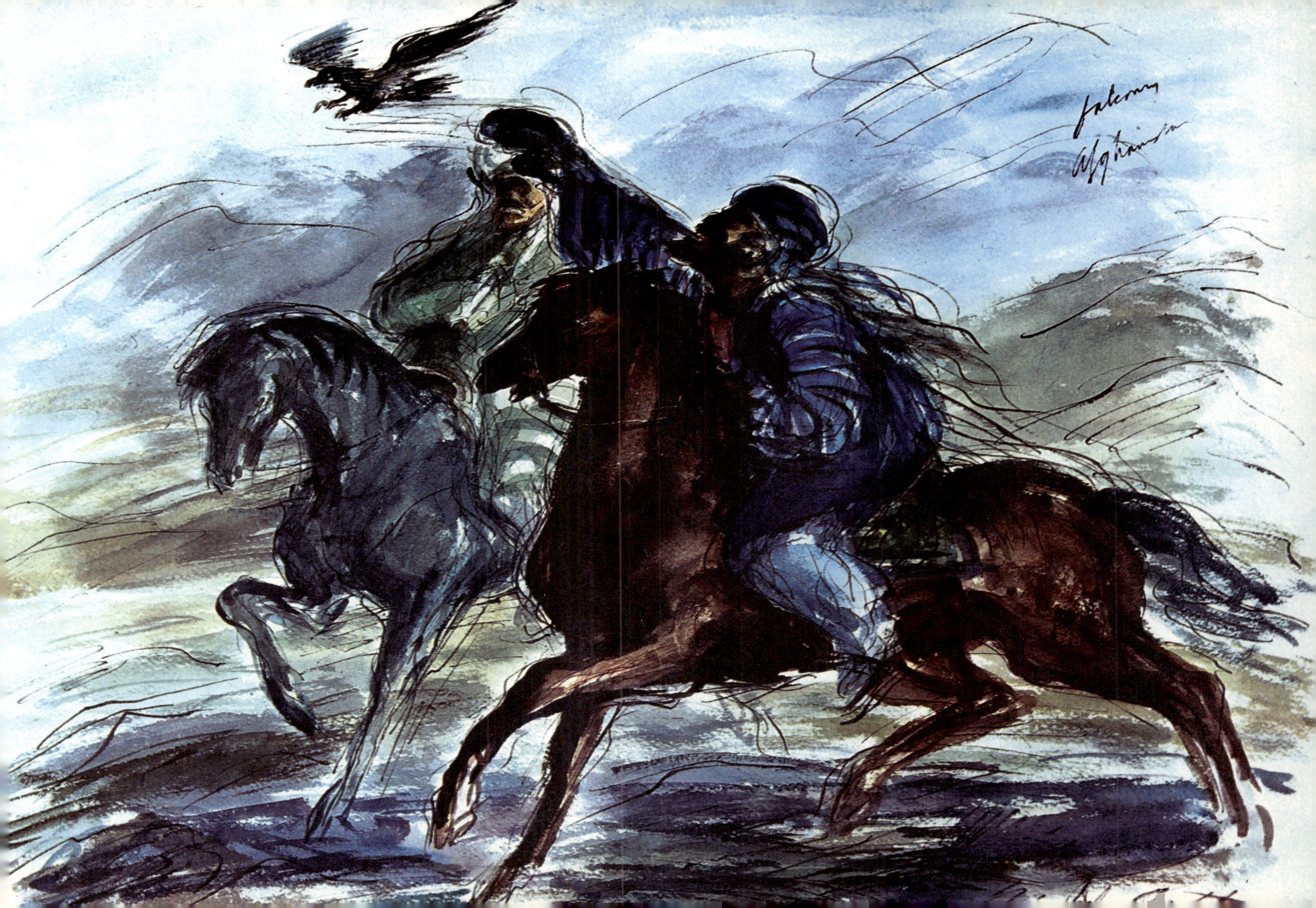

falconry
Afghanistan

Afghan Sports

I found more unusual sports for my portfolio in Afghanistan than in any other country. A few were gentle, some cruel—all of them worth recording.

The typical Afghan's lifestyle has changed relatively little since the bloody days of the Khyber Pass. He still weaves his brillant rugs by hand; he still herds his goats and sheep across the great plains in search of good water and lush grazing; he still transports his wares by camel—from bazaar to bazaar—along trails blazed by his ancestors. He is truly a nomad, this Afghan, a drifter whose only roots are his restlessness. And his country is a planned community devised by ancient Agrarian tradition—a sacred land that he maintains with the infinite finesse once practiced by the American Indian.

But for all this preordained order the Afghan's life is not an easy one. He is constantly battling to stay alive. From the frozen slopes of the Hindu Kush to the Desert of Death, Afghanistan is a country that bends to no man—and neither do its people. Long before Genghis Khan's Golden Horde laid siege to the land in the thirteenth century, the Afghan has had to closely surveil his national borders—to the north, Mongolia; to the south, Pakistan and India—in constant fear of attack. It is hardly difficult, therefore, for anyone to understand why the Afghan enjoys his sports of violence. He himself is necessarily violent.

One popular sport that would shake the sensibilities of the average Westerner is ram fighting. Staged during the peak of the rutting season, ram fighting is simply a duel between two males for the favors of the female—and the honor and financial status of their owners. At any ram bout the betting is fast and furious: owners, in fact, have been known to wager their fortunes on a single match.

Though it lacks the romantic trappings of an Arthurian joust, a ram fight nevertheless follows a similar ritual. It is usually held in a rink near a marketplace or, on formal occasions, in the 30,000-seat Ghazi Stadium in Kabul. The two males are paraded before the gallery of turbaned shepherds just as the mounted knights were presented for the inspection of the king. Tethered to a nearby stake is the prize —a female, awaiting the outcome of combat with a quivering display of anxiety the likes of which the fabled Lady Guinevere could only have dreamed.

Following the wagers and the usual repartee between owners, the rams are released. For a moment or two the horned warriors size up one another, snorting and pawing the turf like a pair of Pamplona bulls. Then, as if by agreement, they drop their heads, zero in and charge. When their heads collide, an ear-splitting crack reverberates through the stadium. A half-dozen such collisions are usually enough to determine a victor, and while his jubilant owner collects the winnings, the top ram is allowed to trot off to a private place with his mewing ewe in tow.

Meanwhile, the losers discreetly take their leave—one carrying a deflated purse and punctured pride, the other nursing a monumental headache and a broken heart.

No more violent perhaps— but considerably nastier—is another popular marketplace pastime, camel fighting. Like rams, camels are at their feistiest during the rutting season. Unlike rams, camels often fight to the death. And if the rams display little style, the camels are downright crude. Once they are unleashed, the shrieking beasts kick, knee and bite for all they are worth, to the delight of the crowd of sportsmen and gamblers. Very often the battles last as long as two hours before one of the camels is done in. As John Groth says, "Camel fighting is not my favorite Afghan diversion."

The most savage sport in Afghanistan—and perhaps in the world —involves a struggle between a freshly caught hyena and a pair of sheep dogs. This diversion is most often found in small villages. When the match is about to begin, one of the villagers loops a short piece of heavy rope around the gray, black-spotted hyena and fastens it to a stake. Then the dogs—often two Asian sheepdogs, as in the drawing— are brought forth, their heavy white coats causing an observer to feel all the more uncomfortable in such heat.

John Groth witnessed one of these vicious fights near the village of Kandahar. After the preliminaries—the betting, the repartee, etc.— the hulking, snarling dogs were unleashed and sicced on the tethered victim. With his retreat limited by the length of the rope, the hyena sprang instantly to the attack, inflicting several severe gashes on the dogs with his fangs. Seemingly spurred on by their wounds, the dogs pounded away at the small animal—butting, pawing and shouldering with the fury of enraged heavyweights. Eventually they decked the hyena and, as he yelped for help, locked their huge jaws on his throat.

Death arrived in seconds.

On the gentler side of the Afghanistan sporting scene are several participant competitions played by children. One game—*ghosai*—is a variation of hopscotch in which two ten-man teams compete on a football-sized field. The object is for one of the players to reach the opposing goal line without being grounded. It seems simple enough, until the crucial rule is explained: the player must get there on his left leg while holding the right behind him. Just as in soccer (until TV commercials changed things), there are no timeouts. The game ends when one team reaches a predetermined point total. The players become amazingly adept at getting around on one leg, and at times the field seems filled with so many whirling dervishes. "After all the bloodshed in the other sports I saw in Afghanistan," says Groth, who watched a *ghosai* match in front of his *serai,* one of many fortlike hotels strung out across the country, "it was a pleasure to watch these kids playing a game that could be popular in any country."

Afghanistan's answer to the shotput is melon tossing. The game is played everywhere—in the northern valleys, where lemon orchards roll all the way to the mountainsides; in the urban marketplaces, where melons are often stockpiled, like small bombs, the lengths of streets; and in the many southern villages that dot the Desert of Death. Wherever, the game is signaled when one of the merchants buys a load of melons—either cantaloupe or watermelons—and places them on the road alongside one of the local strong-boys. Then the challengers arrive, buy their melons and place their bets. Meanwhile, the ubiquitous local beggars position themselves about 100 feet down the road. Each in turn the players heave the melons—and the winner, of course, is the one who tosses his melon farthest. Aside from a few heavy losers, the beggars are delighted when the match is over— when they are treated to a refreshing feast of shattered melons. In a country like Afghanistan, food is seldom allowed to go to waste.

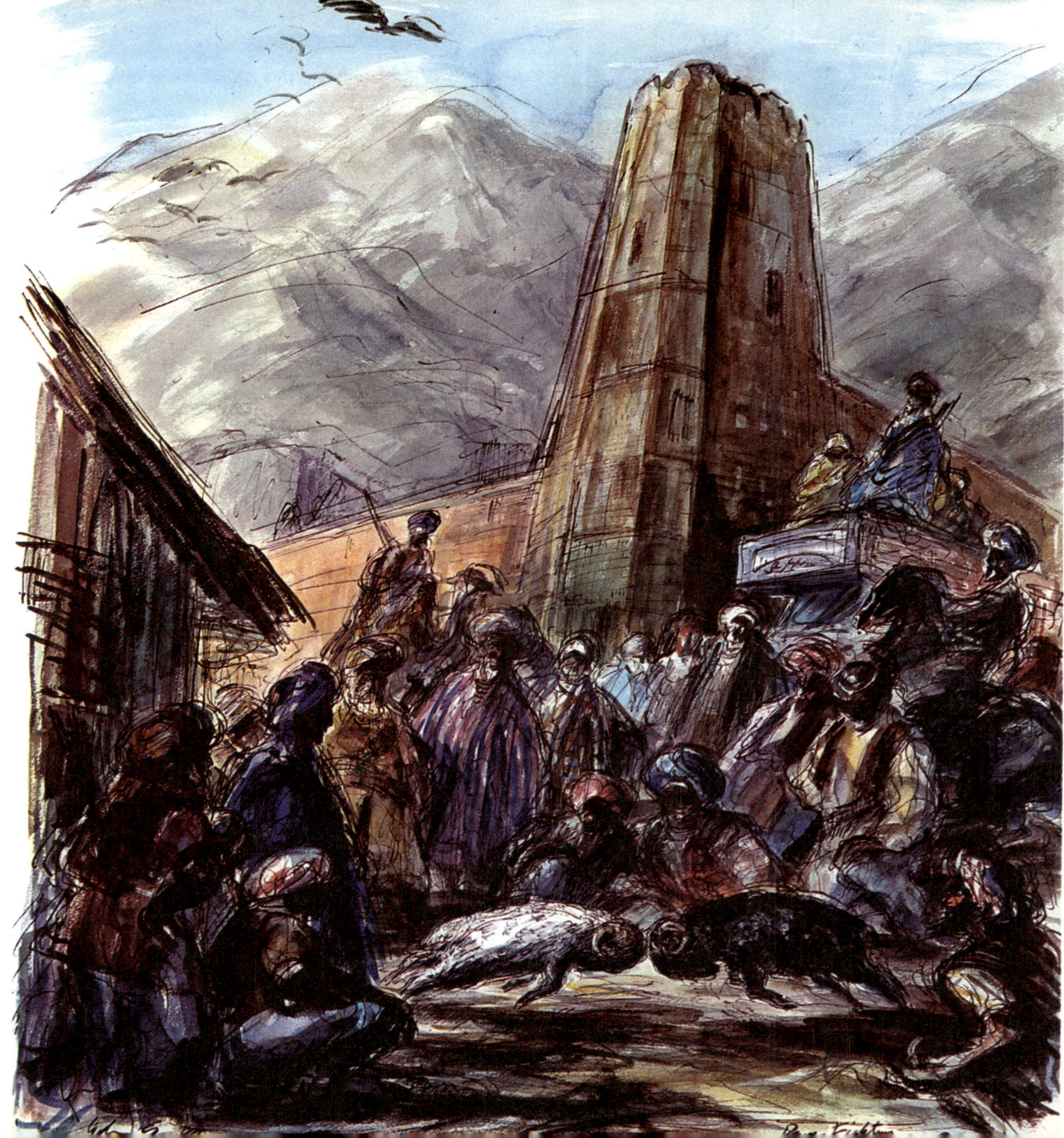

Moment of Impact.

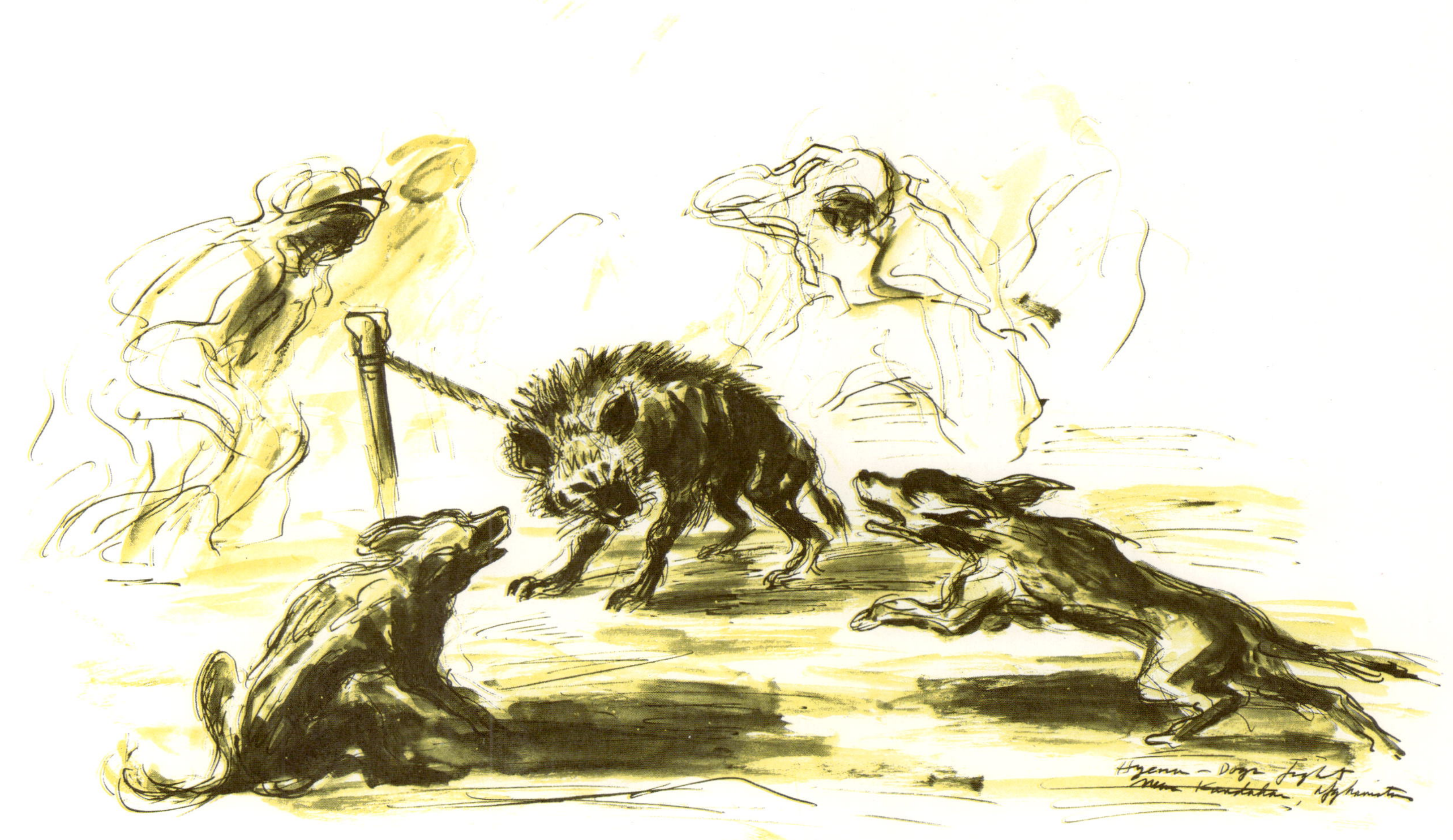

Hyena vs. Dogs.

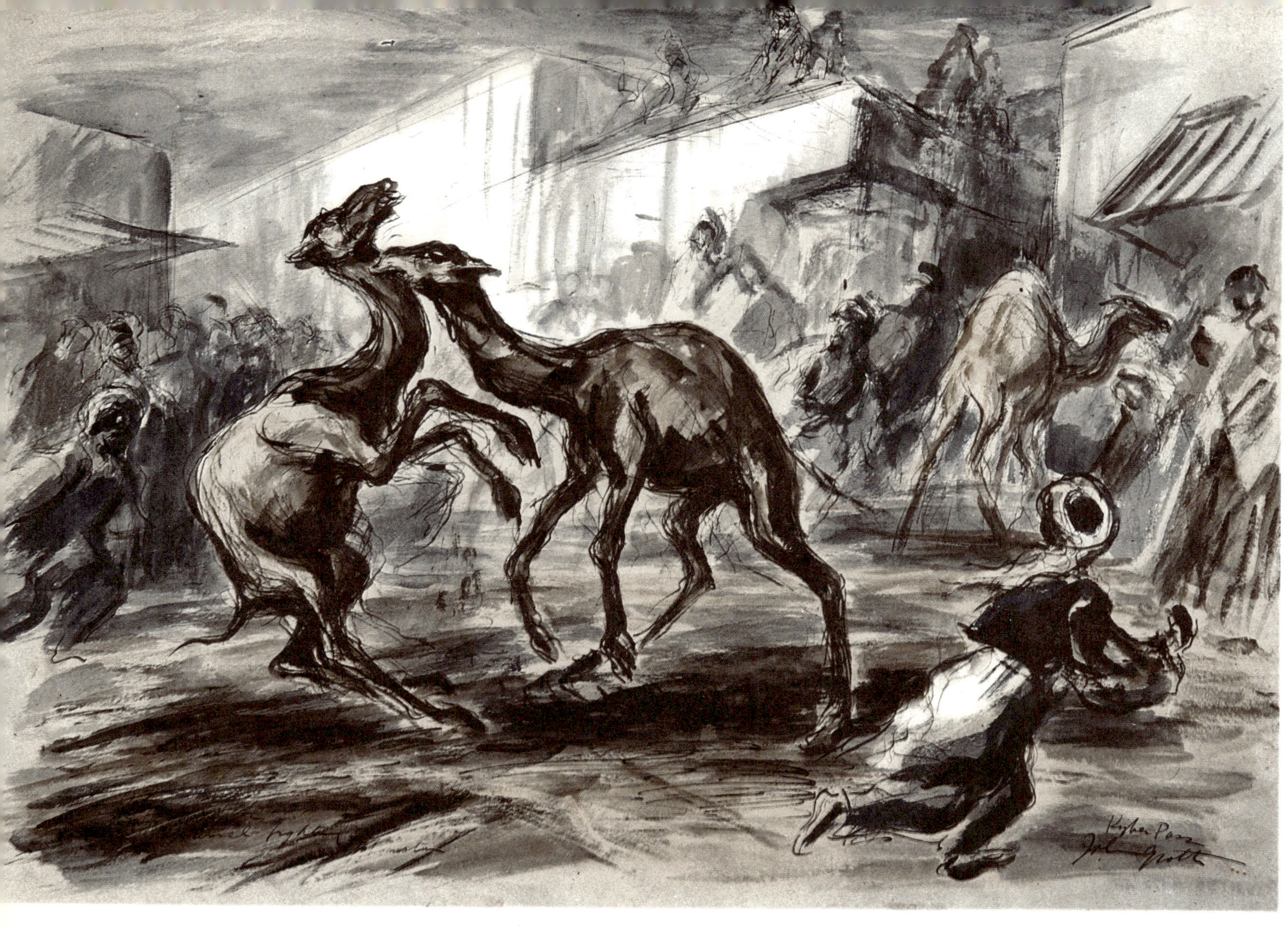

Savage Encounter.

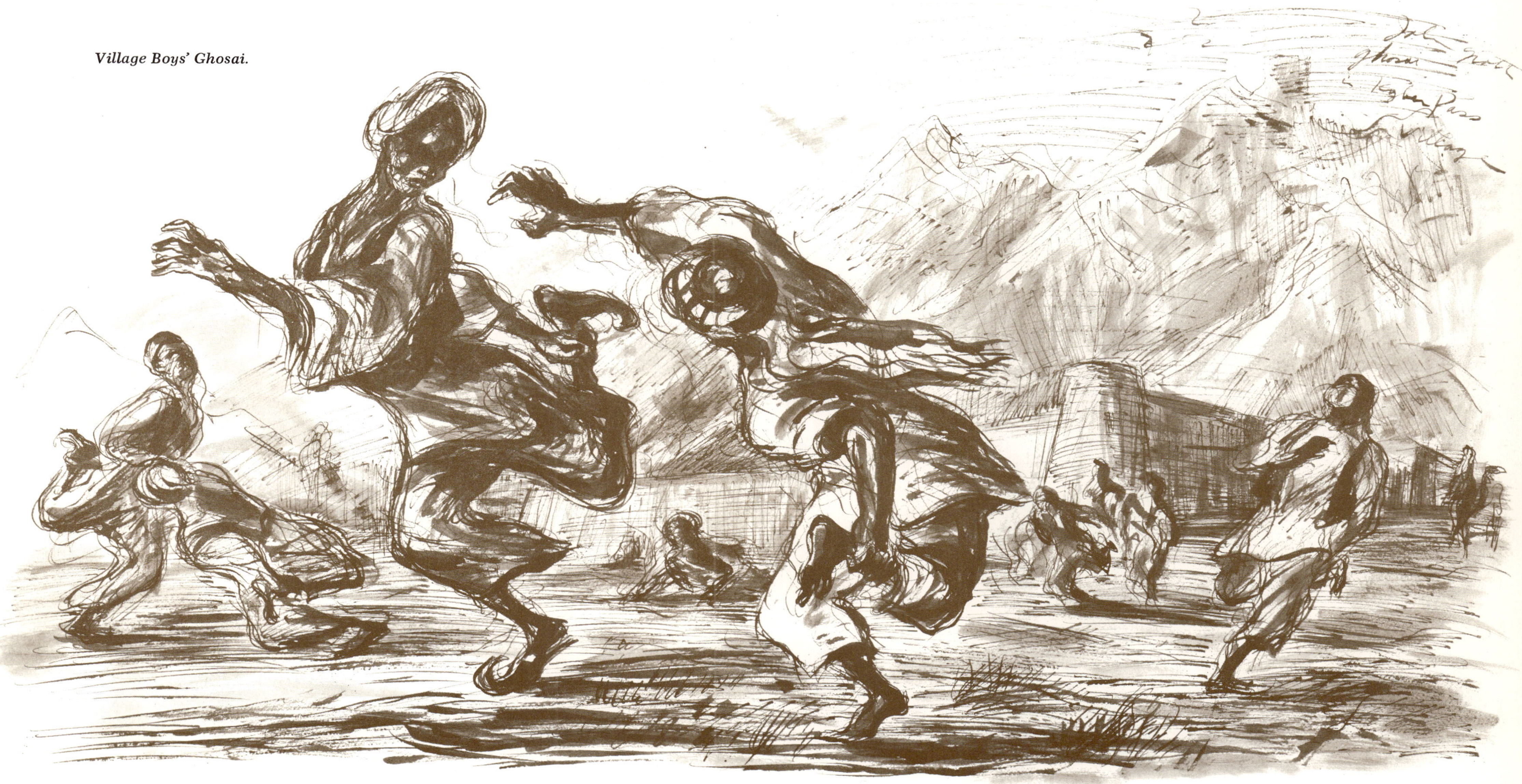

Village Boys' Ghosai.

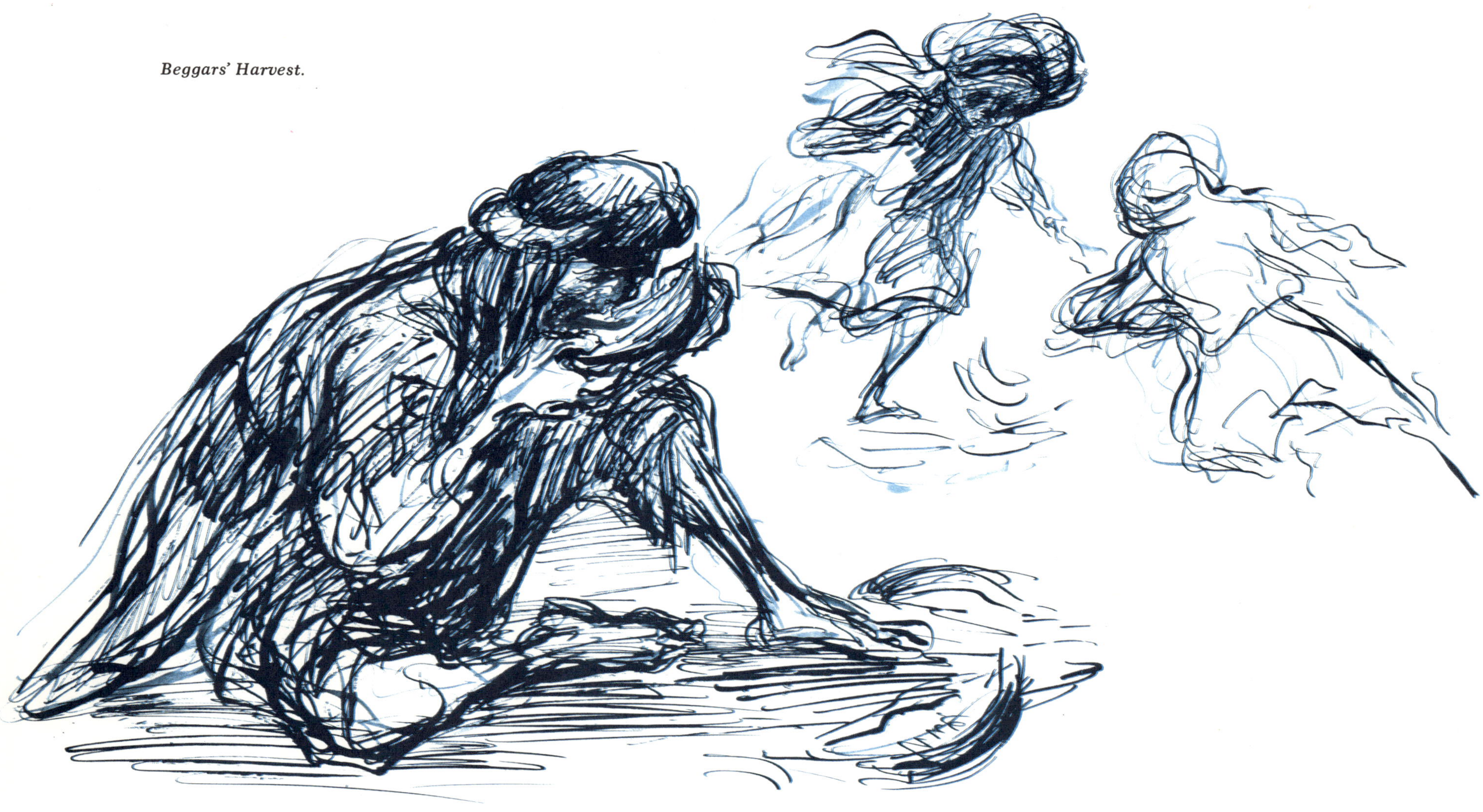

Beggars' Harvest.

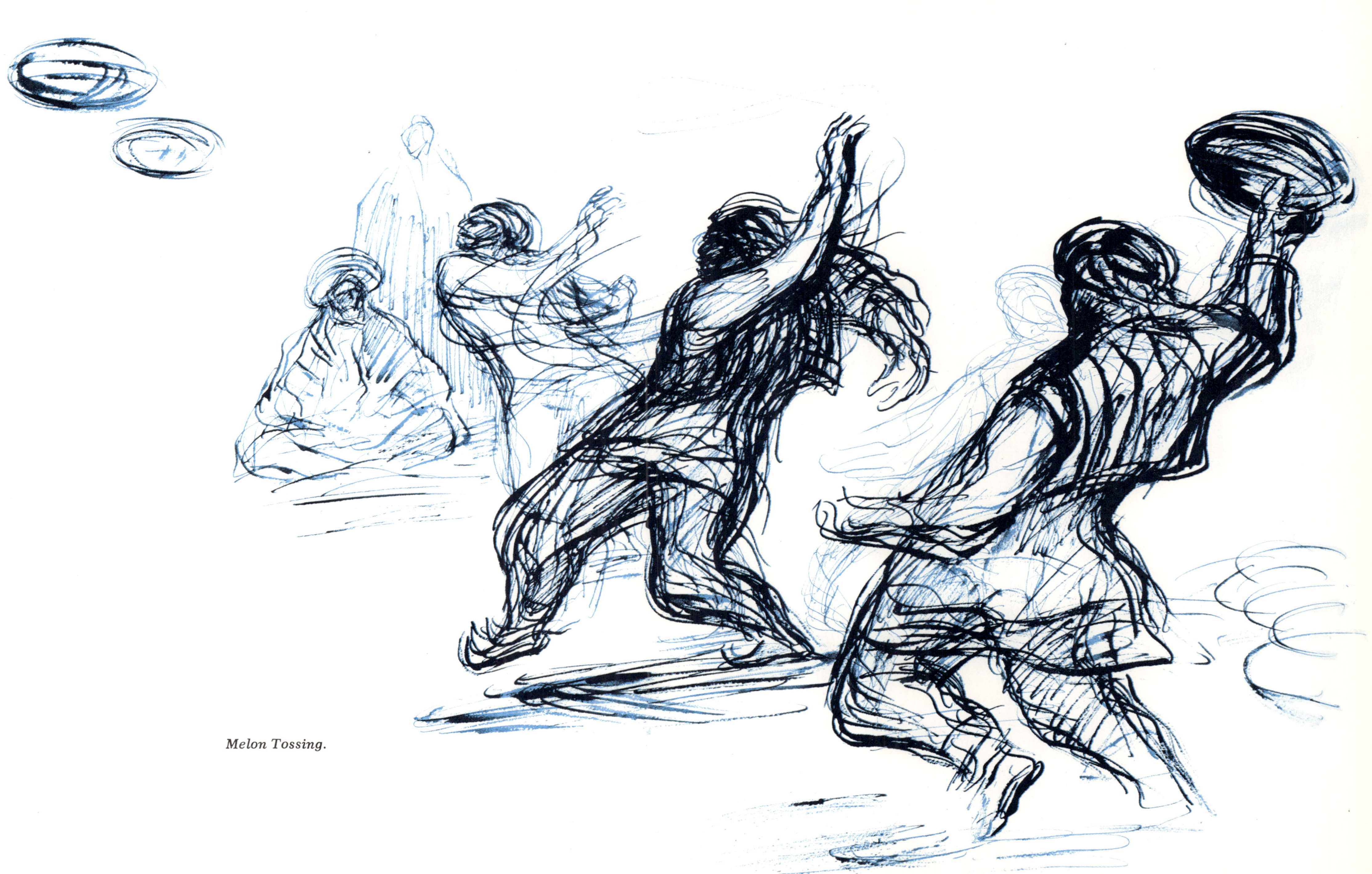

Melon Tossing.

Kushti

The kushti *wrestlers begin their daily training in the coolness of dawn. The combinations of the figures moving in the half-light appealed to me as an artist.*

Nearly ever young Pakistani boy has a single, driving dream—to one day become a *kushti* wrestler. Of course, only a handful realize such a dream, for the road to *kushti*—a professional sport as popular in Pakistan as *sumo* is in Japan—is a narrow one strewn with countless hurdles and harsh disciplines. Yet so great is the honor that each morning in Kim's Lahore—Pakistan's capital of *kushti*—some forty arenas are jammed with thousands of young wrestlers, battling one another in a style very similar to the U.S. collegiate sport, sharpening themselves for future team tryouts as crucial to them as the Olympic trials are to Europeans. "Kushti," says one former practitioner, "is a life unto itself. To be a *kushti* wrestler is to be like a priest."

Indeed, more like a monk. When he is but 10, a scrappy Pak showing promise is presented by his parents, along with a heavy supply of clothes, sweetmeats and money, to a *khalifa* (teacher) for evaluation. The *khalifa* appraises the boy's build, observes him in action and, much as a seminarian would, talks with him to determine the depth of his commitment to the almost monastic life. More often than not, the *khalifa* discreetly turns down the applicant. But if the youngster is accepted, the *khalifa* and the parents decide on a proper tuition fee and the beaming boy is ceremoniously issued a pair of tights known as

a *langota* and the sacred amulet of Ali—the wrestling brother of Mohammed and the patron saint of the sport.

From that moment the boy's life becomes a spartan series of disciplines designed to toughen his mind as well as his body. It is the purest of lives: no candy, no toys, no books except those devoted to his future craft. And when he enters manhood, the deprivations increase: no drinking, no smoking, no tea—and especially no women. "Woman," maintains a noted *khalifa*, "drains a man of his spirit."

Each day the young wrestler gets up with the sun, pulls on his *langota*, dons his amulet and reports to the arena where he trains until dusk—hoisting weights, running and practicing various holds. He stops only for a fattening lunch of milk, meat, butter and almond paste, and in the evening he listens intently to his teacher's remarks on his progress, then prays to Ali and goes to bed, immediately sinking deep into sleep. For all the confinement the young students seem extremely content. Their days are planned. There are no doubts, few temptations. They're shut off.

Finally, at age 16, comes the golden moment—the day the student emerges as a full-fledged *kushti* wrestler. From that point on he will be wrestling for keeps. No longer will he pass his days in the training arena, no longer will he have the benefit of evening counsel from his *khalifa*, no longer will there be mock battles with fellow students. From now on the hip rolls, hammerlocks and Balinese trips will be painfully real—and if he loses, some 30,000 spectators will bear witness from their seats in the stands. If he succeeds, however, the rewards are many: large sums of prize money (to support his family in payment for their trust in him), limitless glory and the finest of all payments—to represent his country in its annual battle against India. "That's like making the all-star team," says Groth. "In fact, it's better."

When the *kushti* warrior grows old and can no longer do battle with sufficient ferocity, he simply retires from the ring and hangs out a shingle—KHALIFA. Then—and only then—he gets a wife. As the proverb goes: All good things eventually come to a successful *kushti* wrestler.

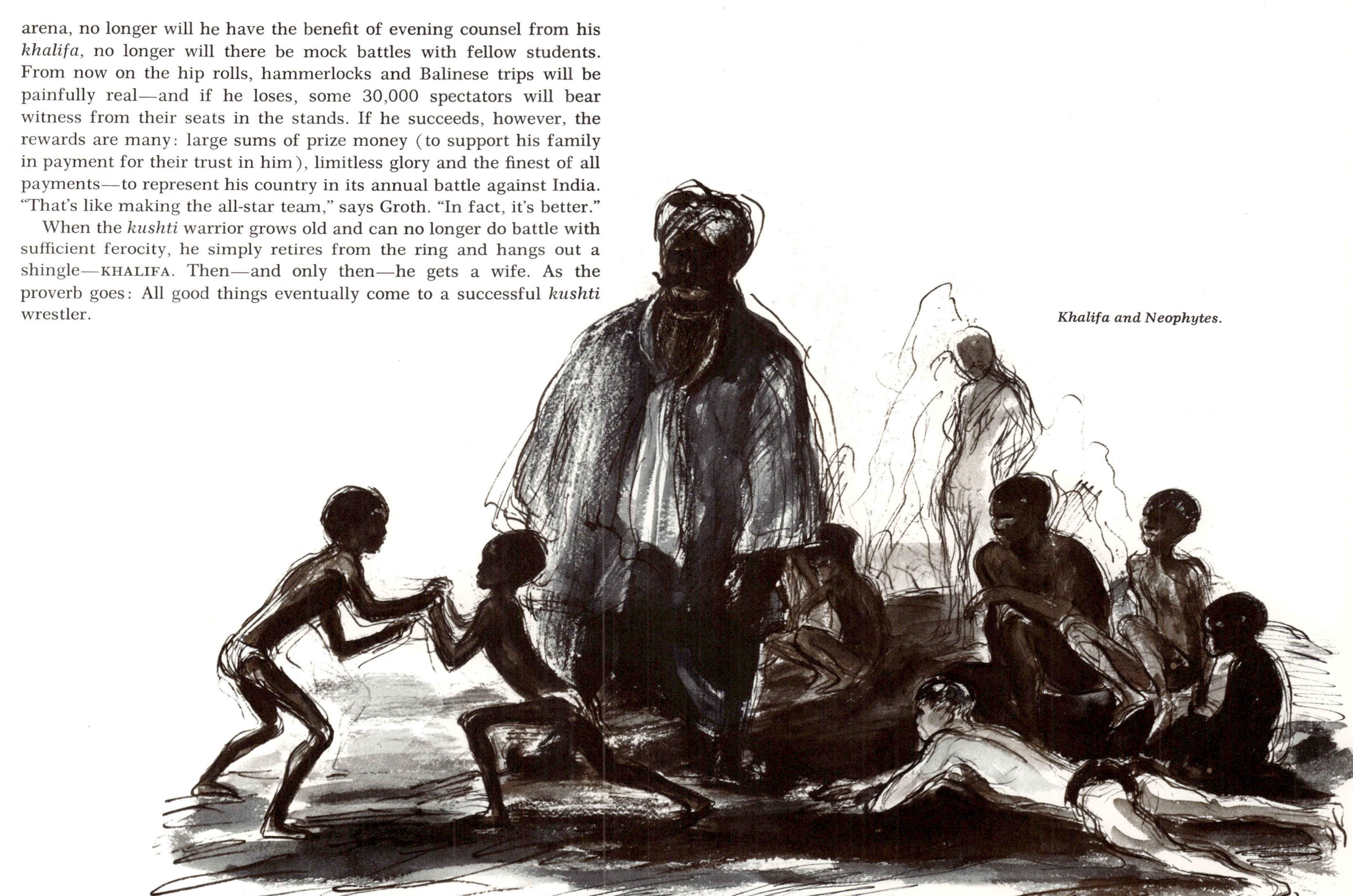

Khalifa and Neophytes.

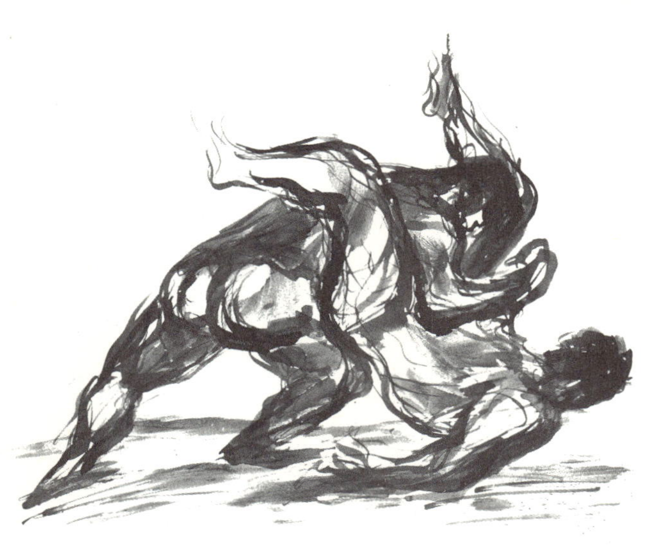

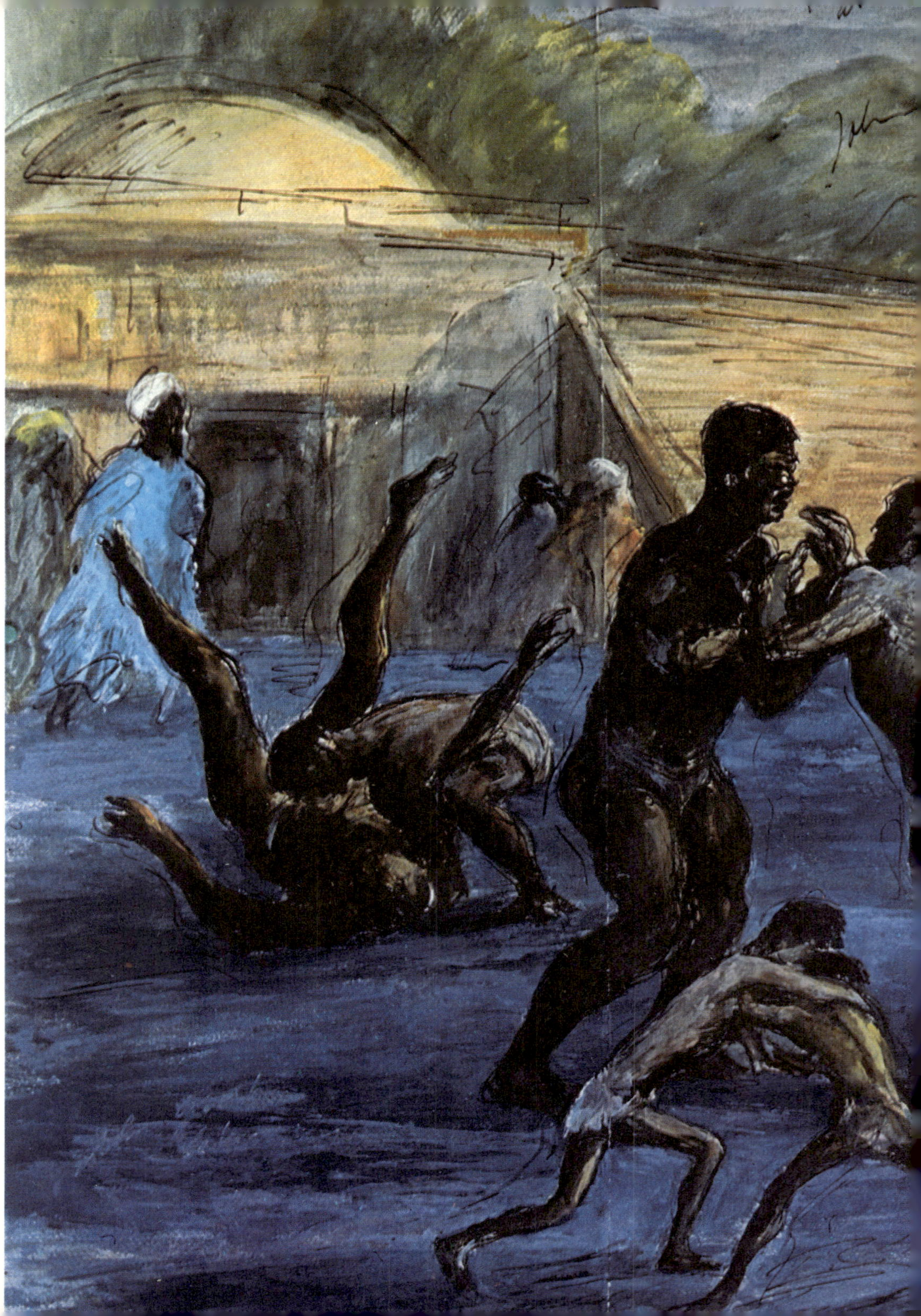

Workout at Dawn, Lahore.

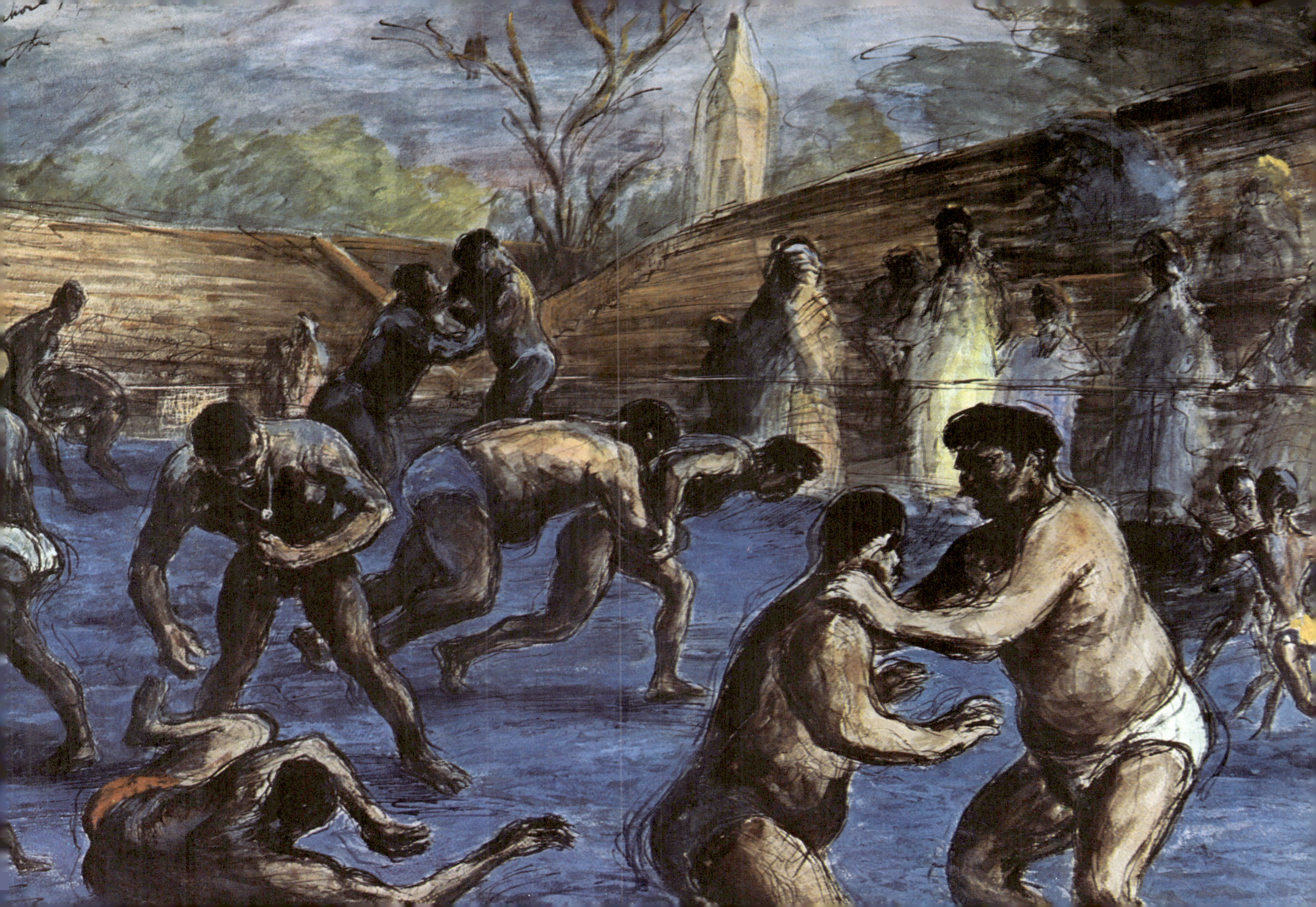

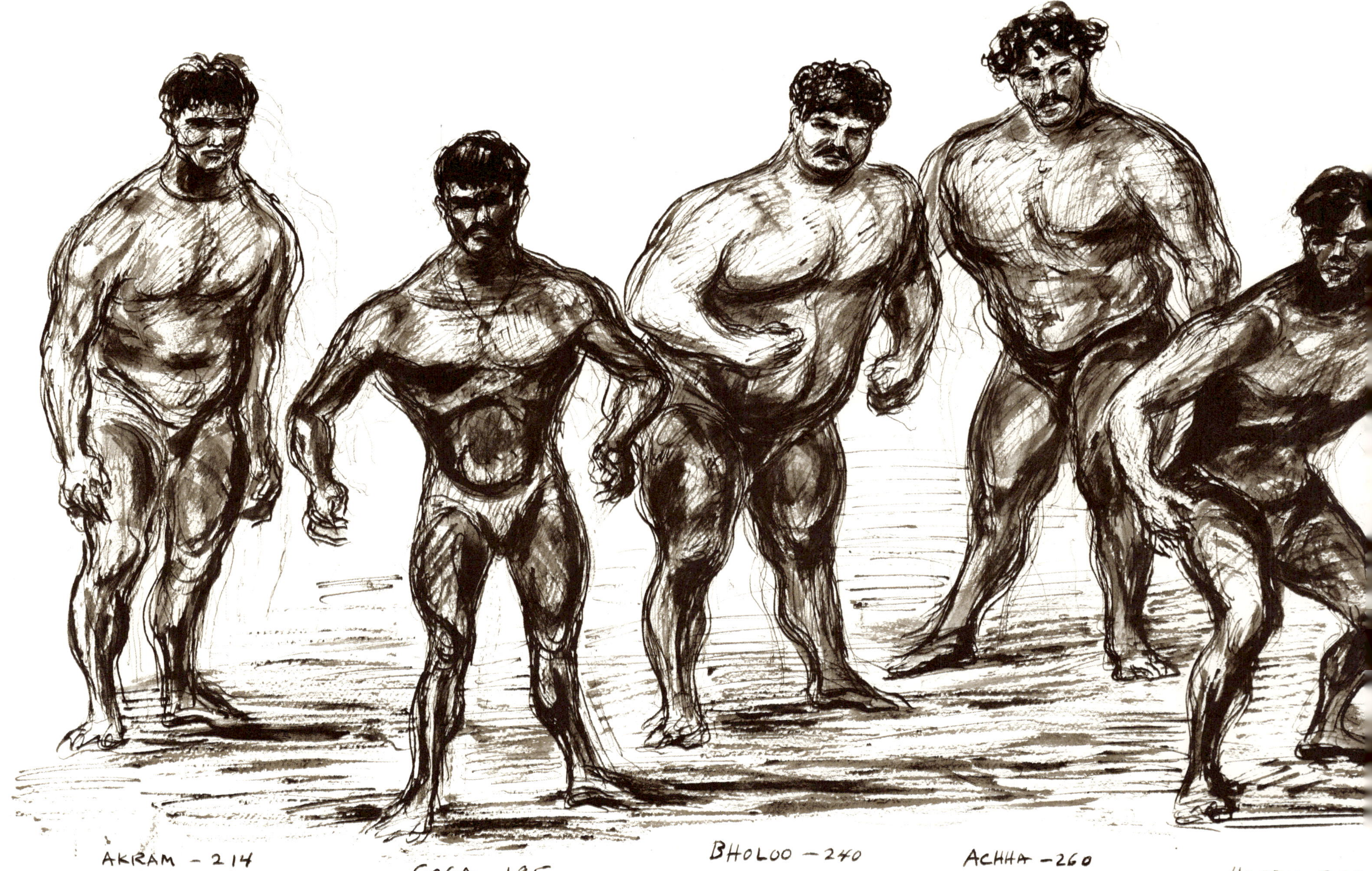
AKRAM - 214
GOGA 195
BHOLOO - 240
ACHHA - 260
HASSU - 200

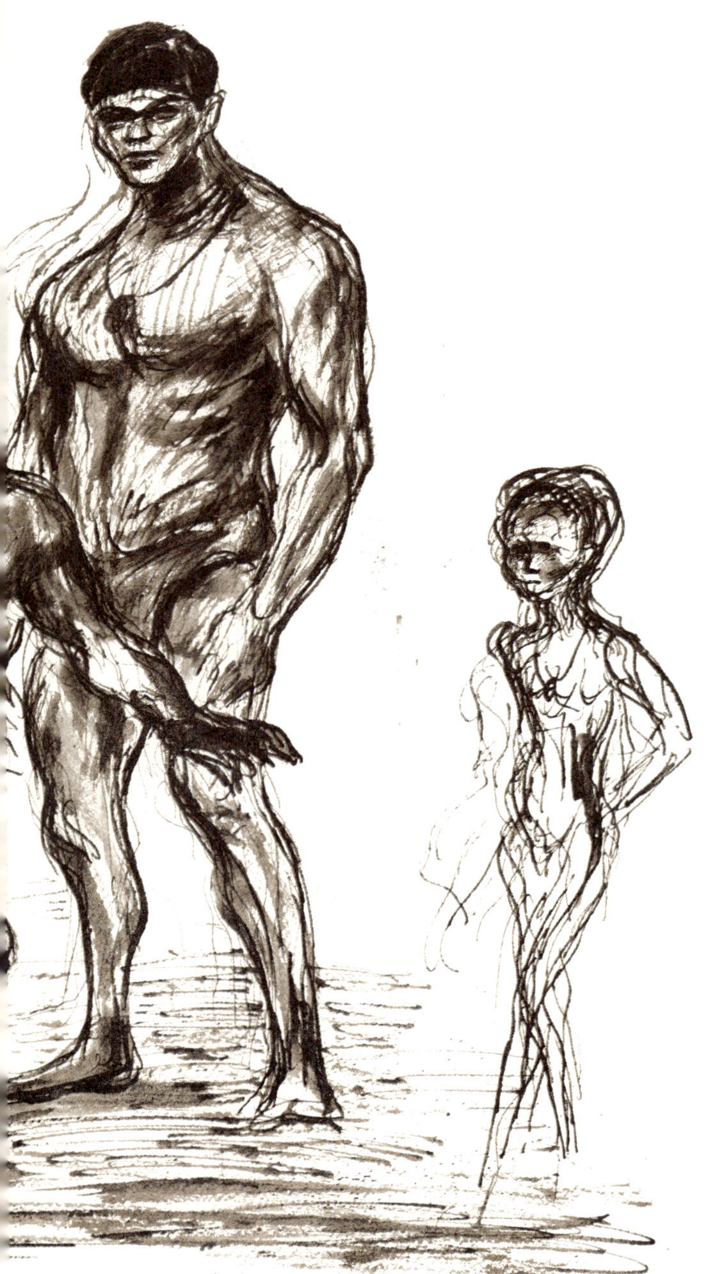

The Family Baksh.

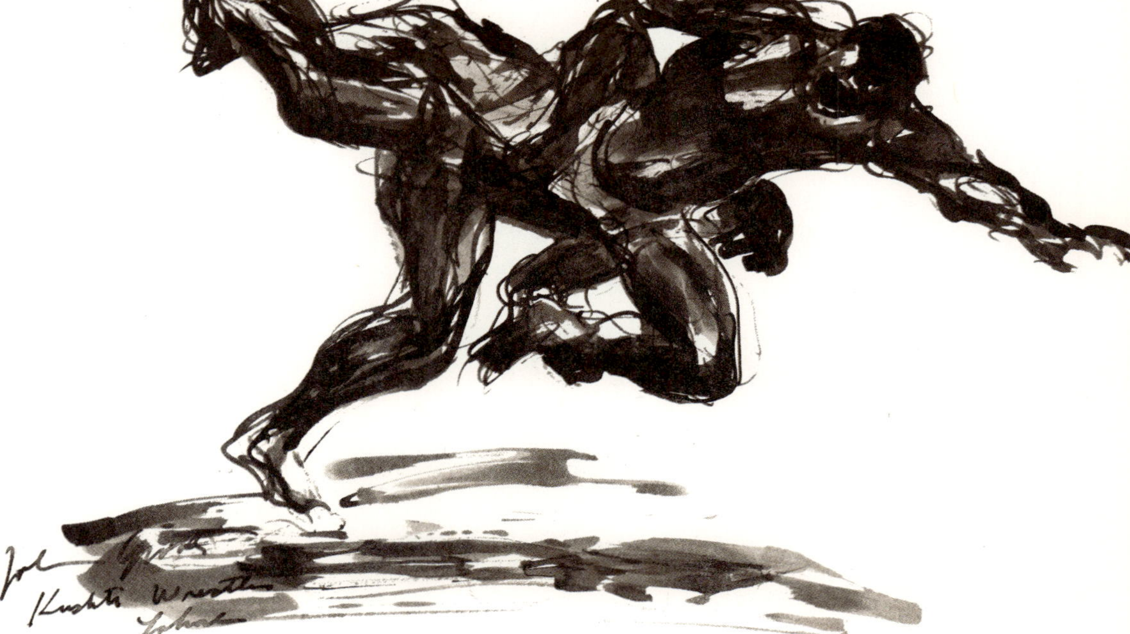

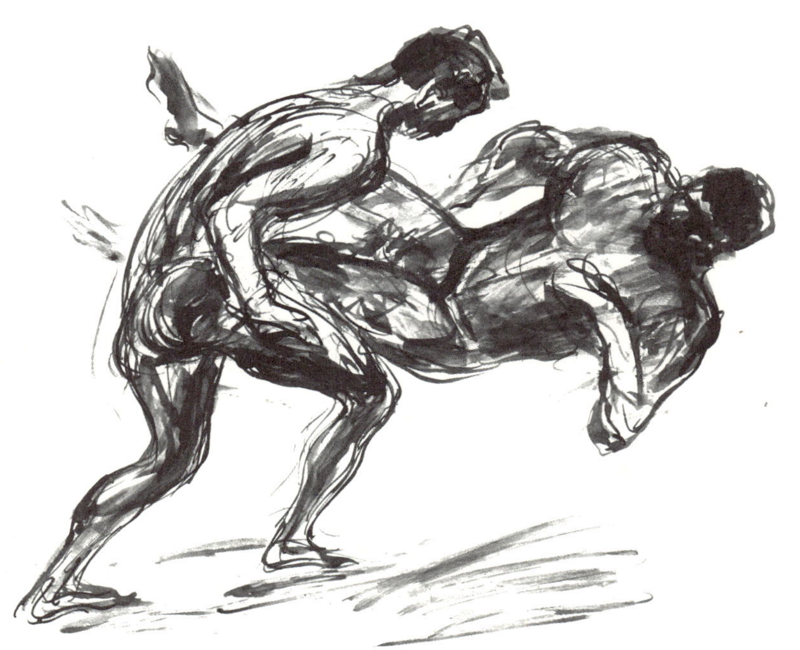

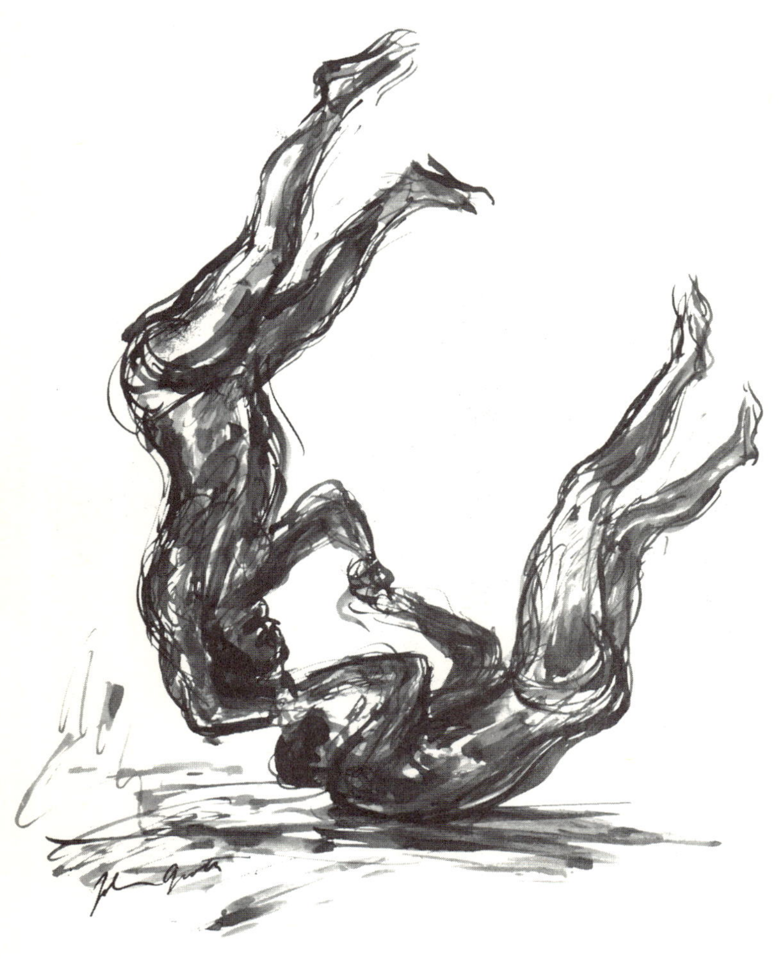

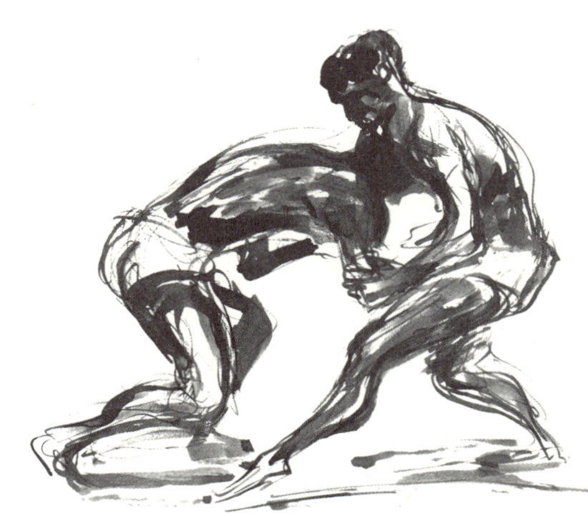

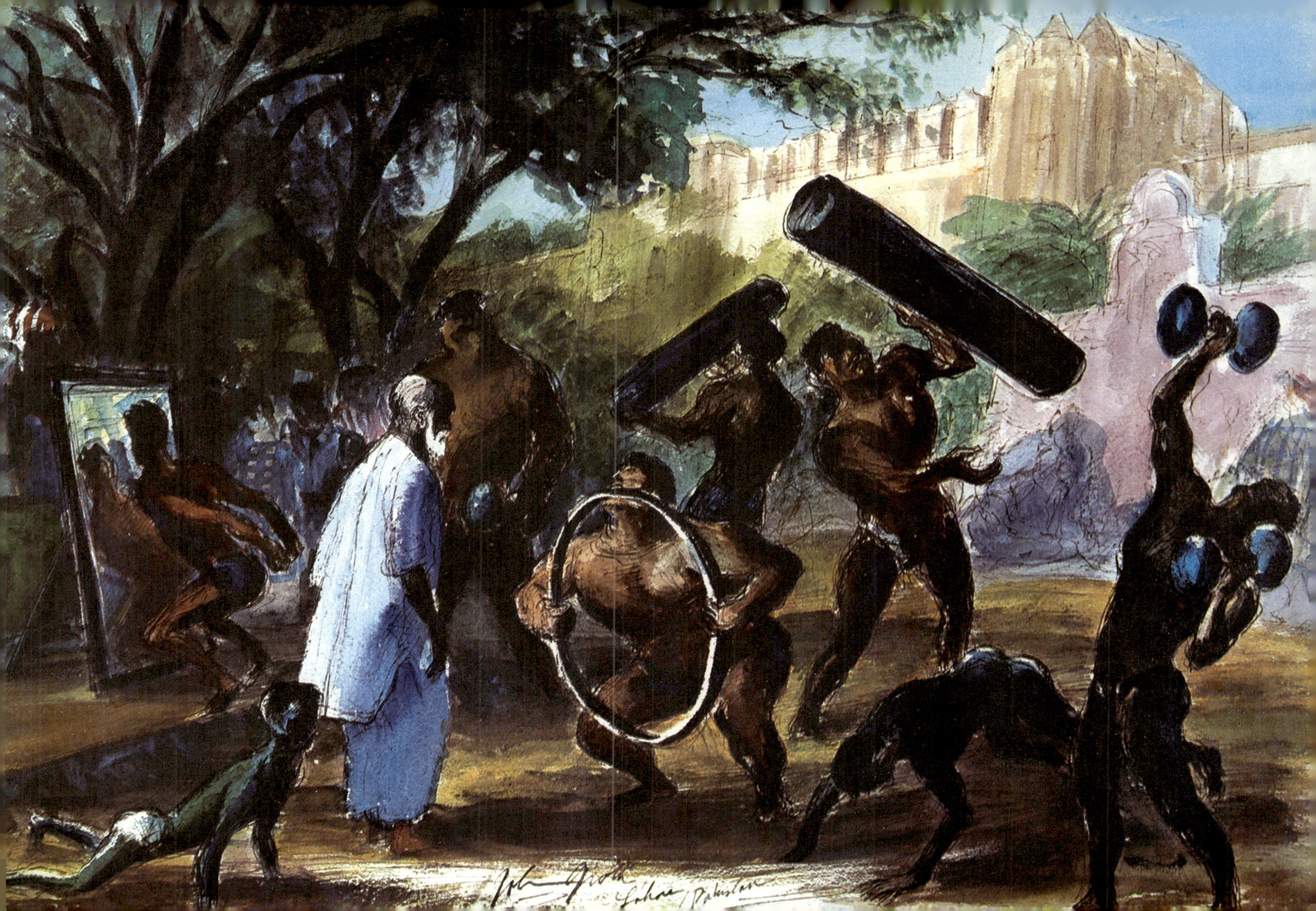

Lahore, Pakistan

Quebec Winter Carnival

For purely panoramic interest, the spectacle of the carnival at Quebec race has everything—the skiers throwing light and shadow on swirling snow, the ice canoes being lifted and hoisted over the heavy ice-floes, and the bright, vibrant color in the tug-of-war contestants' faces, all moving against a winter landscape of grays, blues and whites.

The power of John Groth's pictures, their inescapable sense of action, is vividly demonstrated in the drawings and paintings he did to illustrate the sports events that highlight the colorful winter carnival in the old Canadian city of Quebec.

With the skilled artist-reporter's eye for detail, Groth covered the entire program of sports, and because each event characteristically involved speed and endurance and physical strain, there is in each picture a feeling of violent, almost reckless action. One sees the tense crouch of the skier pitching down a dark slope, flaming torches in each upraised hand, feels the icy wind that assails the drivers of the dog teams as the racing sleds careen around a curve in the course, hears the grunts of the ponderous participants in the tug-of-war (five men to a team), laughs with the rollicking barrel-roll racers, shares the desperation with which the curling sweepers clear paths for the granite weights their teammates have sent twisting toward the target.

Perhaps the most exciting event of all is the ice-canoe race on the broad sweep of the St. Lawrence. Certainly no performers are more disdainful of peril, more rugged or more skilled. The boat, built usually of oak and cedar braced with steel or aluminum, does not conform to the popular conception of a canoe but resembles more the French *bateau*, weighing nearly 400 pounds. The crew is composed of five men who train for months for the carnival.

Even though generally fewer than a dozen boats compete in the event, and even though the St. Lawrence is no mill stream, there is little room to spare between the ice floes that all but choked the river. It is the floating ice, of course, that makes the race so frightening a competition. The rules say that the winner is the boat and crew that traverses the distance from start to finish first—no matter how the trick is turned—so the oarsmen and helmsmen have no patience with such nonsense as skirting as a floe just to keep in open water. When a hunk of moving ice looms ahead, the oarsmen put on all possible speed and the helmsmen drives the boat straight into the mass. The boat smashes into the ice, leaps high into the air and, if it has not capsized at the shock, skids up onto the floe. The crew leaps out to shove and haul the craft to the far edge, where they push off for the clear water again. In the course of a race it may be necessary to repeat this grueling procedure a half-dozen times. Almost never does a boat manage to cover the course in open water.

While the ice-canoe races excite most attention from thrill-seekers, the winter festival (which was started in 1894 when Quebec officials decided to "enliven the monotony of our dull season") is the quaint city's version of pre-Lenten festivities like the New Orleans Mardi Gras and the colorful carnival in Rio de Janeiro. Bonhomme Carnival, a "king" who is elected at the opening of the Quebec festival, is empowered to throw anyone in jail who fails to wear a smile. This coercion has never been necessary. "Everybody has a ball," says John Groth, "even the poor souls who are dunked in the icy water after a race."

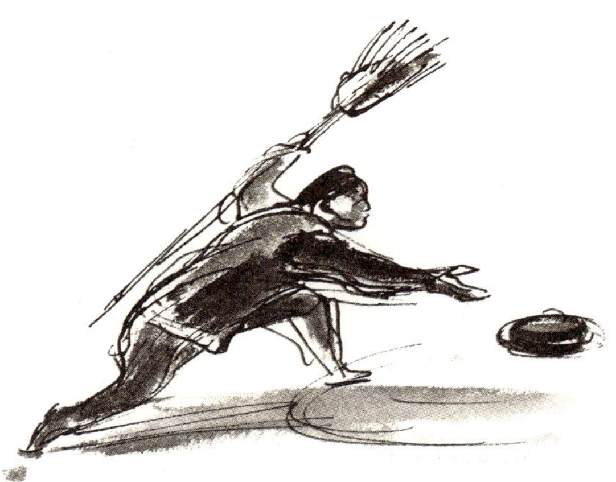

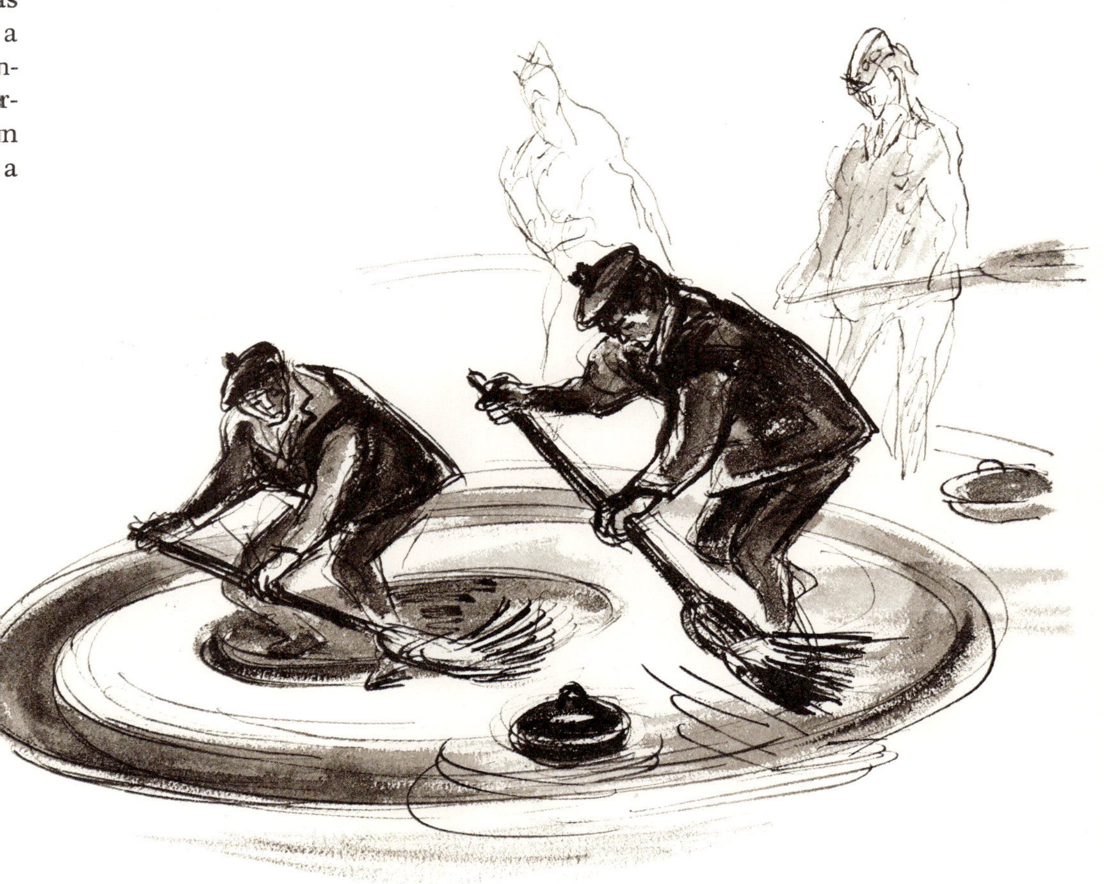

145

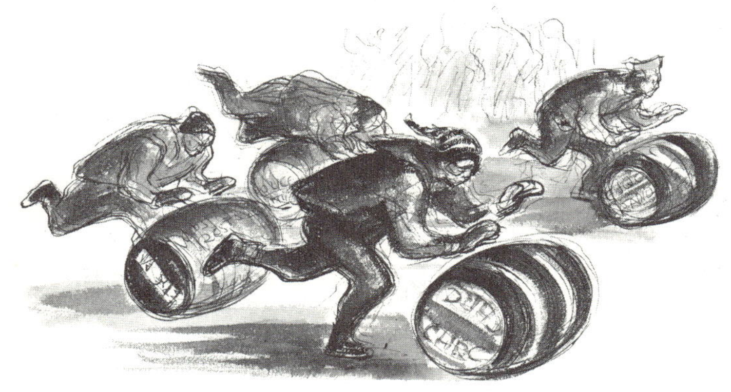

Barrel Rolling.

Ice Canoe Race, Quebec.

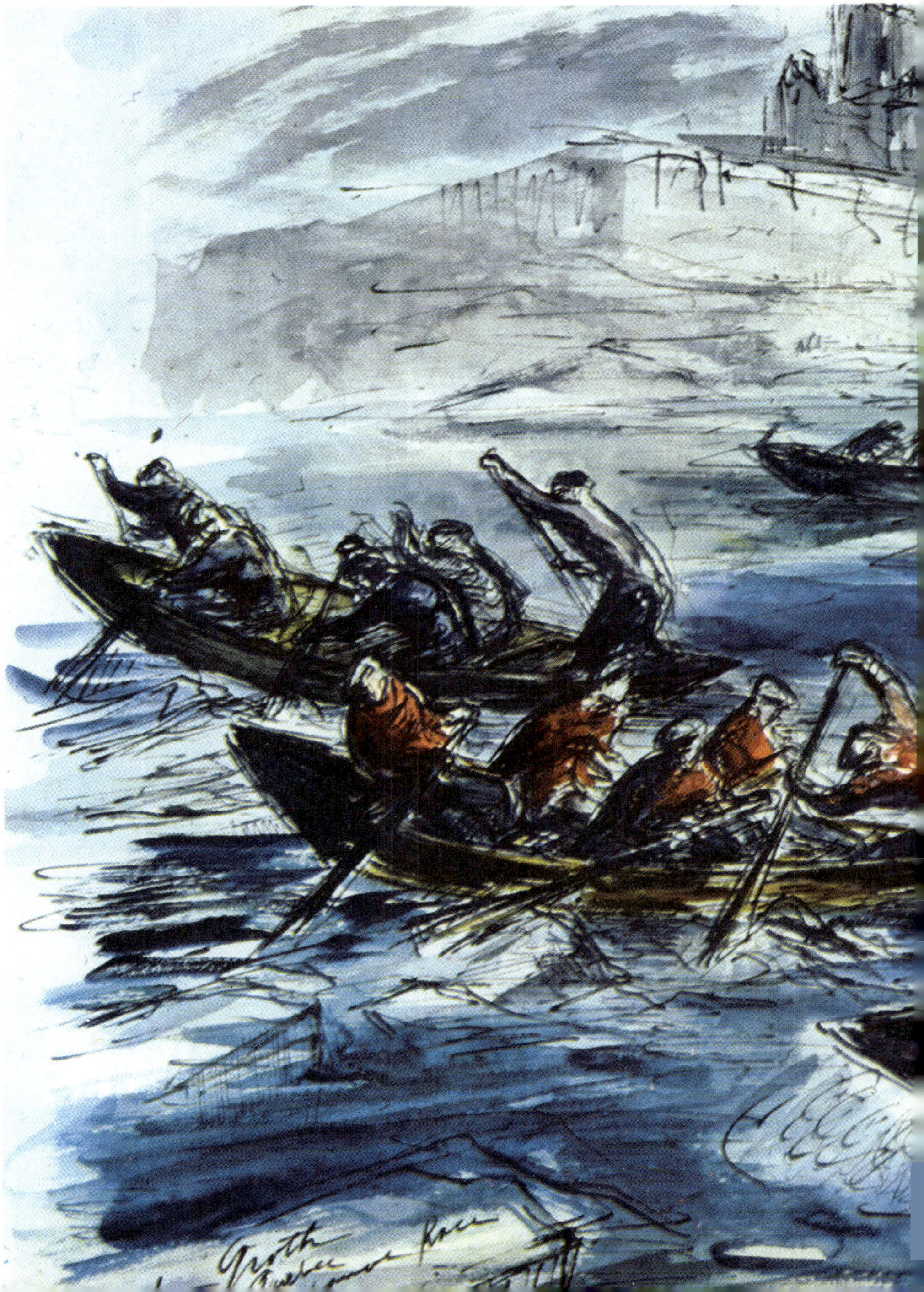

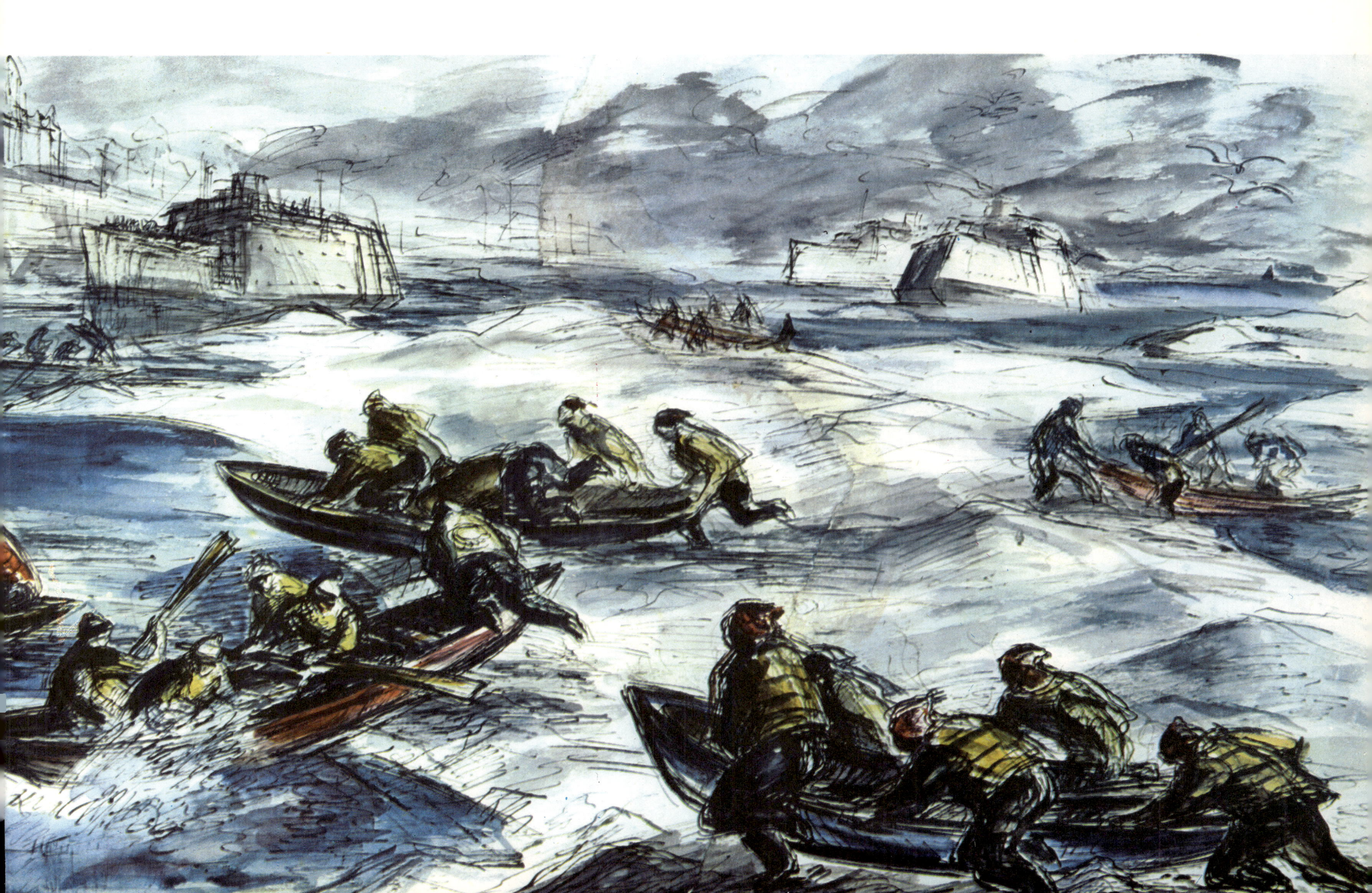

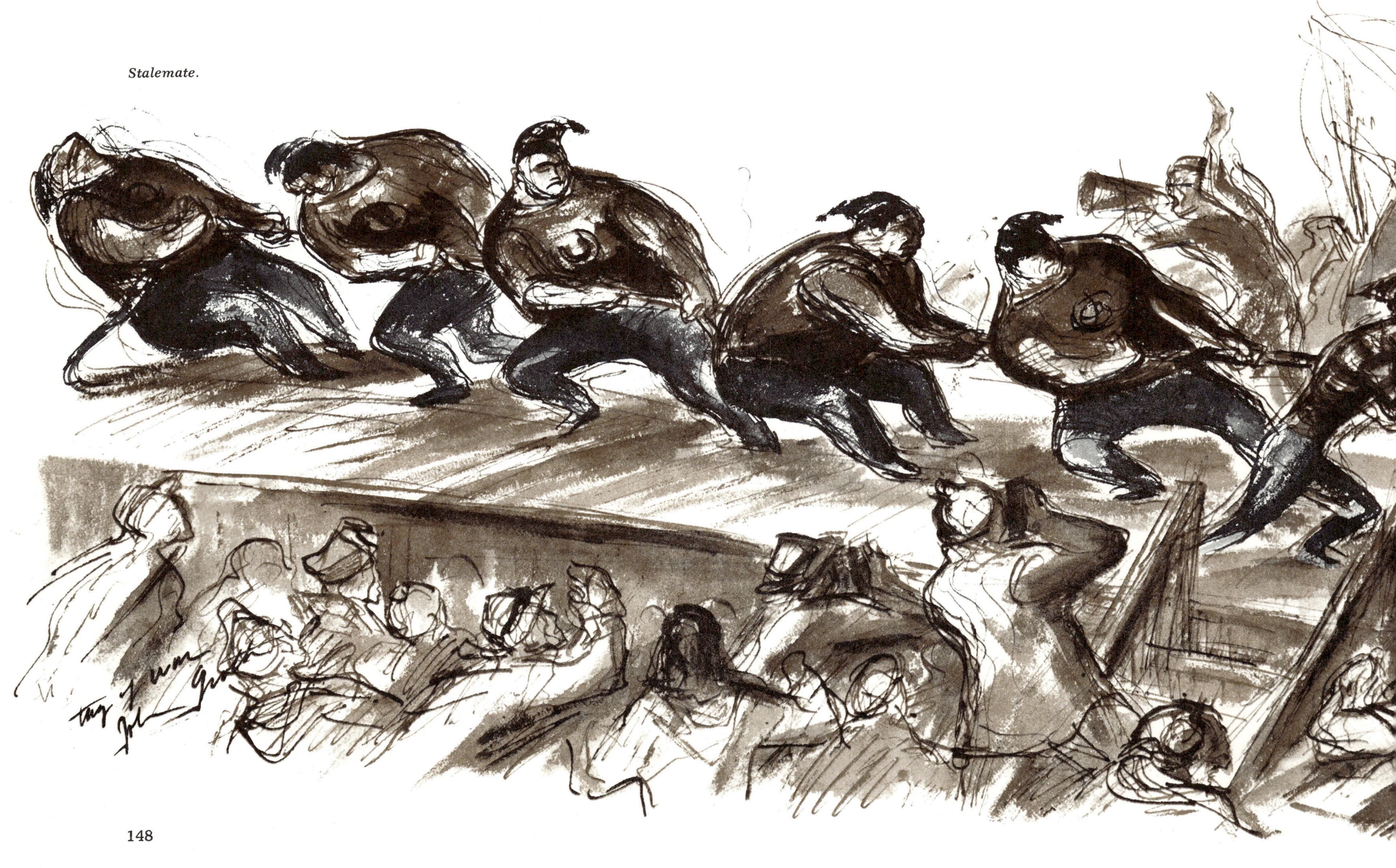

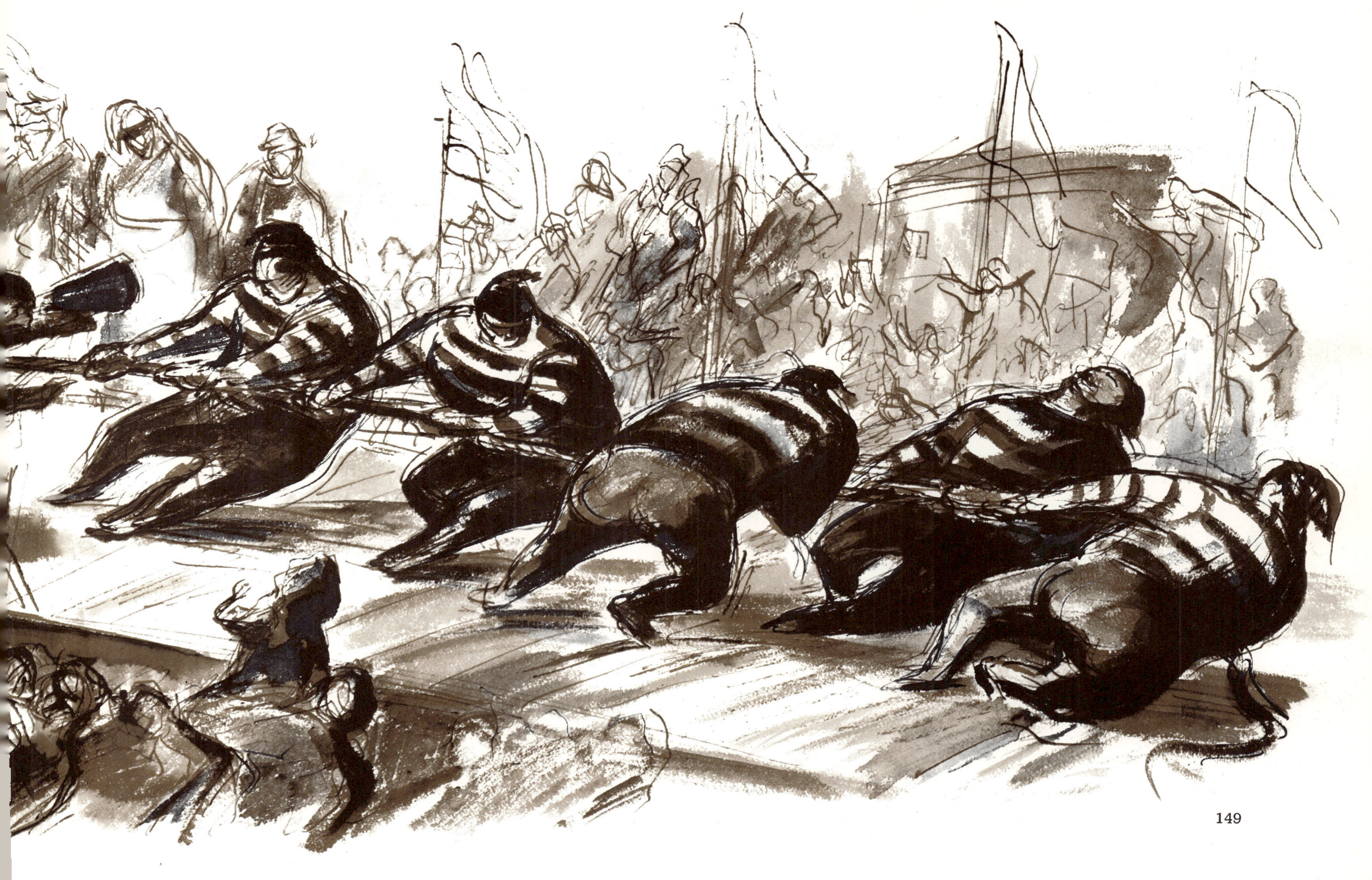

Paintings

Drawings

JOHN GROTH'S biography could be written with quotes from men like Arnold Gingrich, Ernest Hemingway, Jimmy Cannon, Heywood Broun, Red Smith and many others who have known and admired this man of many facets. Born on Chicago's West Side, he became art director of *Esquire* while still in his twenties. His career as an artist-war correspondent began in World War II and continued through Korea, French Indochina, Santo Domingo and Vietnam. Sports has been his other major field of interest. In all the stories he's covered John Groth has always been at the heart of the action . . . sometimes too much so. "I've had more narrow escapes covering sports than I've had as a war reporter," says Groth. He's been run down by the Notre Dame backfield, felled by a line drive off the bat of Brooklyn Dodger Cookie Lavagetto, kicked by a horse in a stall at Churchill Downs, and nearly had his head taken off by a ten-pound hammer head at the Aboyne Highland Games. But John Groth is first of all an artist. His paintings and drawings are in the collections of the Chicago Art Institute, Metropolitan Museum of Art, Museum of Modern Art, Library of Congress, Brooklyn Museum, University of Texas and many other public and private collections. He has written two books, *Studio: Europe* and *Studio: Asia,* and illustrated scores of others, including fine editions of *War and Peace, Gone with the Wind* and most recently Mark Twain's *The War Prayer*. He also teaches at the Art Students League of New York. When he's not traveling on assignment, John **Groth** lives and works in his midtown Manhattan **studio.**